The Art of Biblical Poetry

Books by Robert Alter

Rogue's Progress: Studies in the Picaresque Novel

Fielding and the Nature of the Novel

After the Tradition

Modern Hebrew Literature

Partial Magic: The Novel as a Self-Conscious Genre

Defenses of the Imagination

A Lion for Love: A Critical Biography of Stendhal

The Art of Biblical Narrative

Motives for Fiction

THE ART OF BIBLICAL POETRY

ROBERT ALTER

BASIC BOOKS, INC., PUBLISHERS
NEW YORK

Library of Congress Cataloging-in-Publication Data

Alter, Robert
    The art of biblical poetry.

    Includes index.
    1. Hebrew poetry, Biblical—History and criticism.
2. Bible. O.T.—Language, style. I. Title.
BS1405.2.A48   1985   809'.93522'44   85–47550
ISBN   0–465–00430–X

For Carol

ʾayelet ʾahavim veyaʿalat ḥen

CONTENTS

PREFACE   ix

    I   *The Dynamics of Parallelism*   3

   II   *From Line to Story*   27

  III   *Structures of Intensification*   62

  IV   *Truth and Poetry in the Book of Job*   85

   V   *Forms of Faith in Psalms*   111

  VI   *Prophecy and Poetry*   137

 VII   *The Poetry of Wit*   163

VIII   *The Garden of Metaphor*   185

  IX   *The Life of the Tradition*   204

NOTES   215

GENERAL INDEX   220

BIBLICAL REFERENCE INDEX   227

PREFACE

As THE TITLE WILL SUGGEST, this book is conceived as a parallel volume to my earlier venture into the literature of the Bible, *The Art of Biblical Narrative.* The parallel is only approximate because differences in the topic under investigation dictated differences in both organization and critical strategy. What I have set out to do here is first to define the workings of the formal system of biblical poetry in three initial chapters, moving from the nature of the poetic line to larger structures. The stress throughout is on the basic convention of semantic parallelism rather than on the phonetic and syntactic elements of the system because the latter two aspects would not be perceptible to anyone reading the poems in translation, and in any case much about the phonetics of biblical Hebrew remains uncertain.

After these three chapters on the system of biblical verse, I try to extend and refine my generalizations by applying them to major poetic texts, and through such application to see something of the difference poetry makes in the Bible. I have not attempted a comprehensive treatment of every subgenre of biblical poetry or of all the various poetic insets in the narrative books, but the main genres and texts—psalms, prophetic poetry, Wisdom poetry from Job to Proverbs, love poetry—are all scrutinized. Indeed, one of the many gaps in the understanding of biblical poetry is a failure of those who generalize about it to make sufficient distinctions among genres, and this study represents an initial effort to correct that tendency of amalgamation. For the most part, I proceed through close readings of specimens of the poetry because that seemed to me the best way to recover a sense of the intricate artistry of the poems. As in my book on narrative, the aim is to illustrate principles of poetics working in the Bible, not to provide exhaustive exegesis of the particular texts considered. If I have succeeded in any degree, I would hope that a reader could put these principles to use to read other biblical poems with heightened understanding and keener appreciation.

I must confess that before undertaking this project I questioned its

feasibility because of the daunting problems of talking about poetry—
the best words in the best order—to readers who, apart from a small
minority, would not have access to the original Hebrew words in their
original order. I became convinced, however, that the job was worth
attempting because poetry is a vitally important aspect of biblical
literature that needs to be better understood, while the recent flowering
of literary studies of the Bible has concentrated on narrative to the
neglect of verse. I offer a partial compensation here for the absence of
the Hebrew originals in the translations I have provided for all the texts
discussed. (Verse and chapter numbers refer to the Hebrew text; there
are occasional discrepancies in verse numeration between the Hebrew
and the Authorized Version.) My versions often ignore considerations of
modern idiomatic fluency in order to give a closer idea than conventional
translations do of such elements of the original as word-motifs, anaphora,
envelope structures, and various kinds of significant syntactic designs. I
have also sought to offer some sense of the rhythmic compactness of the
Hebrew, though compactness is sacrificed when fidelity to meaning
requires. No doubt in some instances, at least in the eyes of some readers,
I will have succeeded only in betraying both English stylistic decorum
and the Hebrew original, but I do think there are artful traits of the
original that will be evident in some of the versions, whatever their
failings, that are not easily detectable in the usual translations.

Let me add that many of the poetic texts of the Bible include formidable
philological problems that I do not pretend to solve, and so I have merely
marked the most egregious of these difficulties with a typographical
symbol (an asterisk) while proceeding to the task of poetic analysis. On
this issue, I would only observe that some supposed textual incoherencies
or anomalies in fact make perfect sense in the light of certain general
(and generally ignored) principles of biblical poetics. Readers familiar
with these scholarly questions will note a few points along the way
where poetic analysis of the sort I propose ought to be carefully weighed
before conclusions are drawn about the need to emend the text.

A word is in order on the relation of this study to previous inquiries
into biblical poetry. In contrast to biblical narrative, which to all intents
and purposes was "discovered" as a subject for rigorous investigation
barely a decade ago, biblical poetry is the subject of a vast scholarly
literature, some of it going back two centuries. But whereas the relatively
modest body of work on narrative includes some incisive studies, it
seems to me that most of what has been written on biblical poetry is in
some way misconceived and, however imposing the intellectual equipment

of the writers, tends to be guided by rather dim notions of how poetry works. It did not strike me as useful to try to contend in detail with this scholarly production, which was for the most part beside the points I was trying to make; and so, with the very limited exception of some ground clearing in the initial chapter, I have kept both notes and references to secondary works to a bare minimum, citing only what I thought was strictly relevant.

Of course, no one could be foolish enough to imagine that what he has to say on a topic so abundantly discussed is entirely new. There are certain local anticipations of my observations about parallelism within the line in the traditional Hebrew commentaries from late antiquity to the Renaissance, but these exegetes work on very different interpretive assumptions, with no real sense that there is a formal system of poetics that defines the operations of units of meaning within the text. Among contemporary analysts of biblical poetics, I am indebted for a general orientation to Benjamin Hrushovski, from whose brief but seminal comments on ancient Hebrew prosody I quote in my first chapter. Certain perceptions about the nature of parallelism proposed in the introductory chapter of James L. Kugel's *The Idea of Biblical Poetry* (1981) proved close to ideas I had worked out in my Berkeley seminars in the late 1970s. It is in a way reassuring that different critical eyes should see the same object, though there is also much in Kugel's general conception of biblical poetry to which I strenuously object, as I try to make clear at the outset.

I believe that criticism, like literature, forms a tradition, and this study therefore must owe various debts, large and small, witting and unwitting, to its many predecessors. At the same time, I would hope it will provide a useful new point of departure for others seeking to illuminate this complex and fascinating subject. The book is addressed, like my study of narrative, to all those curious about the Bible, whether their motives are religious, cultural, or specifically literary, and I would like to think that it contains things that will be instructive to specialists and general readers alike. Since the poetry of ancient Israel is, moreover, one of the wellsprings of Western literature, this inquiry may hold some interest for anyone concerned with poetry, even without a special involvement in the Bible.

It gives me great pleasure to express my gratitude to the Institute for Advanced Studies of the Hebrew University of Jerusalem, under whose generous auspices I completed the first half of this book in 1982–1983. The Institute gave me not only a year free of teaching obligations in which to begin the project in a very congenial setting but also the weekly stimulation of my colleagues in the group on biblical studies. Sections of the early chapters were first tried out on that learned audience, and I am sure that my formulations benefited from their questions and suggestions. I was also very fortunate to be able to discuss many of these poetic texts with a graduate seminar in biblical poetry at the University of California, Berkeley, in the spring semester of 1984, and to learn from the alert comments of my students. Typing and incidental research costs were covered by the Committee on Research of the University of California at Berkeley. The typing itself was done by Florence Myer, as always with exemplary precision. Chapter 1 and abridgments of chapters 2 and 4 appeared respectively in *Hebrew University Studies in Literature and the Arts, Poetics Today,* and *Commentary,* and I would like to thank the editors of those journals for their receptivity.

Berkeley
August 1984

The Art of Biblical Poetry

I

The Dynamics of

Parallelism

The detail is everything.
—VLADIMIR NABOKOV

WHAT ARE the formal elements that make up a poem in the Hebrew Bible? The incorrigible naïveté of common sense might lead one to suppose that the rudiments of an answer would be self-evident, but in fact there is no aspect of biblical literature that has elicited more contradictory, convoluted, and at times quite fantastical views, from late antiquity to the latest scholarly publications. To many it might have seemed that after Robert Lowth's *De sacra poesi Hebraeorum* (1753) semantic parallelism between the two (or sometimes three) components of a line was firmly established as the chief organizing principle of the system; but questions have been raised about the actual prevalence of such parallelism, about how it is to be conceived if it is really there, and about whether it might not be an entirely secondary feature of biblical poetry. One influential contemporary theory imagines syllable count to be the defining characteristic of ancient Hebrew verse, with parallelism appearing, as one adherent of this notion rather lamely puts it, when the poet (thought of, without much evidence, as an oral-formulaic composer) needs more syllables to pad out his idea to the end of the line.[1] A still newer theory proposes a bewilderingly elaborate system of "syntactic constraints" as the basis of biblical verse, though this analysis entails, among other intrinsic difficulties, an arbitrary chopping up of poetic lines into units that will confirm the proposed pattern.[2] Others have argued for a combination of syntax and stress as the basis of versification.[3]

The Art of Biblical Poetry

The dismaying range of discussion on this topic is vividly illustrated by two extremes. At one end of the spectrum, an Orientalist in the 1930s, Paul Kraus, set out to show that the entire Hebrew Bible, once properly accented, could be demonstrated to have been written in verse (a project in which he had been anticipated three decades earlier by the German Old Testament scholar Eduard Sievers). When he discovered two-thirds of the way through his analysis that the texts no longer bore out his thesis, he took his own life. At the other end of the spectrum, an ambitious recent study, James L. Kugel's *The Idea of Biblical Poetry*,[4] after a splendid first chapter full of incisive comments on what happens in semantic parallelism, comes perilously close to concluding that there is no poetry in the Bible, only a "continuum" from loosely parallelistic structures in what we think of as the prose sections to a more "heightened rhetoric" of parallelistic devices in what we misleadingly label verse.

Despite the grim fate of Paul Kraus, I don't think the attempt to describe the system of biblical poetry need be a suicidal enterprise, and it is obviously important to get some handle on the system in order to understand what kinds of meaning, what representations of human and divine reality, are made possible by this particular poetic vehicle. But it does seem wise to state clearly at the outset what we do not know and are unlikely to recover. The actual sound of biblical poetry will remain at least to some extent a matter of conjecture. Certain distinctions among consonants have shifted or blurred over the centuries, and what is worse, we cannot be entirely sure we know where accents originally fell, what the original system of vowels and syllabification was, or whether there were audible changes in these phonetic features during the several hundred years spanned by biblical poetry. (The indications of stress and vocalization of the Masoretic text were codified well over a millennium after the composition of most of the poems and centuries after Hebrew had ceased to be the vernacular.) On the level of meaning, although comparative Semitic philology in a remarkable age of archaeological discovery has done heroic work in restoring the original sense of poorly understood words, it would be foolhardy to imagine that we can always recover the real nuances of biblical terms, or the relation between poetic diction and colloquial diction (of which there is no record) or between poetic diction and other specialized usages of the ancient language. Moreover, because the language of poetic texts presents a higher concentration of rare locutions and other stylistic difficulties—difficulties even, apparently, for an ancient Hebrew scribe—one encounters in the poetry phrases, lines, or sometimes whole sequences of lines that look thoroughly corrupted and that read as little more than gibberish unless one has sufficient faith to accept someone's radical emendation of the text. To these problems of sound and meaning, one must add a formal problem: because the poems are not set out as poetry in the traditional Hebrew text, there are sometimes serious questions as to where the line breaks should come and, especially in some of the Prophets, ambiguities about the boundaries between prose and poetic passages.

All these puzzlements should be kept in mind, for there are aspects of the system of biblical poetry, and certainly features of individual poems, that will continue to elude us from where we stand, two and a half millennia—and, in the case of a few texts, perhaps three millennia—after the creation of the poems. The difficulties, however, need not be overstated. There remains much that can be understood about biblical verse; and sometimes, as in the text I am about to quote, even where there are doubts about the poem's meaning, it may exhibit perfectly perceptible formal patterns that tell us something about the operations of the underlying poetic system. My initial example, then, Genesis 4:23–24, is an instructive enigma, and only the second instance of clearly demarcated formal verse in the Bible (the first being the two-line poem in Genesis 2:23 that Adam uses to name his helpmate Woman). It is a poem, addressed by Lamech to his two wives, that would seem to be almost entirely dependent on context, some obscure story of an injury or insult perpetrated on Lamech and the vengeance he exacts. The trouble is that no context whatever is offered. All we know about Lamech is that he is the fifth linear descendant of Cain, of whom God had said, "Whoever slays Cain will be avenged sevenfold," and that he begat with his two wives the inaugurators of the archetypal civilized activities of flock tending, music making, and metal forging, and a daughter with no designated archetypal role. This frustrating lack of context for the poem, however, can be taken as the occasion to look without distraction at the formal configuration of meanings and rhythm and word order that constitute its three lines:

ʿadáh vetziláh shemáʿan qolí   neshéi lémekh haʾzénaʾimratí
ki ʾísh harágti lefitzʾí   veyéled leḥaburatí
ki shivʿatáyim yúqam-qáyin   velémekh shivʿím veshivʿáh

Ada and Zilla, hear my voice.   Wives of Lamech, give ear to my speech.

A man I have killed for my wound,   a boy for my bruising.
If sevenfold avenged is Cain,   Lamech then seventy-seven.

5

The Art of Biblical Poetry

Since doubts have now been raised, at least by James Kugel, as to whether it is justifiable to speak of poetry in the Hebrew Bible, let me begin with a brief consideration of the most fundamental question: Is this text indisputably a poem? To answer that question, we need some notion of what it is in general that enables us to distinguish poetic from nonpoetic discourse, and I should like to cite as a helpful point of reference Barbara Herrnstein Smith's apt proposal on this issue in her book on poetic closure. "As soon as we perceive," she writes, "that a verbal sequence has a sustained rhythm, that it is formally structured according to a continuously operating principle of organization, we know that we are in the presence of poetry and we respond to it accordingly . . . , expecting certain effects from it and not others, granting certain conventions to it and not others." We shall soon be concerned with precisely what those expectations and conventions might be in the case of biblical poetry, but first we need to reflect on the presence or absence in this and other biblical texts of a "sustained rhythm" that works as "a continuously operating principle of organization." Barbara Smith, as she goes on to make clear, has in mind a model of perceptual psychology in which a relatively structured pattern is perceived as a figure against a ground of more random data. "One of the most significant effects," she concludes, "of meter (or, more broadly, of principles of formal structure) in poetry is simply to inform the reader that he is being confronted by poetry and not by anything else. . . . Meter serves, in other words, as a frame for the poem, separating it from a 'ground' of less highly structured speech and sound."[5]

The term "meter," because of its associations with a Greco-Roman system of carefully regulated sequences of vowel quantities, may not be the best one to apply to our text, but the continuously present frame of formal structure of which Barbara Smith speaks is quite conspicuous here. To be sure, there are also certain elements of symmetry and repetition in the surrounding prose, but, set against the tight formal organization of these lines, the narrative text all around is surely perceived by reader or listener as a "ground" of nonpoetic discourse. And it will not do to argue, as Kugel does, that the syntactic, rhythmic, and semantic strategies of biblical verse are simply part of a "continuum" with what we designate as prose because roughly analogous configurations of language can be discovered in the prose. In fact, it is rare to find anywhere a poetic style that does not bear some relation to the literary prose of the same culture; or rather, it turns out in many instances that literary prose is influenced by contemporary or antecedent poetry in the same language, often seeking knowingly or unwittingly to achieve for itself a quasi-poetic status without the formal constraints of verse. Fielding's splendid satiric style, with its pointed antitheses and poised symmetries, surely owes something to his experience of Pope's handling of the heroic couplet, and Melville, striving to shape a prose of the sublime, is famous (or notorious) for his Miltonic and Shakespearian effects, sometimes producing whole passages that almost scan as blank verse; but neither of these instances is evidence that readers and writers of English make no sharp generic distinction between poetry and prose.

Now, what clearly sets our text off from the surrounding prose is the strictly observed principle of parallelism on which it is organized, something perfectly apparent even in translation, but it is important to recognize what is involved in the parallelism and where parallelism begins to turn into something else. The most obvious thing is the parallelism of meaning, observed by the poet with what seems almost schematic regularity in the opening line, every component of the first half of the line being precisely echoed in the second half: Ada and Zilla / wives of Lamech, hear / give ear, my voice / my speech. This semantic parallelism is reinforced by a perfect syntactic parallelism, the word order in each of the half-lines exactly mirroring the other, with each corresponding term in the same syntactic position. The syntactic parallelism continues in the second line, with the minor modification that the verb ("I have killed") does double duty for both halves of the line. (This very common configuration of ellipsis, usually of the verb but sometimes of another part of speech, opens certain poetic possibilities to which we shall presently attend.) The last line of the poem, which also has a double-duty verb ("is avenged"), exhibits a further deviation from parallel word order: "If sevenfold avenged is Cain, / Lamech then seventy-seven." This is a careful maneuver by the poet: embedding in his poem a precise citation from the preceding narrative (Gen. 4:15) about the sevenfold vengeance that will be exacted for Cain, he then reverses the word order for Lamech, thus producing a chiastic structure in which Cain and Lamech are set back to back and bracketed by "seven" at the beginning and "seventy-seven" at the end of the line. This neat chiasm underscores the contrast between Cain and Lamech (more of which in a moment) while providing, through the switch from the regular syntactic parallelism of the two preceding lines, a sense of closure at the end, terminal variation of repeated structure being a common closural device in many kinds of poetry. Finally, the poem reflects a parallelism of stresses between the half-lines. If the Masoretic text can be taken at least as an approximate guide to the original stress system, the distribution of accents would be as follows: 4/4, 3/2, 3/3, with perhaps some margin of flexibility to "regularize" the middle, rhythmically asymmetrical line by giving weight to the secondary stress in the word I have translated as "for my bruising" (lehaburatí).

Any reader of biblical poetry ought at this point to object that I have made things far too easy for myself by choosing such an untypically neat example, even if it happens to be one of the first poems in the Bible. Such a perfect accord of parallel meaning, syntax, and rhythm as we find in the first line of Lamech's poem is not, after all, so very common: syntax often changes from one half-verse to the next, the number of stresses is often not duplicated, and worst of all, there are many lines of biblical verse, and in Psalms sometimes whole poems, where semantic parallelism appears to be very weak or entirely absent.

Such discrepancies between the theory of parallelism and the variegated evidence of the poetic texts have led, as I indicated at the outset, to the most dizzying feats of critical acrobatics in the effort either to "save" parallelism or to replace it with some other principle. But perhaps there is no real need for acrobatics. Benjamin Hrushovski, in a synoptic article on the history of Hebrew prosody[6] whose extraordinarily compact paragraphs on biblical versification have unfortunately been ignored by biblical scholarship, offers an account of the system that seems to me thoroughly convincing precisely because of its elegant simplicity and its lack of strain. Hrushovski proposes a "semantic-syntactic-accentual rhythm" as the basis of biblical verse. "In most cases," he observes, "there is an overlapping of several such heterogeneous parallelisms [that is, semantic, syntactic, prosodic, morphological, phonetic, and so on] with a mutual reinforcement so that no single element—meaning, syntax, or stress—may be considered as purely dominant or as purely concomitant." The result is what Hrushovski defines as a "free rhythm," which is to say, "a rhythm based on a cluster of changing principles," but this does not imply, as Kugel would have it, that poetry in the Bible is not a formally distinct mode of expression, for the freedom of the rhythm "is clearly confined within the limits of its poetics." These limits are in part numerically demarcated, as Hrushovski goes on to note: "[Since] by rule no two stresses are permitted to follow each other, . . . each stress dominates a group of two, three, or four syllables; there are two, three, or four such groups in a verset; and two, three, or four parallel versets in a sentence."[7]

The Dynamics of Parallelism

Some analysts, with an eye to the number of stresses in a verset, have sought to detect a system of "meters" in biblical poetry. It is true that in many poems a particular count of stresses in each of the matched versets tends to predominate, the most common combinations being 3:3 and 3:2, but there is little evidence that the counting of stresses was actually observed as a governing norm for a poem, in the way a Greek or Roman poet watched his iambs or hexameters throughout a poem, and so the term meter should probably be abandoned for biblical verse.

The rhythmic and to some extent the syntactic aspects of the system will be invisible in translation, and so in what follows, while assuming the general validity of this account, I will be concentrating on the operation of semantic parallelism. I will also emulate Hrushovski in designating the line-halves, or the line-thirds in the case of triadic parallelism, "versets," because the older scholarly term "hemistich" and the current "colon" (plural "cola") both have misleading links with Greek versification, the latter term also inadvertently calling up associations of intestinal organs or soft drinks. In place of Hrushovski's concept of the "sentence," which seems to me a little problematic to decide on for biblical verse, I will speak simply of the two or three parallel versets constituting a poetic line.

Let us then consider more closely the operation of semantic parallelism as it is illustrated in Lamech's chant. There would seem to be some satisfying feeling of emphasis, for both the speaker and his audience, in stating the same thing twice, with nicely modulated variations. Like rhyme, regular meter, and alliteration in other poetic systems, it is a convention of linguistic "coupling" that contributes to the special unity and to the memorability (literal and figurative) of the utterances,[8] to the sense that they are an emphatic, balanced, and elevated kind of discourse, perhaps ultimately rooted in a magical conception of language as potent performance.

But the recognition of such repetition in biblical verse has unfortunately led to a view of it as essentially a system for the deployment of synonyms or, as it is sometimes put, "thought-rhymes." A characteristic expression of this prevalent understanding of parallelism is the following observation by T. H. Robinson in a standard handbook on biblical poetry: "So the poet goes back to the beginning again, and says the same thing once more, though he may partly or completely change the actual words to avoid monotony."[9] This view has not gained in conviction by being recast conceptually with the apparatus of more recent intellectual trends,

9

as one can see from a lively and ultimately misconceived description of the mechanism in Structuralist terms by Ruth apRoberts in an article entitled "Old Testament Poetry: The Translatable Structure."[10] She proposes that biblical poetry has proved so remarkably translatable because self-translation is the generative principle within the text itself, the way one verset leads to the next, and thus the clear manifestation of the "deep structure" of the text. What this and all the conceptions of biblical parallelism as synonymity assume[11] is a considerable degree of *stasis* within the poetic line: an idea or image or action is evoked in the first verset; then forward movement in the poetic discourse is virtually suspended while the same idea, image, or action is rerun for the patient eye of the beholder, only tricked out in somewhat different stylistic finery. What I should like to propose, and this is the one respect in which my own understanding of the phenomenon is close to James Kugel's, is that a diametrically opposite description of the system— namely, an argument for dynamic movement from one verset to the next—would be much closer to the truth, much closer to the way the biblical poets expected audiences to attend to their words.

Literature, let me suggest, from the simplest folktale to the most sophisticated poetry and fiction and drama, thrives on parallelism, both stylistic and structural, on small scale and large, and could not give its creations satisfying shape without it. But it is equally important to recognize that literary expression abhors complete parallelism, just as language resists true synonymity, usage always introducing small wedges of difference between closely akin terms. This general principle was nicely formulated early in the century by the Russian Formalist critic Viktor Shklovsky in "Art as Technique," an essay that has proved to be one of the seminal texts of modern literary theory: "The perception of disharmony in a harmonious context is important in parallelism. The purpose of parallelism, like the general purpose of imagery, is to transfer the usual perception of an object into the sphere of a new perception— that is, to make a unique semantic modification."[12] What I should like to suggest in the case of the semantic parallelism on which so many lines of biblical verse are constructed is that, with all the evident and at times almost extravagant repetition of elements of meaning from one verset to the next, "semantic modifications" of the sort Shklovsky has in mind are continually occurring. This operation was nicely perceived two centuries ago by J. G. Herder in a response to Bishop Lowth's path-breaking theory, but scholarship by and large has sadly neglected Herder's observation that "the two [parallel] members strengthen, heighten, empower each other."[13]

It may be easiest to see how this dynamics of repetition operates in our poem by working back from the last line to the first. What does a poet do with numbers in semantic parallelism? If the system were really based on a principle of synonymity, one would expect to find pairings on the order of "twelve" and "a dozen," but in fact this never happens. The invariable rule, as scholars have long recognized without making the connection with an underlying poetic principle, is that if you introduce a number in the first verset, you have to go up in the second verset, either by adding one to the number or by moving to a decimal multiple of the first number or a decimal multiple plus the number itself. A paradigmatic instance occurs in Moses' valedictory song (Deut. 32:30): "How could one pursue a thousand / and two put a myriad to flight?" Thus the logic of numbers in parallel versets is not equivalence but an assertion of *a fortiori*, "how much more so," and this impulse to intensification is also the motor force in thousands of lines of biblical poetry where no numbers are present.

The first verset in the concluding line of Lamech's chant rehearses a grimly monitory notion apparently already proverbial in this world of dim beginnings—that sevenfold vengeance would be exacted for the murder of Cain. The second verset uses that piece of familiar lore as the springboard for a more startling statement—that Lamech's vengeance will be seventy-seven-fold. It should be observed, moreover, that the pattern of intensification is not limited to the two versets but is interlinear, which, as we shall see, is an extremely common feature of biblical verse and will have important implications for the structure of longer poems. The logic, that is, of "how much more so" goes back from the numbers of the third line to the "wound" and "bruising" of the second line. Manifold vengeance, we recall, was to be exacted for the *killing* of Cain, but Lamech's boast is that he will be avenged many times more than Cain for a mere injury. There is clearly also a movement of intensification between the two versets of the second line, although with such scanty context for the poem we may be a little uncertain about what precisely is involved. Some commentators have construed "boy" as "young man," which would yield a meaning something like this: it is not any man I have killed, but a young fellow at the height of his powers. The trouble with this reading is that *yeled* in the sense of "young man" occurs quite rarely and mostly in later biblical usage; in the vast majority of instances it means "child," or even "newborn baby," with a stress on the tenderness and vulnerability of the child. The more philologically likely, if also more morally unpalatable, meaning—Lamech is, after all, an archaic figure, long before the Mosaic dispensation!—would be: there is no limit to my vengeance; I have killed not only a man for wounding me but even a child for bruising me. I have tentatively assumed, perhaps quite falsely, that *ḥaburah*, "bruise," is less serious than *petz'a*, "wound," and so participates in the heightening of assertion from the first verset to the second. This is a minor illustration of how we sometimes cannot be certain about the precise differences between semantically related terms, but I would like to emphasize a general principle that would indicate there is no absolute necessity to insist on a differentiation here: it is by no means expected or obligatory that every paired set of terms in parallel versets reflect development or intensification. Poets may sometimes choose to step up all the parallel terms in a line, but in the majority of instances it is rather one key set of matched terms that carries the burden of development.

Development of what and for what? The manifold and necessarily qualified answer to that question will take us to the heart of biblical poetics, but before broaching the general issue, I should like to move upward to the opening line of Lamech's chant, which, in contrast to the second and third lines, would seem perfectly to confirm the synonymous conception of parallelism: "Ada and Zilla, hear my voice. / Wives of Lamech, give ear to my speech." Anyone familiar with biblical poetry will recognize this as a formulaic beginning of a poem, following a convention in which the poet/speaker calls attention to his own utterance and invokes an audience—or more often a witness—for his utterance. (This very convention, by the way, and other formal introductions to poems like "Then Moses sang" and "He [Balaam] took up his theme and spoke" are clear indications that the original framers of the lines regarded them and ostentatiously presented them as poetry, set off in its formal organizing principles from the surrounding prose.) The line is formulaic not merely in invoking a convention of poetic beginnings but also in being made up of conventionally fixed pairs: voice/speech, listen/give ear.

The presence of such fixed pairs in biblical verse, a good many of them apparently inherited from the same Syro-Palestinian tradition reflected in Ugaritic poetry, several hundred years earlier than most of the biblical texts, has led some scholars to conclude that the poems were oral-formulaic compositions. That is, the fixed pairings were ready-made rhythmic-semantic units that the improvising bard could build with as his Homeric counterpart is presumed to have introduced formulaic epithets as part of a repertory of formulaic devices that helped him retell his familiar tale in regular hexameters. There are several intrinsic problems in this hypothesis, but even if it could be demonstrated to obtain for what we know of the Syro-Palestinian poetic tradition antecedent to the Bible, the elaboration and variegation of supposedly fixed pairs in biblical verse lead one to suspect that oral composition was at most a fact of the prehistory of our texts. A telling difference is that the *sequence* of bracketed terms appears to have been fixed in Ugaritic, whereas biblical poetry reveals a good deal of flexibility in this regard as well as in the substitution of a new term in ostensibly formulaic pairings. In any case, the idea of stock pairings should not lead to the misconception—a misconception, in fact, for oral-formulaic as well as other kinds of verse—that there was something automatic and mechanical in the way the Hebrew poets bracketed synonyms.[14]

But are they ever altogether synonyms, even in a formulaic case like the one before us? In the strictest sense, of course, no language has entirely true synonyms, and imaginative writers in both poetry and prose, by virtue of their necessary sensitivity to their chosen medium, have always been keenly conscious of this. Six inches and half a foot may be exact quantitative equivalents, but they are not true synonyms, as the eighteenth-century novelist Tobias Smollett was perfectly aware when in *Peregrine Pickle* he described a character with a grotesque face overshadowed by a nose half a foot long—which for the affective reader is a good sight longer than six inches. In other words, what is constantly exploited in literary expression is not merely the definable referendum of the word but also the frame of reference to which the word attaches (in the example from Smollett, feet as against inches), the related semantic fields toward which it points, the level of diction that it invokes, the specialized uses to which it may be put. The predominant pattern of biblical poetry is to move from a standard term in the first verset to a more literary or highfalutin term in the second verset. That happens in our formulaic line (from *qol*, "voice," to *'imrah*, "speech," or, perhaps better, "utterance," and from *shema'an*, "hear," to *ha'zena*, "give ear," though elsewhere, in keeping with what I said about the flexibility in the use of conventional formulas, "give ear" precedes "hear"). Admittedly, there are no remarkable consequences here of this slight shift in diction. Nevertheless, the general pattern in which this movement from standard to literary term participates is an especially instructive one, and I should like to pursue it before returning to Lamech's wives, whom I, in proper patriarchal fashion, have left standing by their tent, still sadly uncommented on.

One might assume that a literary synonym is simply a fancier or more *recherché* way of saying the same thing, and I would guess that this could be the case in some of the pairings of this sort we find in the Bible—as, say, in some of the uses of *kos/quba'at* (cup/chalice), *ra'oh/ shur* (see/behold), *rosh/qodqod* (head/poll). But the more one looks at this phenomenon of "doubling" ordinary words by poetic equivalents, the more one sees a dynamic of meaning emerging from one verset to the next. Thus the Psalmist (Ps. 88:12–13): "Will Your steadfast care be told in the grave, / Your constancy in Perdition? // Will Your wonders be known in the darkness, / Your bounty in the land of oblivion?" In these two lines, as is quite typical, one set of matched terms remains stable, being a complementary series of linked concepts: steadfast care, constancy, wonders, bounty. The other set of matched terms, on the other hand, carries forward a progressive imaginative realization of death: from the familiar and localized "grave" to *'avadon,* "Perdition," a poetic synonym that is quasi-mythic and grimly explicit about the fate of extinction the grave holds; then, to another everyday word, "darkness," which is, however, a sensory realization of the experience of death, and then to a second poetic term for the underworld, "the land of oblivion," which summarizes and generalizes the series, giving emphatic closure to the idea that death is a realm where human beings are utterly forgotten and extinct, and where there can be no question of God's greatness being recalled. We ought to note as well in passing that the parallelism is conspicuously interlinear (in fact, the line that precedes these two is also part of the pattern), another very frequent feature of sequences of lines, despite the claim some have made that a line of biblical poetry is semantically self-contained and prosodically end-stopped.

Let us look at a second pair of lines, where we can observe how the movement from ordinary to literary term is associated with an allied developmental pattern. Here, too, we will see emphatic interlinear parallelism, which goes on to an intriguing third line, but I must resist the temptation to use the third line as well because it hinges on a word found only here that is uncertain in meaning. The verses are from Isaiah 59:9–10: "We hope for light and look! darkness, / for effulgence, and in gloom we go. // We grope like blind men a wall, / like the eyeless we grope." The first line follows the pattern of moving from ordinary to poetic term for both the nouns in each verset—from simple "light" and "darkness" to the more literary *negohot* and *'afelot,* "effulgence" and "gloom," which moreover are cast in the feminine plural form, elsewhere used to give nouns an abstract or adverbial force, and which seems to endow the words here (I would guess) with an aura of vastness. The second line intensifies the assertion of the first line by making the outer darkness an inner darkness, the total incapacity to see, and transforming the general image of walking in the dark of the preceding verset into a more concrete picture of a blind man groping his way along a wall. The "blind men" of the first verset become "no-eyes" (*'eyn 'eynaim*) in the second verset, which is the substitution not of a term from literary diction but of a kind of kenning or epithet. The effect, however, is like that in the move from "grave" to "Perdition"—a realization of the first term (or, as Shklovsky would have put it, a defamiliarization of it) that calls our attention to its essential meaning.

Again and again, the biblical poets will introduce a common noun in the first verset and match it with a kind of explanatory epithet—or, more interesting, a metaphorical substitution—in the second verset. Sometimes, the substitution would appear to be rather automatic and not particularly strong in expressive effect, as in these two separate lines from the prophet Joel (Joel 1:5 and 13): "Rise, drunkards, and weep, / and wail all *drinkers of wine.*" "Gird yourselves and keen, you priests, / wail, you *ministrants of the altar.*" In other instances, it is hard to be sure whether the term in the second verset represents a "realization" of its counterpart in the first, because we don't know to what extent a particular kenning may have become an automatized substitution for the Hebrew listener. Thus, when Micah (6:7) says, "Shall I give my firstborn for my trespass, / *the fruit of my loins* for my own sins?" perhaps the kenning of the second verset communicates nothing more than the idea of offspring, though I would be inclined to suspect that it reinforces the sense of intimate bodily connection between parent and child. A similar pairing occurs in Job (15:14), where, however, the likelihood of dynamic progression from the first term to the second may be somewhat higher. "What is man that he should be guiltless, / that he should be in the right, *he born-of-woman?*" At any rate, the replacement of the general term *'enosh,* "man," by the kenning *yelud 'ishah,* "born-of-woman," would seem to stress man's creaturely frailty, his dependence upon the cycle of biological reproduction, which fits in with the emphasis the speaker (Eliphaz) goes on to make, that the very heavens are guilty before God, and how much more so lowly man.

A kenning, one recent study has suggested,[15] is a riddle transformed from the interrogative into the declarative, which one can see by turning it back into a riddle: What is a whale-road? The sea. What is fruit of the loins? A child. Kennings are minimal metaphors, usually, as in the examples I have cited, more or less self-explanatory. In other words, the metaphorical vehicle of a kenning may often have rather limited saliency in relation to the tenor to which it refers. Sometimes, however, either context or the intrinsic formulation of the kenning or a combination of the two will lead to a greater actualization of the metaphor, and in such instances in biblical poetry the substitution of kenning for literal term in parallel versets is manifestly an instrument for the forceful development of meaning that I have described. In Jacob's blessing of Judah, for example, we encounter these parallel terms: "He washes his garment in wine, / in *the blood of grapes* his cloak" (Gen. 49:11). However much "blood of grapes" might have been a formulaic equivalent of "wine," going back to Ugaritic precedents, it does not call up the same image or associations as the prosaic term. It immediately brings to mind the crushing of the grapes (as opposed to the finished product, wine), something reinforced in context because the preceding line has twice mentioned a vine. The paradoxical intimation of violence embedded in a pastoral image is also exploited in the poem: the already extravagant action of laundering in wine (as a demonstration of affluence?) threatens to become, without quite becoming, a still more extreme action of laundering in blood, and this suggestion is contextually reinforced by the following line, which sets in counterpoint wine-bright and milk-white. The effect, in any event, is clearly to introduce a "new perception" through the device of parallelism.

Finally, one encounters in biblical poetry this sort of replacement of a literal term not merely by a kenning or explanatory epithet but by an original metaphor. Let me cite just one elaborate instance, where a metaphor is worked out through three lines. The passage is from Jeremiah 48:11:

Moab has been placid from youth,	settled in his lees.
Never emptied from vessel to vessel,	in exile never gone.
And so his taste has kept,	his fragrance has not changed.

The elegance of the formal structure is also a subtle instrument for the development of meaning. The first line moves from the literal statement, Moab's state of unruffled security, to a metaphorical elaboration, the settled lees. The next line reverses the order of literal and figurative so as to develop the metaphor—"never emptied from vessel to vessel"—

before returning to explain its historical tenor, that Moab has never been exiled. Thus the two lines are built on a chiastic structure of literal/figurative//figurative/literal. The poet/prophet, moreover, plays with the ambiguity of whether the figurative condition of being like unstirred wine is a good or a bad thing. The first two lines, beginning with a possibly ambiguous word, *sha'anan* ("placid," "secure," but sometimes with overtones of "complacent"), and the image of the lees, which are undrinkable, might lead us to a negative inference. The third line, devoted entirely to a further elaboration of the figure with no literal assertion, would appear to turn this inference around by stressing that it is a happy circumstance for wine to be undisturbed, as all its desirable qualities are thus preserved. This sets us up (perhaps in a way inviting us momentarily to adopt the Moabite perspective) for a final reversal, as the prophet will proceed to pronounce grim doom on Moab, now seen in fact to have been complacently settled into its lees and foolishly oblivious to the imminent smashing of vessels that is to befall it. One sees that the progression from literal to figurative and back to literal again, far from being a matter of juggling semantic equivalents, can become the means for setting in motion a delicate dialectic interplay of meanings.

Let me emphasize that the cognate patterns of movement from prosaic to poetic and literal to figurative locution are simply one recurrent instance of a more general developmental impulse of biblical verse, and it will be important to get a bearing on some of its other major manifestations. All this has taken us rather far afield from Lamech's simple chant, but I have been concerned to show that the underlying principle of poetics that could issue in these rather complicated examples is already detectable in our first three-line poem.

The time has now come to return to Ada and Zilla and say something about what may have happened to those two neglected ladies between the first verset and the second. By now it should be evident that they fall under the rule of substitution of epithet for simple designation: having been addressed by their proper names in the first verset, they are called "wives of Lamech" in the second half of the line. (Elsewhere, a person's name in the initial verset is followed by his patronymic in the second verset.) The substitution seems automatic enough, but I would like to raise the possibility, as a kind of limiting case of this definition of semantic parallelism, that even here there might be at least a minor "semantic modification" in the introduction of the parallel term. Biblical narrative, we might remind ourselves, is exquisitely deliberate in its choice of relational epithets: Michal is called the daughter of Saul precisely when the narrator wants to stress her connection with the jealous king and is referred to as the wife of David when that link is thematically appropriate. It is certainly possible that the poets exercised similar selectivity, though I must admit that in the example before us it is hard to think of another relational epithet for Ada and Zilla—unless they, like Leah and Rachel, had the same father—that would have worked rhythmically. Be that as it may, it does not seem far-fetched to hear some new emphasis in the second verset. First, Lamech calls Ada and Zilla by name; then he summons them as wives of Lamech, and it is in their capacity as his wives that they are invited to attend to his chant—for this is, after all, a song of triumph, and he wants them as his consorts to recognize what a man of insuperable strength and implacable principle they have in their husband. Admittedly, my attempt to recover a differentiation of meaning in the vocatives that begin Lamech's poem could be a wrong guess, but the evidence of line after line of biblical verse suggests that we are too quick to infer automatic and formulaic rhetorical gesture of repetition when more than that is going on. In any case, my purpose in scrutinizing each set of paired terms in this rather rudimentary instance of biblical verse is not to offer exegesis but to suggest how precisely the flow of meaning is channeled in the system of poetic parallelism.

Let me now sketch out a more general account of the related varieties of semantic development that typically occur in biblical parallelism. My understanding of what happens semantically is in some respects similar to that of James Kugel, an indefatigable opponent of the synonymous conception of parallelism, who speaks of the *"emphatic* character" of the second verset, its function "as a kind of strengthening and reinforcing." His generalization about the relation of second verset to first is apt, if far from exhaustive: "B was connected to A, had something in common with it, but was not expected to be (or regarded as) mere restatement . . . for it is the dual nature of B both to come *after* A and thus to add to it, often particularizing, defining, or expanding the meaning, and yet to harken [sic] back to A and in an obvious way connect to it."[16] Before I go on to amplify and illustrate this general pattern, a couple of important qualifications should be made. Kugel speaks of A and B rather than of bicola or hemistichs or versets because he is unwilling to grant that these two members constitute a line of poetry. Once one recognizes that there is a formal system of biblical versification distinct from the prose, the nuances of relation between parallel formulations come into sharper focus and, equally important, it is easier to see the interplay between lines as well as the possibilities of relation between the internal structure of the line and the structure of the poem. The formula, moreover, of B "going beyond" A, as Kugel puts it, is extended by him to include all those lines of biblical poetry in which there is no semantic parallelism between first and second verset (to offer my own example, Psalm 137:2, "On the willows there / we hung our lyres."), whereas to me it seems less forced to assume with Hrushovski that such instances are manifestations of the "free rhythm" of biblical versification in which the semantic component of the parallelism is dropped. In fact, the relatively late poet who composed Psalm 137 virtually avoids semantic parallelism throughout the poem, and when the relation between versets turns out to be one between adverbial phrase and main clause, or between subject and object, it hardly makes sense to speak of the second verset as a "going beyond" or a "seconding" of the first.

In the abundant instances, however, in which semantic parallelism does occur in a line, the characteristic movement of meaning is one of heightening or intensification (as in the paradigmatic case of numerals), of focusing, specification, concretization, even what could be called dramatization. There is, of course, a certain overlap among these categories, but my concern is to point to the direction in which the reader can look for meaning, not to undertake an exercise in taxonomy. The rule of thumb, then—and in all of what follows I shall be talking, necessarily, about rule of thumb, not invariable law—is that the general term occurs in the first verset and a more specific instance of the general category in the second verset. "Your granaries will be filled with *abundance*, / with *new wine* your vats will burst" (Prov. 3:10). (The verbs in this line reflect a movement not of specification but of intensification, from being filled to bursting.) "His heart is as solid *as stone*, / as solid as *the nether millstone*" (Job 41:16).

If the first term is spatial or geographical, the second is usually a smaller spatial entity contained within the first (thus an instance of what I call focusing): "I shall put an end *in the cities of Judea* / and *in the streets of Jerusalem* // to the sound of gladness and joy, / the sound of bridegroom and bride" (Jer. 7:34). (The second line, of course, reflects the movement from general category to specific instance.) "Who gives rain *to the earth* / and sends water over *the fields*" (Job 5:10). (If the sequence of "rain" and "water" here does not follow the pattern of specific term after general, that is because the water in the fields is the *result* of the rain, and the relation between process and consequence of process often obtains between first verset and second.) Deutero-Isaiah, in a beautiful piece of interlinear parallelism, twice in succession illustrates this tendency to offer first the spatial field and then something contained within it: "I made *the earth* / and *man* upon it I created. // I, my hands stretched out *the heavens,* / and *all their host* I mustered" (Is. 45:12).

Another strategy, which illustrates the connection of all this to the movement from literal to figurative that we reviewed earlier, is to use first the general term and then a synecdochic substitution, which is still another variety of focusing: "Your *lot* you will throw in with us, / let us all have *one purse* together" (Prov. 1:14). Not surprisingly, in many instances it is hard to separate the parallelism of specification from the parallelism of intensification because as the general term is transformed into a specific instance or a concrete image, the idea becomes more pointed, more forceful. Thus Isaiah (17:1), in an initial verset, announces, "Look, Damascus *will cease to be a city,*" then goes on to say, "will become *a heap of ruins.*" One finds elsewhere this pattern of a verb or verbal phrase paralleled by a nominal or adjectival phrase that is a concretization or crystallization of the verbal process: "She *weeps on* through the night / and *her tears are on her cheek*" (Lam. 1:2). "My son, *eat* goodly honey, / nectar is *sweet on your palate*" (Prov. 24:13). Perhaps more commonly, a verb appearing in the first verset will be matched with one in the second verset that is more specific, more extravagant, or even explanatory of the initial verb. Here is a two-line example from that most elegant of biblical poets, Deutero-Isaiah: "God *has redeemed* His servant Jacob, / and they *did not thirst* in the wastelands where He led them. // Water from a rock He *made flow* for them. / He *split* the rock and water *gushed*" (Is. 48:20–21).[17] Note how the interlinear parallelism carries on this movement of specification in what amounts to an explanatory chain: What does it mean that God "redeemed" Israel (first verset)? They were not thirsty in the desert (second verset). How could they not have been thirsty?—because He made water flow from a rock (third verset). How did He make water flow from a rock?—by splitting it so the water gushed (fourth verset).

The greater specificity of the verbal activity in the second verset can be a way of dramatically realizing the initial verset, as is evident in these lines from Isaiah or, more compactly, in Balaam's formula of poetic self-introduction: "Who *beholds visions* from the Almighty, / *falls down with eyes unveiled*" (Num. 24:4), where the general visionary capacity is transformed into an image of ecstatic seizure. And not infrequently the heightened specificity becomes a hyperbolic stepping-up of the initial verb: "Face to the ground they *will bow to you,* / they *will lick the dust of your feet*" (Is. 49:23). A similar parallelism occurs in Psalm 72:9: "Before him the desert dwellers *will kneel,* / his enemies *will lick the dust.*" Job 30:10 offers another instance of the bracketing of two physical actions expressing the same relation, with the second action more extreme than the first: "They *despised* me, *drew away* from me, / and from my face they *did not hold back their spittle.*" Or, the movement toward the extreme may be coordinated with the characteristic swing from general to specific and from literal to figurative, as in Job 29:23: "They *waited* for me as for rain, / they *held their mouths wide open* for the showers." Here, the simile "as for rain" of the first verset is carried into the verb of the second verset and turns the activity of waiting into the hyperbolic gaping of the mouth for drops of water.

I have illustrated the movement of heightening or focusing through verbs and their attendant adverbial phrases, but other syntactic configurations and parts of speech can be used to the same effect. A noun in the first verset can be focused adjectivally in the second verset: "For I was a *son* to my father, / a *tender only child* to my mother" (Prov. 4:3). (In the Hebrew "only child" is adjectival in form.) A pair of nouns where focusing occurs may be bracketed with a pair of verbs that reflect intensification: "For You *smote* all my foes **on the cheek,** / **the teeth** of the wicked You *smashed*" (Ps. 3:8). The pattern of a large spatial image followed by a smaller entity contained within it may be coordinated with the tendency to concretization, creating a similar kind of mutual reinforcement within the line: "They *will lay waste* his **land,** / his **cities** *will be razed without inhabitants*" (Jer. 2:15). Intensification can also be achieved by the introduction of a simile or metaphor in the second verset that brings out the full force of meaning of an image occurring in the first verset. "You will smash them with an iron mace, / *like a potter's vessel* shatter them" (Ps. 2:9). Here, the simile of the fragile vessel compounds the violence of the initial image of the iron mace in an almost startling way. Or, an image may be taken to the "second power" in a similar fashion by introducing a hyperbole in the second verset: "Your light will shine in darkness, / and your gloom *like noon*" (Is. 58: 10). This last instance illustrates with special deftness the raising of meaning to the second power: the naturalistic shining of light in darkness of the first verset becomes a supernatural event (in rhetorical terms, a figure compounding a figure) when Israel's very gloom is to shine like noon; and the progression is reinforced by an implied temporal image from dawn to midday because the verb for "shine" in the first verset, *zaraḥ*, is associated with the beaming of dawn.

All that I have said is meant to orient the reader of biblical poetry, but I do not want to mislead by overstating the case. In a few very exceptional instances, one actually encounters a reverse movement from specific to general or from figurative to literal, as in "Their tongue is *a sharpened arrow*, / they *speak deceit*" (Jer. 9:7) and "*My innards seethed* and were unquiet, / days of *affliction greeted me*" (Job 30:27). But these instances are so rare (I have been able to find only half a dozen clear-cut examples) that they hardly disprove the general rule. Much more commonly, however, there are semantically parallel versets where only tortured ingenuity would infer development and where it looks as though the line has really been shaped on a principle of relatively static synonymity. "A false witness will not get off, / a lying testifier will not escape" (Prov. 19:5). "Did my lips speak iniquity, / did my tongue utter deceit?" (Job 27:4). (It is instructive, however, for the general case of parallelism that the line from Proverbs just cited also appears in a variant form, Prov. 19:9, in which the change of the final verb makes it a paradigmatic instance of inter-verset intensification: "A false witness will not get off, / a lying testifier *will perish*.") Static parallelism may work with close synonyms, as in these two examples, or with a combination of synonyms and complementary terms (often formulaically linked), as in this line from Isaiah (10:2): "For widows to be their booty, / and they plunder orphans." But even in many instances such as these the stasis proves to be relative. In this line from Isaiah, for example, though "booty" and "plunder" are bound synonymous terms, only the second verset has a transitive form of the verb. It is worth noting that the bracketing of complementary notions—that is, two coordinate items belonging to the same category, like "green pastures" and "still waters"—is at least as common a form of static parallelism as synonymity.

There would seem to be differences between one poet and the next and one poem and the next, and perhaps also between different periods, in regard to the preference for heightening and focusing within semantic parallelism. In some texts, such as Moses' valedictory song and the Book of Job, this intensifying tendency of biblical verse is entirely dominant; elsewhere, as in some of the Psalms, the poet seems to have preferred relatively static semantic parallelism. Interestingly, however, where static parallelism prevails, one may discover that developmental movement is projected from the line to the larger structure of the poem, as in Psalm

145, where the poet moves through a series of relatively synonymous lines in a progression from the general praise of God to an affirmation of His compassion, His kingship, His daily providing for those who truly call unto Him. And, as one might expect, many of the poets are alive to the aesthetic possibilities of counterpointing a predominant intensification or specification of meaning in parallelism with lines founded on synonymity or balanced complementarity. In any case, the system of versification as a whole definitely encourages dynamic interplay between versets in which feelings get stronger, images sharper, actions more powerful or more extreme. This predominant tendency of biblical poetry has important consequences in regard to both what listeners or readers are expected to attend to within the line and how the poem is articulated as a developing structure from line to line. That process of articulation deserves careful attention in its own right, but before we undertake that, it may be instructive to look at one final recurring pattern that takes place within the line and that illustrates how the formal constraints of the system are used to produce a certain movement of meaning and imaginative experience.

In showing how semantic modifications are introduced through seemingly equivalent terms, I have said nothing of the role of literal repetition from one verset to the next, although a couple of our examples (Is. 59: 10 and Job 41:16) exhibit such repetition. The most common pattern in this regard is one of incremental repetition: something is stated; then it is restated verbatim with an added element. The Song of Deborah makes repeated use of this device: "Curse Meroz, says the Lord's angel. / Curse, O curse *its inhabitants. //* For they came not to the aid of the Lord, / to the aid of the Lord *among the warriors"* (Judg. 5:23). This pattern in itself illustrates the general tendency I have been describing, for as the restatement is made, an emphasis of meaning is introduced in the increment that was no more than implicit in the original statement.

But far more prevalent in biblical poetry than incremental repetition is what might be characterized as "hidden" repetition—that is, the very common maneuver of ellipsis in which a word in the first verset, usually a verb, governs the parallel clause in the second verset as well. (Very occasionally, one also finds retrospective ellipsis, in which the double-duty term occurs in the second verset rather than in the first.) I would suggest that it is useful to recognize this device as a hidden or implied repetition because despite its prosodic difference from incremental repetition, it is closely related to the latter in the way it is used to introduce an increment of meaning.

Now, the conventional scholarly description of what occurs in elliptical parallelism is that the semantically corresponding term in the second verset is a "ballast variant" of its counterpart in the initial verset. For example: "He suckled him with honey *from a rock* / and oil *from the flinty stone*" (Deut. 32:13). That is, since the verb *vayeiniqeihu*, "He suckled him," does double duty for the second verset, a whole rhythmic unit with its governing stress is absent from the second verset and so must be replaced by a kind of periphrastic substitution for "rock" *(selʿa)* that will restore the otherwise lacking accent, and thus we have *ḥalmish-tzur* ("the flinty stone"). Such an account strikes me as a serious misconception of what goes on in lines like this and is therefore a warrant for misreading them. The parallel term in the second verset, as I have sought to show through a wide variety of examples, is by no means merely a "variant" of its counterpart, and it is certainly not "ballast," that is, deadweight or padding brought in to fill out the metrical requirement of the line.[18] In the example just quoted from Deuteronomy, "flinty stone" follows the rule of a specific instance of the category coming after the general term and by so doing effects an intensification or focusing of meaning. The first verset might even be read "naturalistically," as a hyperbolic poetic allusion to the discovery of honeycombs in rocky crags, but no such construal is allowable in the second verset, both because here it is oil that is provided and because the focusing effect of "flinty stone" leaves no alternative to a recognition of the miraculous character of the event.

Let me spell out the general principle involved. Every literary tradition converts the formal limitations of its own medium into an occasion for artistic expression: the artist, in fact, might be defined as a person who thrives on realizing new possibilities within formal limitations. In a system of semantically corresponding versets, it is understandable that quite frequently a single verb or noun would do double duty for two parallel utterances. But from the viewpoint of the poet, what is accomplished through this simple syntactic maneuver is a freeing of space in the second verset (through the absence of one whole rhythmic unit out of two or three or four), which can then be used to elaborate or sharpen meaning. This freeing of space, moreover, nicely accords with the formal focusing effect of the absence of the verb in the second verset, which has the consequence of *isolating for attention* this second object of the verb. Often what happens is that the second term, where the poet has room for introducing a compound form or a compact cluster of nouns or nouns and qualifiers, is an elaboration of the first term that makes its meaning more vividly present to the imagination, as in this prophetic image of the return from exile: "They shall renew ruined cities, / the desolations of generations untold" (Is. 61:4). The general idea, that is, of cities laid waste becomes an emphatic picture of ruins that have stood in their desolation from time immemorial. In some cases, the second, elaborated term is a striking dramatization of the first, as in another line from Moses' valedictory song: "He found him in a desert land, / in an empty howling waste" (Deut. 32:10). It is clear that the general geographical indication "desert land" ('*eretz midbar*) undergoes a forceful realization in the second verset, with its intimation of howling winds, jackals, or whatever; its onomatopoeic alliteration, *yeleil yeshimon;* and its oblique allusion to the primal void and chaos *(tohu)* in the word rendered here as "empty."

Elsewhere, the room opened up for elaboration through ellipsis in the second verset leads to a kind of development that might almost be thought of as incipient narrative. "The ox knows its owner," Isaiah (1:3) pronounces, and then goes on in the second verset, "the ass its master's crib." Now, there may be a progression here on an axis of increasing closeness of connection from the ox, a beast of the field, to the ass, which you ride and which might be tethered at your door. What is clear, however, is the difference in *concreteness* and thematic insistence between simply knowing a master and knowing a master's crib, the feeding-trough through which the palpable benefits flow from owner to owned. The image in the second verset of the ass at the crib begins to look like a miniature illustrative dramatic scene.

Or again, in one of those vivid warnings in the Book of Proverbs against the wiles of the seductress, we find this line: "To save you from a foreign woman, / from an alien woman who talks smoothly" (Prov. 2:16). (In my translation I have not used the more felicitous "smooth-talking," because I wanted to preserve the verbal force of the Hebrew, and I have rendered her foreignness literally to keep the synonymity, though the reference is actually to her sexual morality, not to her national identity.) Since the verb "to save" does double duty for both versets, the poet has space in the second verset to make the dangerous temptress the subject of a brief subordinate clause. We see her, that is, in both the literal and the figurative sense of the term, going into action, and thus we begin to understand why it is that the young man who is addressed in the poem must be warned away from her. This "going into action" that is the elaboration of the parallel term in our elliptical line then *generates* a recognizable narrative in the next three lines (Prov. 2:17–19), a monitory tale in which the forbidden woman, whether because of the addictive dissipation she offers or the venereal diseases she may conceal, becomes a mythic figure of the all-consuming female:

Who leaves the friend of her youth,	the pact of her God forgets.
Her house inclines toward death,	her steps to the shades.
All who come to her will not return,	will never regain the paths of life.

The "smooth-talking," that is, of our first line, which at first might have seemed like mere adjectival "filler," proves to be a characteristic action introducing a compact narrative sequence: the woman's initial betrayal of husband and God, the dangers of her home and company, the irrevocable fate of those who fall victim to her.

By this point, the consideration of the dynamics of the line have brought us to the brink of two more "macroscopic" aspects of biblical poetics: How do elements of narrative emerge in a verse form that is used overwhelmingly for nonnarrative purposes, and what sorts of larger structures are produced, or at least encouraged, by this kind of poetic line? Each of these issues deserves separate treatment.

II

From Line to Story

PERHAPS the greatest peculiarity of biblical poetry among the literatures of the ancient Mediterranean world is its seeming avoidance of narrative. The Hebrew writers used verse for celebratory song, dirge, oracle, oratory, prophecy, reflective and didactic argument, liturgy, and often as a heightening or summarizing inset in the prose narratives—but only marginally and minimally to tell a tale. This absence of narrative is all the more striking against the background of the surrounding and ante-cedent literatures of the ancient Near East that have been uncovered by archaeological research. To cite the most apposite example, the literature of the city of Ugarit, on the Mediterranean coast of present-day Syria, written until about 1300 B.C.E. in a language closely cognate to biblical Hebrew and according to the same general conventions of poetic paral-lelism, includes long verse narratives that have recognizably epic features: in an interplay of narration and dialogue, the formal burden of the poetry is the telling of a traditional tale; and the narrative tempo is leisurely enough to allow for detailed descriptions of feasts, of hand-to-hand combat, even to some degree of the physical appearance of the actors, human and (for the most part) divine.

There is nothing like this in the Hebrew Bible, and supposedly "epic" elements like the historical psalms (Psalms 78, 105, 106) are actually exceptions that confirm the rule, for they turn out to be versified summaries or catechistic rehearsals of Israelite history, with no narrative *realization* of the events invoked, their intelligibility dependent on the audience's detailed knowledge of the events. Even the rare biblical poems that have explicit narrative segments, such as the Song of the Sea and the Song of Deborah, are not, strictly speaking, narrative poems, because they lack the defining feature of independent narrative—exposition—

27

and instead respond to an event or set of events presumably already known to the audience through other means.[1] Although it is not very likely that the biblical writers specifically knew the Ugaritic corpus, there are persuasive grounds for concluding that a good many of them were familiar with a now lost Canaanite literature to which Ugaritic essentially belongs: biblical poetry not only repeats the system of parallelism and dozens of actual word-pairings found in the Ugaritic but also abounds in allusions to elements of the Canaanite-Ugaritic myths, and occasionally even borrows a whole line of verse from its pagan predecessors ("For lo, thine enemies, O Baal, for lo, thine enemies shall perish . . .").

It may well be, as the Israeli biblical scholar Shemaryahu Talmon has suggested,[2] that the ancient Hebrew writers generally avoided verse narrative precisely because of its associations with pagan mythology. In considering the resourcefulness of prose in biblical narrative, I have had occasion to propose that there may also have been a positive attraction of the prose medium for the Hebrew teller of tales: the suppleness and subtlety of prose as it was handled by the biblical writers made possible a more nuanced and purposefully ambiguous representation of human character, liberated from the fixed roles, the hieratic and hyperbolic perspectives, of ancient Near Eastern verse narrative.[3]

The perception, however, of this decisive shift of narration from poetry to prose should not lead us to conclude that biblical verse is chiefly a poetry of assertion and reassertion, "purified" of narrative elements. On the contrary, I would contend that the narrative impulse, for the most part withdrawn from the prominent structural and generic aspects of the poems, often resurfaces in their more minute articulations, from verset to verset within the line and from one line to the next. Recognizing the operation of such a narrative impulse in the poems may help us see their liveliness more fully, may help us understand the links in modes of expression between the typical nonnarrative poems and the occasional poems with explicit narrative materials. Before looking at how these principles might work in the texts, let me briefly recapitulate the description I have proposed of semantic parallelism.

Following Benjamin Hrushovski's cogent account of biblical prosody as a "free rhythm" in which, within fixed quantitative limits, there are shifting parallelisms of meaning, accentual stress, and syntax, with a coincidence of all three elements of parallelism always possible but by no means obligatory,[4] I would observe that semantic parallelism, though sometimes actually avoided by poets either locally, for reasons dictated by context, or even throughout a poem, remains a very prominent feature of most biblical verse. Prevalent notions of the second verset of a line as an "echoing" or "variant" of the first verset involve several difficulties, one of which is a failure to explain how the poet in his series of allegedly synonymous, end-stopped utterances develops the momentum to move from line to line—how, in other words, the poem has a structure that is more than a jerky progression from one repetition to the next. If, however, one recognizes that the semantic orientation of the system of apparent repetitions—let us say, cautiously, in two-thirds of the cases— is toward a focusing, a heightening, a concretization, a development of meaning, it is possible to see that movement generated between versets is then carried on from line to line into the structure of the poem. In a preliminary way, I would propose that there are two fundamental kinds of structure in biblical poems, both of them following from what happens between versets within the line. On the one hand, one frequently encounters, especially in the Prophets and Job, a structure of intensification, a sort of crescendo development, in which certain images and ideas introduced in the first parallel versets—they often may be binary oppositions—are stepped up from line to line and brought to a certain climax. On the other hand, a good many poems are worked out through a consequentiality of images and ideas that is incipiently narrative and may include brief sequences of explicit narrative development.

In order to establish a broader and more shaded picture of the variety and interplay of semantic relations between versets, I should like to quote in full one relatively long biblical poem, David's thanksgiving or victory hymn. Of course, no single poem in a variegated corpus can be entirely typical, but I have chosen this text in particular because it is not stylistically one-sided in its handling of semantic parallelism and illustrates a range of possibilities in its use of the convention. The poem is duplicated, with certain prominent textual variants, between Psalm 18 and 2 Samuel 22, but though the version in Psalms offers at least a couple of attractive readings at difficult junctures, it is somewhat less compact than the version in 2 Samuel, containing certain elements that look suspiciously like glosses, and so I will translate from 2 Samuel 22 as the probably more authentic text. I shall use the following typographical symbols to make efficiently clear the shifting semantic relations between versets: = synonymity; ⊜ synonymity with verbatim repetition; { } complementarity; > focusing, heightening, intensification, specification; → consequentiality. "Consequentiality," I am aware, is a concept that requires some explaining, but that will be the burden of much of my general analysis of the movement from line to story. In just a few instances I have superimposed two symbols, and of course there is no reason why a semantic relation cannot be partly one thing and partly another. In one case I have left a question mark because the relation between versets did not seem to me decidable, perhaps as a result of a philological problem in the line. Since our concern here is with poetic lines, the numeration I offer is according to lines and does not reflect the traditional verse numbers, there being fifty-one verses in the accepted division of this chapter but fifty-three lines of poetry as I scan them.

1	The Lord is my crag and my fortress	=>	and my deliverer.
2	God my rock where I shelter	=	my shield, my saving horn.
3	My stronghold and my refuge,	>	my savior, Who saves me from havoc.
4	Praised I called the Lord,	→	and from my enemies I was saved.
5	For the breakers of death washed round me,	>	the torrents of the underworld terrified me.
6	The snares of the Pit encircled me,	=	the traps of death sprung on me.
7	In my strait I called to the Lord,	=	to my God I called.
8	From His abode He heard my voice,	>	my cry in His ears.
9	The earth heaved and shuddered,	{ }	heaven's foundations shook, →

they heaved, for He was incensed.

10	Smoke went up from His nostrils,	→	consuming fire from His mouth, →

coals blazed forth from Him.

11	He bent the heavens, came down,	→	dense mist beneath His feet.
12	Mounted a cherub and flew,	→	soared on the wings of the wind.
13	Set darkness pavilions around Him,	>	a massing of waters, looming thunderheads.
14	From the brilliance before Him	→	fiery coals blazed.
15	The Lord thundered from heaven,	<→	the Most High sent forth His voice.
16	He let loose arrows and scattered them,	>	lightning, and routed them.
17	The channels of the sea were exposed,	{>}	the world's foundations laid bare.
18	From the Lord's roaring,	>	the blast of His nostrils' breath.
19	He reached from on high and took me,	>	He pulled me out of the mighty waters.

20	He rescued me from my strong enemy,	>	from my foes who were too much for me.
21	They overtook me on the day of my disaster,	→	but God was my support.
22	He set me out in an open place,	>	He freed me for He was pleased with me.
23	The Lord dealt with me by my merit,	>	the cleanness of my hands He requited.
24	For I kept the ways of the Lord,	>	I did no evil before my God.
25	All His statutes are before me,	>	I swerved not from His laws.
26	I was blameless before Him,	>	and kept myself from sin.
27	He requited me by my merit,	>	my cleanness in His eyes.
28	With the loyal You deal loyally,	{ }	with the blameless warrior, blamelessly.
29	With the pure You deal purely,	{ }	with the perverse, deviously.
30	A lowly people You save,	{ }	on the haughty Your eyes look down.
31	You are my lamp, O Lord,	>	the Lord lights up my darkness.
32	With You I rush a barrier,	{ }	with my God I vault a wall.
33	God's way is blameless,	→	the Lord's word pure, →

He is a shield to those who shelter in Him.

34	For who is god besides the Lord,	=	who a rock besides our God?
35	The God, my mighty stronghold,	→	Who kept my way blameless,
36	Made my legs like a gazelle's,	→	and stood me on the heights.
37	Taught my hands combat,	>	made my arms bend a bow of bronze.
38	You gave me Your saving shield,	?	Your answering power* made me great.
39	You helped me take broad strides,	→	and my feet did not trip.
40	I pursued my enemies, destroyed them,	→	turned not back till I finished them off.
41	I finished them off, smashed them beyond rising,	→	they lay beneath my feet.
42	You girded me with might for combat,	→	brought my adversaries low before me.
43	Made my enemies turn tail before me,	→	my foes, and I wiped them out.
44	They looked—there was none to save them,	>	to the Lord—He answered them not.
45	I crushed them like the dust of the earth,	>	like street mud, I ground them, trampled them.

* Here and henceforth this symbol indicates a philological obscurity or possible textual difficulty in the Hebrew.

46 You delivered me from the strife → kept me at the head of nations,
of peoples, →
a people I knew not served me.

47 Aliens cowered before me, → at the mere report became my
vassals.

48 Aliens shrank, → came trembling from their
forts.*

49 The Lord lives, blessed is my ˜{ } exalted is God my saving rock.
rock,

50 The God Who grants me > and lays low peoples before
vindication, me.

51 Frees me from my enemies, => lifts me over my adversaries, =
saves me from wreakers of havoc.

52 For this I sing Your praises, Lord, = and chant Your name.
among the nations,

53 Saving tower to His king, = performing kindness to His
anointed.

Translation inevitably presupposes interpretation, but I have tried to minimize the tendency to doctor the evidence by hewing as close as possible to the actual idioms and the lexical values of the original, even to the point of awkwardness. Like many biblical poems, and in consonance with the regular practice of the prose writers, David's victory hymn uses certain reiterated *Leitwörter* as focal points for its thematic argument—the most important is "saving" or "salvation," *yesh'a*, which is even sardonically punned on in line 44, *yish'u ve'eyn moshi'a*, "they looked—there was none to save them"—and with this in mind I have kept the same English equivalent for the same Hebrew root throughout, again at the cost of some awkwardness. There are, to be sure, certain philological problems in the poem, and specialists may debate some of my construals, but I do not think such problems are extensive enough to affect the generalizations about the poetics of these lines that I should now like to propose.

The poem is long enough that a statistical breakdown of the varieties of semantic relation between versets may be instructive. In fact, the proportions here are fairly typical of the corpus of biblical poetry. In thirty-six of the fifty-three lines there is a clear element of dynamic movement from the first verset to the second: in nineteen lines this involves some sort of intensification or specification; in another seventeen lines, some relation of consequentiality. Twelve lines reflect a relatively static relation between versets—six of these through the deployment of synonyms, the other six through the bracketing of complementary terms, which may be similar in meaning, as in line 28, or antithetical pairs, as in lines 29 and 30. The five lines not yet accounted for include the philologically problematic line 38 and four lines where the semantic modification from verset to verset is weak enough to leave some doubt whether the line should be thought of as static or dynamic. The triadic line 51, for example, lists three overlapping and perhaps virtually synonymous actions of deliverance; but it is also possible to infer a developmental or intensifying sequence: first He frees me, then He lifts me up over my enemies, and, what is more, He saves me from wreakers of havoc. In any event, it is hardly necessary to insist on such borderline cases in order to preserve the clear statistical preponderance of dynamic over static lines, here and elsewhere in biblical poetry. We might note, moreover, that of the eight essentially synonymous lines here (adding two now from the ambiguous column), two occur at the very beginning and three at the very end of the poem, leading one to suspect that the poet reserved this paradigmatic form of static parallelism for the purposes of framing, while parallelism in the body of the poem is preponderantly dynamic.

Turning to the dynamic lines of the poem, let me rapidly indicate the typical maneuvers through which intensification or focusing is effected, and then we can go on to the relation I have labeled consequentiality, which will have more direct implications for the presence of narrative elements in this and other biblical poems. The simplest strategy of intensification is the introduction in the second verset of one parallel term that is obviously stronger than its counterpart in the first verset, as in line 5, where the breakers of death merely "wash round" (or "encompass") while the parallel torrents of the underworld "terrify." Specification of place, action, agency, and cause in the second verset achieves a similar effect, as in line 19: "He reached from on high and took me, / He *pulled me out of the mighty waters*." There is a kinship between such lines and the sort of development that occurs in incremental repetition, as one can see by comparing with the line just quoted the triadic line 9, where, after a complementary link between the first verset and the second, there is incremental repetition between the first verset and the third: "The earth heaved and shuddered, / heaven's foundations shook, / they heaved, *for He was incensed*." The departure from syntactic parallelism while parallelism of meaning is preserved (as in the subordinate clause of the last verset just cited) can be a means of adding to or at least heightening meaning. One of the most common patterns in this regard is for the poet to place nouns or a nominal phrase in the first verset and make them more active through verbal development in the second verset, as in line 3: "My stronghold and my refuge, / my savior, *Who saves me from havoc.*" Or again, in line 31: "You are my lamp, O Lord, / the Lord *lights up my darkness.*"

A more general term in the first verset may become more specific and/ or more concrete in the second verset, whether as a verbal transformation of a noun or as a matched noun. Thus, in line 50: "The God Who grants me *vindication,* / and **lays low peoples** before me." Or, less conspicuously, in line 23: "The Lord dealt with me *by my merit,* / the **cleanness of my hands** He requited." Another variation of this pattern appears in lines 24–26, where all the first versets affirm generally that the speaker has been faithful to God's laws while the second versets stipulate that he has actually avoided evil. (Such rhetorical bracketing of x and not-the-opposite-of-x, which is fairly common in biblical poetry, is, approximately, a strategy for creating ad hoc synonyms, but it usually involves some element of specification or activation of the initial term, as our example illustrates.) More impressively, the focusing of an idea can also become the focusing of an image, as in line 8, "From His abode He *heard my voice,* / **my cry in His ears,**" or the awesome effect of line 18, "From the Lord's *roaring,* / **the blast of His nostrils' breath.**" Focusing an image can also involve a hyperbolic stepping-up of the idea, as in line 37: "Taught my hands *combat,* / made my arms **bend a bow of bronze.**" Finally, if, as I have intimated, many of the maneuvers of intensification ultimately derive from an archaic matrix of incremental repetition, it is not surprising that we should find lines where the heightening of meaning is achieved through an appositional elaboration or piling-on of associated images or acts, as in line 13, "Set darkness pavilions around Him, / a massing of waters, looming thunderheads," and line 45, "I crushed them like the dust of the earth, / like street mud, I ground them, trampled them."

There is a single line in our poem that would seem to be one of those very rare instances in biblical verse that run directly counter to the principle of semantic development from first verset to second: "The Lord thundered from heaven, / the Most High sent forth His voice" (line 15). "Thundered" is obviously the stronger as well as the more specific term, "sent forth His voice" the weaker and the more general one. There is a reason, however, for this reversal, which will lead us into the issue of consequentiality. I would assume that thunder precedes the voice of the Lord because that is the way it was experientially for the ancient Near Eastern imagination: first the awestruck observer heard the peal of thunder; then he realized that God must be speaking. In rhetorical terms, the relation between the two utterances is between the vehicle and the tenor of a metaphor, but in logical terms, which may be more strictly relevant for the biblical imagination of the natural world, it is a relation of effect and cause. We will repeatedly find that an utterance in the second verset, whether or not it is parallel in meaning to the first verset, occurs there because it *follows* from the initial utterance, either in our human perception of the phenomenon invoked or, far more frequently, as an objective event in a chain of events. This is perhaps most obvious when there is no semantic parallelism, as in line 4: "Praised I called the Lord, / and from my enemies I was saved." The relation between the two statements is one of both narrative sequence and cause and effect. First, the speaker, presumably in straits, praised God and/or called upon Him in supplication (the Hebrew syntax is somewhat ambiguous), and then, in vindication of this faith and in response to this prayer, God rescued him from his enemies. Even where an ear lulled by the illusion of synonymity might pick up nothing but a series of equivalent images, there often proves to be sequential movement in time and consequential movement in a chain of causality. In our text, the extraordinary passage describing the Lord's descent, amidst cosmic fireworks, to scatter His enemies, provides the most powerful case in point. Let me quote again for analysis three central lines of this segment, lines 10–12.

Smoke went up from His nostrils,   consuming fire from His mouth,
              coals blazed forth from Him.
He bent the heavens, came   dense mist beneath His feet.
down,
Mounted a cherub and flew,   soared on the wings of the wind.

Since the first of these lines is triadic, we might pause a moment to note the function of triadic lines in a system of versification that is predominantly dyadic. One can think of approximate analogies in other prosodic systems, such as the occasional use of a triplet amidst heroic couplets in English Augustan verse. In that instance, however, the practice was rare and a purist like Pope considered it bad form, whereas in biblical verse many poets move back and forth freely between two-verset and three-verset lines. In some of the relatively long poems, like this one, triadic lines appear to have been used with purposeful selectiveness to mark some special emphasis or to indicate the beginning or conclusion of a segment within the poem (compare the placement of lines 9 and 10, 33, and 51). The triadic lines 9 ("The earth heaved . . .") and 10 begin the great sweeping movement of cosmic upheaval in which

God is carried from His heavenly abode (line 8) down to the scrimmage of the battlefield (line 16). The earthquake imagery of line 9 leads metonymically—from the poet's viewpoint, from effect to cause—to the volcanic depiction of the Deity in the first of the three lines quoted above. The link between versets in line 10 is not a simple bracketing of conventionally associated complementary terms, as we have in the preceding line. That is, "earth" and "heaven" or (line 17) "sea" and "world" are parts, even halves, that make a whole, whereas the series smoke-in-the-nostrils, fire-in-the-mouth, blazing-coals-all-around is a more dynamic progression. To begin with, the series presents a paradigmatic instance of intensification (smoke > fire > blazing coals). More important for what will follow in the poem, the series embodies a powerful sense of *process:* the smoke rises, then consuming fire leaps out, then there is a terrific incandescence all before the Lord as He prepares to come down to do battle.

The forward rush of process may be even more evident when semantic parallelism is abandoned, as in line 14, which depicts divine incandescence in similar language but is shaped on the causal movement from a prepositional phrase in the first verset to the main clause in the second verset: "From the brilliance before Him / fiery coals blazed." Something similar happens in the second of our three lines ("He bent the heavens, came down, / dense mist beneath His feet"), where the second verset is no longer a semantic parallel to the first but an adverbial modifier of it that quite beautifully carries our eye downward with God's descent toward earth. The flight earthward is then dramatically realized in the next line, as God mounts His battle steed and swoops down toward the fray. (Modern readers should be warned that the biblical cherub, *keruv*, is not the dimpled darling of Renaissance iconography but a celestial winged beast, majestic and probably rather fierce in aspect.) I have cheated slightly at this one point by adopting the more plausible reading of Psalm 18, "soared," rather than the 2 Samuel 22 text, which says "was seen" (a difference of just two, barely distinguishable letters in the Hebrew), but even if one uses the reading from 2 Samuel, the narrative movement between versets remains clear: first God mounts His cherub and takes off; then He soars, or is seen, on the wings of the wind. These two versets are, I would suggest, not alternative images but equivalencies, the cherub conceived figuratively by the poet as a representation of the wind. (The Hebrew imagination, we might note, was unabashedly anthropomorphic but by no means foolishly literalist.)

The last comment I would like to make on these three lines is about the way they at once overlap and move forward—a pattern thoroughly characteristic of narrative in biblical poetry. Earlier, we had occasion to note the frequency of interlinear semantic parallelism. There are vestiges of that here too, as between lines 11 and 12, where there is first a general account of God's descent, then a more specific depiction of downward flight. But the most essential relation of the lines to each other (to look now over the whole sequence from 9 to 18) is as a series of linked events following one another in time: the earth heaves; God glows with fire (an action "cued" by the final clause of line 9, "for He was incensed," the Hebrew verb for anger here clearly suggesting heat); He tips down the sky and descends; He soars earthward; He surrounds himself with ominous clouds; burning fiercely within them, He hurls His thunderbolts and scatters the enemy; and, finally, in the closure of an envelope structure that takes us back to the seismic beginning in lines 9–10, the seabed and the earth's foundations are laid bare by His fiery breath.

In all this, it is important to recognize the underlying connection between the movement within the line, from one verset to the next, and the movement from one line to the next. At first thought, semantic parallelism would seem to be preeminently an operation along what Roman Jakobson calls the paradigmatic axis, or axis of selection, of language. That is, the poet introduces a particular term, like "orphan," in his first verset; then he selects another term, like "widow," from the same general category for the second verset, or, more synonymously, having invoked "voice" in the first verset, he chooses a counterpart like "utterance" from the same linguistic paradigm for the second verset. But the evidence we have reviewed ought to suggest that this is a very incomplete and misleading description of what actually goes on in biblical parallelism. In point of fact, the links between versets are often what Jakobson would call syntagmatic—that is, proceeding along the axis of contiguity, which is transformed by the poet into actual concatenation— rather than the axis of selection. Or perhaps it would be better to put aside the Jakobsonian imagery of axes, with its suggestion of movements set at right angles to each other, because what we very frequently find in biblical verse is the emergence of the syntagmatic from the paradigmatic: as the poet offers an approximate equivalent for an image or idea he has just invoked, he also begins, by the very logic of specification or intensification of the system in which he works, to push the initial image or idea into action, moving from one image to another that is temporally subsequent to and implied by the first. Narrativity, in other words, asserts itself at the heart of synonymity. If the second verset, as I have argued, is very often a spatial, experiential, or thematic focusing of the first verset, it can also be a focusing in a temporal chain, where initial and rather general actions lead to sharper or more extreme or more dramatically vivid consequences. (At least to the observing eye, causes tend to seem less concrete and particular than their effects.) In many instances, such syntagmatic links are confined within the line to the two or three versets; in many other cases, as in the one we have just examined from 2 Samuel 22, the incipiently narrative momentum within the line is carried over from one line to the next and becomes the propelling force for a small-scale narrative within the poem.

Before attempting to follow the workings of this principle in verse narrative proper, I should like to offer a few examples in single lines of the pronounced general orientation of biblical poetry toward a focusing that is at once thematic and temporal. To begin with, when a line brackets two nonsimultaneous actions, even where there is no difference in intensity or specificity between them, the chronologically later action will appear in the second verset, as in Psalm 22:10, "You drew me out of the womb, / made me safe on my mother's breasts," or Psalm 100:4, where we have two subsequent stages of the same action, "Enter His gates in acclamation, / His courts in praise." Often, the movement from general to specific is also at least implicitly a movement in temporal sequence, as in Proverbs 1:16, "Their feet run to evil, / they hurry to shed blood." Bloodshed is of course a specific and extreme instance of the general category, evil, but the line also intimates sequentiality: they go running to do evil and end up shedding blood. Temporal sequence is more explicit in a common pattern where a single verb in the first verset is followed by a small chain of verbs in the second verset that develop the initial action. Thus Isaiah 26:17: "As a pregnant woman draws near to give birth, / she shudders, she screams in her pangs." Here the second verset conspicuously *focuses* the first verset, but at the same time it follows it: first the woman's time draws near; then we see her writhing in labor. A similar development is observable in Jeremiah 46:10: "The sword shall consume, / shall be sated and drunk from their blood." Or again, in Isaiah 28:13: "But they shall trip backward, / shall be broken, ensnared, and entrapped."

Another common configuration of sequentiality is a movement from cause to effect, which is necessarily also a temporal movement and hence implicitly narrative, as in this line from Jacob's blessing (Gen. 49:17):

"He bites the horse's hooves / and its rider falls back," or in the image of fire that plays across two lines in Isaiah 1:31: "The mighty tree[5] shall turn to tow, / its attendant a spark. // And the two shall burn together / with none to extinguish." The swerve away from semantic parallelism in the last verset here in order to follow the curve of "plot" is a characteristic procedure that reflects how narrative momentum can begin to take over in the articulation of a rhetorical figure. One sees the same pattern in this triadic line from Psalm 11:2: "For look, the evil bend their bow, / string their arrow, / to shoot from the gloom at the upright."

I should like to stress that in all these instances, as well as in the next two we shall go on to consider, what the poets give us is not narrative but narrativity—which is to say, the narrative development of metaphor. One might even apply that characterization to David's victory hymn, where, despite the strong narrative indications of the closely sequenced verbs in the perfect tense (as in biblical prose narrative), the anthropomorphic "plot" of God's descent to do battle is, ultimately, a metaphor for His sustaining power, not an account of a discrete event that literally took place.

As these small-scale examples may suggest, narrative movement forward in time is typically generated by the establishing of a series of linked actions that, according to the poetics of parallelism, are approximate equivalents but prove to be, on closer inspection, logically discriminated actions that lead imperceptibly from one to the next. A sense of temporal progression is thus produced in a manner analogous to the illusion of movement created in the cinema, where a series of still photographs flashes on the retina with sufficient speed so that one seems to flow into the next, each frozen moment in the visual sequence fusing into temporal flux. A slightly longer passage will be necessary to illustrate how this principle works. Here is Job (16:9–14), in the midst of one of his harrowing protestations of anguish, recounting his tale of woe, which even without the expository and concluding verses I have omitted, is clearly a tale with a beginning, a development, and a climax:

His anger rent and pursued me.	He gnashed his teeth against me.
My foe stabbed me with his eyes.	
They opened their mouths wide against me.	In scorn they struck my cheeks.
They were inflamed against me.	
God gave me over to the wicked.	In the hands of the evil He thrust me.

I was untroubled and He broke me.	He smashed me, set me up as a target.
His archers surrounded me,	He pierced my kidneys mercilessly,
spilled to the ground my bile.	
He breached me, breach upon breach,	rushed at me like a warrior.

Formally, one might describe these lines as a continuous series of interlinear semantic parallelisms, one image of assault piled onto another, with a unifying metaphor of tearing or rupture: in the first line here, God "rends," *taraf*, the verb used for the ravening action of beasts of prey; He goes on to stab, pierce, break, and smash, and in the last line breaches, "breach upon breach." The logic of the parallelism, then, is preeminently the logic of intensification we have observed in so many other biblical texts, but it is important to note that the process of intensification here is projected onto a temporal axis, which is to say that it becomes narrative—or, to be more precise, the narrative development of a metaphor (God as implacable assailant). First we have the hostile approach of the wrathful God, gnashing His teeth, glaring from a distance. Then He lets loose His baleful emissaries of destruction, who threaten Job, strike him, seize him, then make him a target for their arrows, and finally reduce him to a mass of gaping wounds. The analogy I have proposed with the cinematic illusion of movement through a sequencing of overlapping stills may be helpful because it suggests that this is, remarkably, a mode of narrative report that works essentially without recourse to summary. The biblical prose narratives, by contrast, constantly make use of the boldest summaries, alternately speeding up narrative tempo through summary and slowing it down (usually through extended dialogue), thus conveying a sense of controlled uneven jumps in time that help embody the narrator's subtle interpretive perspective on his own materials. The verse narrative, on the other hand, is a sort of past continuous—with the ambiguity of the Hebrew verbs even allowing construal as a virtual present tense—in which the sequence of overlapping actions catches us up experientially in the reported events, leaving no space for an obtrusively manipulative narrator to stop the action, change its pace, or summarize a whole temporal segment.

I do not mean to suggest that what I have just described is, in this precise form, the invariable narrative strategy one encounters in biblical verse, though I do think it is instructively typical. Obviously, any poet will to some extent adapt his intimation of temporal progression to the particular kind of process or action he is representing. In the tremendous evocation of the Day of the Lord at the beginning of Joel 2, the poet is much more interested in imparting the rhythm of an inexorable march to his description of the advancing enemy army, and to that end he takes advantage of certain expressive possibilities of formal repetition. The whole powerfully interlinked passage has to be seen (again, the numeration reflects my line divisions, not the traditional verse numbers):

1	Blast a horn in Zion,	sound the alarm on My holy mount.
2	Quake all who live on the earth,	for the Day of the Lord has come, is close.
3	Day of darkness and gloom,	day of cloud and dense mist.
4	Like soot spread out on the mountains,	a vast immense people.
5	Its like there never was	and never will be again
	to years without end.	
6	Before it consuming fire	and after it blazing flame.
7	Like the Garden of Eden before it,	after it desolate waste,
	nothing escapes it.	
8	Like the look of horses their look,	like steeds they run.
9	Like the sound of chariots on hilltops they dance,	like the sound of fiery flame consuming straw,
	a vast people arrayed for battle.	
10	Before it peoples tremble,	every face turns ashen.*
11	Like warriors they run,	like fighters they scale a wall.
12	Each man on his own track goes,	they swerve* not from their course.
13	No man jostles his fellow,	each goes on his own path,
	though they fall through a loophole they are unscathed.*	
14	Through the city they swarm,	they run to the wall.
15	They scale the houses,	come in at the windows like thieves.
16	Before them the earth quakes,	heaven shakes.
17	Sun and moon grow dark,	the stars pull in their brightness.
18	And the Lord sounds His voice before His army,	His camp is immense,
	vast are His agents.	
19	For great is the Day of the Lord, very awesome—	who can endure it?

This poem does impressively convey through its parade of "parallel" actions a sense of forward movement in time, but the narration is formally framed and formally punctuated by a deployment of symmetrical repetition not observable in the passage just quoted from Job. Lines 1–4, which introduce the Day of the Lord, are beautifully mirrored, image for image and even word for word, by the formal conclusion in lines 16–19. At the beginning, the warning trumpet is sounded; at the end, the Lord sends forth His voice. At the beginning, those who dwell on the earth quake; at the end, the earth itself quakes, and heaven as well. The darkness and gloom of the opening lines become a cosmic darkness at the end (line 17), and the epithets "vast" and "immense" for the destroying army that are introduced at the beginning are reiterated at the end, as is the key-term, "Day of the Lord."

But what of temporal progression in the poem? Initially, the invading army is seen as ominously inert, "spread out" like soot (or, if one prefers the more conventional interpretation of this word, oxymoronically, like dawn) on the mountains, with no verb directly attached to it. The poet allows us at first to see not so much the army as its effects—consuming fire before and behind it, weirdly counterpointing the deep darkness that the enemy exudes. The first two versets of line 7 are a brilliant exploitation of the possibilities of surprise inherent in the system of parallelisms. Expecting a complementary or synonymous utterance to follow "the Garden of Eden"—as in the "before it/after it" pairing of the preceding line—we are shocked by the image of devastation ("Like the Garden of Eden before it, / after it desolate waste"), and thus made witnesses to the army's annihilating advance without the action itself being directly narrated. The poet exercises a stark economy in both his figurative language and his choice of vocabulary. Apart from the reiterated image of consuming fire (to which *shaḥar* of line 4, whether it means "soot" or "dawn," would be associatively linked), all the similes for the army turn out to be metonymies intimately bound to the actual army or in fact literal designations rhetorically masquerading as similes. The troops are like horses, which at least some of them presumably would be riding; they run like warriors and fighters, which is what they are. To be sure, if the whole description of the army is a metaphorical representation of the plague of locusts already invoked in Joel, that would explain this peculiar literalness.

More relevant to the issue of narrative is what happens with the verbs. The first verb for the movement of the invaders—"run"—is not introduced until the end of line 8. Then we have an overlap from "run" to "dance," followed by a repetition of "run," which moves on to "scale," then "go" repeated in two successive lines, then the addition of the vivid "swarm," followed by another occurrence of "scale" and "run," and finally, "come in." (In this recapitulation, I have omitted verbs that have a subject other than the army and also the verbs in lines 12–13, which indicate not the invaders' forward movement but the fact that they make no lateral movements.) This sequence of verbs is, of course, a pattern of overlapping actions, but a more pointed way of describing it would be to say that it reverts far more directly than is common to what I have called the matrix of incremental repetition of biblical verse. The poet here is less interested in an illusion of seamless temporal progression than in a steady, solemn advance—spatially, from the distant mountains up to and over the walls of the city and into the houses—marked by a mounting drumbeat, and for this the model of incremental repetition is particularly apt: they run, they dance, they run, they scale a wall, they go; indeed, they go, they swarm, they run, they scale, they come in at the windows like thieves. A narrative tempo like this brings us close to the mesmerizing rhythms of the Song of Deborah, to which it now behooves us to turn.

The Song of Deborah is too long to be analyzed here in its entirety, but the remarkable concluding section (Judg. 5:24–31), which recounts the Canaanite general Sisera's death at the unflinching hands of Jael, is in itself an illuminating instance of the artistic possibilities of Hebrew verse narrative, and is all the more instructive because the way it shapes its materials can be handily compared with the prose version of the same events that precedes the Song. Here is the complete passage, to the very end of the poem, again with local line numeration rather than verse numbers:

1 Blessed above women be Jael,   wife of Heber the Kenite,
          above women in tents be she blessed.
2 Water he asked, milk she gave,   in a princely bowl she brought
                                                       him curds.
3 Her hand reached for the tent peg,   her right hand for the workman's
                                                       hammer.
4 She hammered Sisera, cracked his   smashed and pierced his temple.
   head,
5 Between her legs he kneeled, fell,   between her legs he kneeled and
   lay,   fell,
          where he kneeled, he fell, destroyed.
6 Through the window she looked   Sisera's mother, through the
   and whined,   lattice.
7 "Why is his chariot so long in   why so late the clatter of his
   coming,   cars?"
8 The wisest of her ladies answer,   and she, too, replies on her own:
9 "Will they not find and divide the   a damsel or two for every man?
   spoil?
10 Spoil of dyed stuff for Sisera,   spoil of embroidered dyed stuff,
          embroidered dyed pairs for each neck as spoil?"
11 Thus perish all Your enemies, O   Be His friends like the sun rising
   Lord!   in might.

No text could make more beautifully clear how far from automatic formulas are both the literal repetitions and the synonymous substitutions of biblical poetry. The passage begins with a formal introduction that blesses Jael, to be matched at the very end of the poem by the line that symmetrically distributes a curse to God's enemies, a blessing to His friends. The middle verset of the triadic line 1, following the convention for names in parallelism, substitutes a relational epithet, "wife of Heber the Kenite." It is, however, a thematically pointed substitution, for it reminds us that this heroine, who is not even an Israelite but a member of a clan loosely allied to Israel and also friendly to Sisera's king, was the one who struck the final blow in a war in which several of the tribes of Israel had failed to rally to the cause. The third verset of line 1 is an incremental repetition of the first, but the seemingly innocuous and automatic increment, "in tents," is crucially significant for what follows— first because of Jael's exceptional departure from the pacific domestic role of tent-dwelling women, and then because the tent will be the scene of Jael's killing of Sisera, the tent peg and hammer being the convenient weapons she seizes.

The relation between versets in the second line is an instance of that combined imagistic and temporal focusing we have observed elsewhere. Asked for water by the battle-weary fugitive, Jael gives, or offers, milk, which is then hyperbolically elaborated as "curds" at the end of the line. But the increment of "in a princely bowl" in the second verset offers us a concrete dramatic image that follows chronologically from the general proffering of milk in the first verset. Even more particularly, it directs our attention toward Jael's hands bearing the bowl and thus becomes an implicit overlap to the next line: "Her hand reached for the tent peg . . ." What is elided through this brilliant transition, though it is assumed, is the prose version's account of Sisera going to sleep after drinking the curds (we will consider this difference between the two renderings of the story presently). In consonance, that is, with both the principle of incremental repetition and that of closely sequenced interrelated pictures, each line of narration picks up something from the preceding line and somehow pushes it further, and so here the hands that would necessarily be bearing the princely bowl are immediately seen reaching for the deadly implements. A separate report of Sisera's sleep is not allowed to intervene, though the audience would surely have presupposed that narrative datum, and without it Jael would scarcely have had the chance to pick up peg and hammer and strike the blow. (For her to use both these instruments, her victim would have had to lie quite still.) In general,

44

the elliptical nature of the narrative—Sisera is not even mentioned by name here until the fourth line—reflects that lack of exposition I referred to earlier in Hebrew narrative verse, its ancillary relation to a preestablished story.

"Hand"/"right hand" (*yad/yamin*), in that order, make a fixed word-pair that goes back to the Ugaritic, but whereas *yad* elsewhere usually means the same thing as *yamin*, here the poet takes advantage of the fact that parallel versets can be complementary rather than synonymous, making *yad* in this case refer to the left hand and so giving us in the two halves of the line a complete image of Jael's preparations for the fatal act. "Hammer" as a noun at the end of line 3 is then transformed into "hammer" as a verb at the very beginning of line 4, in accord with a general tendency of nominal constructs to generate verbal chains, of actors or agents to produce actions. Line 4 is a strong instance—not only between versets but even within each verset—of the use of a sequence of seeming synonyms that in fact are related to each other syntagmatically, each term closely following the preceding one in time, like movie frames: she hammered, cracked, smashed, drove the stake all the way through the enemy's head. Line 5 exploits emphatic incremental repetition to achieve an entirely new effect. Moving in a contrastive overlap from Sisera's head to Jael's legs, or feet ("from foot to head" is a fixed collocation in biblical idiom), the verbatim repetition produces an effect of slow motion that mimics Sisera's death agony, the middle verset of the triadic line exceptionally giving us repetition with one element of the initial utterance ("lay") deleted, heightening the sense of almost suspended motion. Presumably, once the blow was struck, he convulsively heaved from the bed, sprawled forward on his knees before Jael, and then lay still—"destroyed," as the line concludes in a finely climactic increment to the repetition "kneeled and fell."[6]

My translation of line 6 reproduces the Hebrew word order, which effects a sharply ironic transition between scenes. If line moves to line by overlap, this is an instance of a false overlap, or what in film would be called a *faux raccord* between different scenes. The unspecified "she" looking out the window in the first verset might momentarily be taken for Jael, the feminine singular who has dominated all the action up to this point, although the presence of a window in a tent would be puzzling. As we move into the new scene, we quickly realize that there is a pointed contrast between the simple Kenite tent and the Canaanite palace, with its bevy of female attendants so interested in the material benefits of war. When the subject of the verb "look," Sisera's mother, is sprung on us at the beginning of the second verset, we at once take in the dramatic irony even before she utters a word—that she is on the lookout for a warrior-son, whom we have just seen lying with a tent peg through his temple, destroyed.

Her words, both the question and the answer, illustrate the expressive power of the kinds of patterns of dynamic relation between versets we have been following. In line 7, she first wonders about the tarrying of his chariot and then, in a wonderful focusing move or dramatic concretization, about why she has not yet heard "the clatter of his cars." (The Hebrew *pe'amim* would refer literally to the pounding or rhythmic sound of the horses' hooves, invoked earlier in the Song—Judges 5:22.) Since the prose narrative in Judges has earlier reminded us that the Canaanite military superiority on the coastal plain is largely due to their iron chariots, this locally effective image also carries a larger historical-thematic irony. In the answer to the question (lines 9–10), the focusing procedure is specification rather than dramatic concretization: the general term "spoil" of the first verset is stipulated initially as captive females, then, in the incremental repetition of line 10 (which is triadic, apparently as part of a closural effect), as dyed stuff, as dyed embroidery (that is, still more valuable), as a pair of dyed embroidered cloths for every neck. All these details, moreover, reverberate ironically against the previous scene in Jael's tent. The poet takes rhetorical pains to introduce a whole circle of Canaanite court ladies (there is no absolute necessity for their presence, since Sisera's mother in fact answers her own question). These women speak with blithe confidence on behalf of a patriarchal warrior culture. The first instance of spoil they mention is the sexual booty they assume the men have coming to them. The rare term that I, like other translators, have represented here with the courtly "damsel" is actually derived transparently from the word for "womb," and so might in ancient usage have meant something much coarser than "damsel." (The Ugaritic cognate is sometimes an epithet for Anat, the warrior-goddess, which could argue for a more decorous connotation and might even suggest an allusion to the fierce goddess in Jael.) Only after invoking the imagined abundance of female slaves do Sisera's mother and her ladies conjure up the lovely embroidery that would be, one gathers, their special share in the booty. All this stands in shocking contrast to the still lingering—or perhaps even synchronous—image of the Canaanite general felled by the hand of a woman, lying shattered between her legs in a hideous parody of soldierly sexual assault on the women of a defeated foe.

With these words of dialogue that are a gloating, illusory anticipation of the spoils of war, the story is sharply cut off, concluding with an appropriate formula of curse and benediction. This very technique, we might note, of leading the reader to draw inferences by abruptly breaking off a story in mid-dialogue, is one frequently employed in the prose narratives (a signal instance is Simeon and Levi's unanswered question to Jacob at the end of the tale of the rape of Dinah, Genesis 34:31, "Will our sister be treated like a whore?").

It would in fact be surprising if there were not occasional carryovers in technique from the prose to the verse as well as the other way around, but a reading of the prose version of Sisera's death (Judg. 4:15–22) suggests that the different formal logics of the two media lead to strikingly different imaginative definitions of the same narrative data. Let me quote the central section of the prose version:

18. Jael went out to meet Sisera, and she said to him, "Come in, my lord, come into my place, do not be afraid." And he came into her tent and she covered him with a blanket. 19. And he said to her, "Please give me a little water to drink, for I am thirsty." And she opened the skin of milk and gave him some to drink, and covered him. 20. He said to her, "Stand at the tent opening, and if a man should come by and ask you, 'Is there a man here?' say there is not." 21. Then Jael the wife of Heber took the tent peg and placed the mallet in her hand. And she came to him stealthily and drove the peg through his temple till it went down into the ground, he being fast asleep from exhaustion. And thus he died.

The obtuseness of a certain academic preoccupation with supposed historical precision is vividly illustrated by the contention of some scholars that there were two different "traditions" about the killing of Sisera, one reflected in the prose and the other in the poetry. One recent commentator, whom in decency I shall leave unnamed, goes so far as to claim that, in the "tradition" transmitted by the poem, Sisera did not go to sleep but was bashed on the head by Jael with the princely bowl and, thus stunned, was finished off with tent peg and mallet! In point of fact, all the differences between the two versions are a matter of the writers' interpretive rendering of the same event. The single "factual" discrepancy between the two accounts is in the minor detail of the container from which Sisera drank: the prose version, with its homey realistic depiction of the tent scene, mentions Jael's opening of the skin bottle, with no hint of pouring the milk into a more aristocratic receptacle; the poem, with its generic tendency toward heightening, stresses Jael's serving the milk in a princely bowl. Which of the two accounts is older—the received

47

wisdom of scholarship has been that the poem antedates the prose—is beside our point, as is the question whether the author of the one text knew the other text as we have it. What seems clear is that both poet and prose-writer possessed the same basic narrative data, though not necessarily in any written version.

The prose account, in keeping with the standard practice of biblical narrative, chiefly defines the action and the relation between the actors through dialogue, even including, characteristically, a snippet of quoted speech embedded within quoted speech (". . . if a man should . . . ask you, 'Is there a man here?' "). This method of presentation opens up certain possibilities of subtlety and complication of characterization not available to the verse narrative. First Jael is seen (verse 18) in an active role coming out of the tent to greet Sisera, politely and reassuringly inviting him in to the hospitality of her tent, also noticing that he hesitates or looks fearful. (The commander of the redoubtable iron chariots has abandoned his vehicle and fled on foot after losing the battle.) It is significant that Sisera is assigned no direct reply to her invitation but simply follows her—silently?—into the tent, speaking only after she has covered him with the blanket to ask for a drink, then again after drinking to ask her to stand guard for him. (His dialogue is all requests, hers all invitation.) The stress he puts in his instructions on there being or not being a man in the tent will be picked up ironically at the end of the story (verse 22), when Jael will say to Barak, the Israelite commander, "Come and I'll show you the man you seek."

This version plays almost teasingly with the expected roles of man and woman. Jael's initial words to Sisera might almost be construed as a sexual invitation, but she at once assumes a maternal role toward her battle-weary guest, tucking him in like a child, giving him milk rather than the water he requested. (One might guess that the poetic version avoids direct representation of Jael putting Sisera to bed partly because the poet does not want to mitigate or complicate with maternal associations the image of Jael the triumphant slayer. It is enough to have the implicit ironic contrast between the lethal Jael and the anxiously waiting mother of Sisera. It is instructive in regard to the way literary form establishes meanings for narrative data that in the poem the very same detail, the giving of milk instead of water, does not seem a "maternal" act, because it is not reported together with Jael's putting Sisera to bed and because, in an intensifying pattern of verse parallelism, it is presented as a gesture of "epic" hospitality that goes beyond ordinary expectations.)

The actual report of the murder (verse 21) has nothing of the poem's crescendo series of smashing and stabbing but instead seeks to define or clearly explain the mechanics of this extraordinary deed. It incorporates, however, a hint of sexual double meaning: Jael "came to" Sisera, a term often used elsewhere in the case of males to refer to sexual entry, and the driving through of the tent peg into the ground on which the narrator dwells seems to be what our own age would call a phallic aggressive act. By intimation, then, Jael here is in turn seductress, ministering mother, and sexual assailant, whereas the sharp focus of the poem is simply on the powerful figure of Jael the hammerer, standing over the body of Sisera, whose death throes between her legs, kneeling, then prostrate, may be, perhaps, an ironic glance at the time-honored martial custom of rape.

I do not mean to suggest that one version is superior to the other, only that they achieve different effects and that they represent character in the midst of portentous action in crucially different ways. The interchange between Jael and Sisera in the prose version is ultimately moral and psychological in nature: the manslaughtering Canaanite oppressor is at first fearful, then reassured, entrusting himself implicitly to Jael's care, even assuming the posture of a child; she prudently knows how to soothe, how to minister, how to kill. By contrast, in the poem, the two figures are kept at a certain distance from us and even from each other (there is, we should note, no dialogue at all between them) in an almost emblematic tableau: Jael standing, hammer in hand, Sisera the would-be conqueror, prostrate at her feet, destroyed. The prose account plays delicately with different values associated with "man" and "woman"; the poem boldly juxtaposes the scene of a woman felling a man with the scene of the enemy women waiting for their men to return bearing captive girls and plundered embroidery, and by so doing it sharpens the edge of triumphal harshness in the story.

This general contrast between the two renderings of the event may suggest a way of expanding our initial assumption about the reasons for the general avoidance of narrative in biblical verse. The semantic momentum of the system of parallelism, as I have tried to show analytically, invites, when it is used for narration, a certain unilinear and powerfully heightened representation of character: as actions proceed from strong to stronger, the imposing, inexorable actors, whether human or divine, go from strength to awesome strength. It is hardly an accident that biblical poetry, when it turns, even episodically, to narration, is particularly at home with the depiction of processes of destruction: God descending amidst lightning and black clouds to rout His enemies; Job assaulted and macerated; armies sweeping like all-consuming fire to engulf Jerusalem; a relentless heroine pounding, smashing, laying low the enemy—all of these actions except the last being figurative or monitory rather than historical events. Biblical Israel was compelled to win a purchase on life in the harshest historical circumstances, first wresting its inheritance by conquest, then surrounded by hostile peoples, at the geographical cross-roads of great and often ruthless empires. The frequent fierceness of the narrative verse, then, expresses a deep and even predictable current of ancient Hebrew sensibility, but, given the imperatives of ethical monotheism, it was not the main current; and in order to show, in story form, the fluctuating and ambiguous behavior of man as a moral agent acting from the peculiarity of his own character, writers had to turn from the emphatic progressive rhythms of parallelistic verse to the freer and more flexible medium of prose.

Since, however, the subject of biblical literature is not man alone but also God powerfully working in history, verse narrative could be appropriately used to represent the terrific and decisive intervention of the Lord in human affairs. In other words, there could be no proper epic poetry, with its larger-than-life human figures and its deities conceived in essentially human terms, but there could be narrative verse on a smaller scale celebrating God's power in the affairs of man, as in David's victory hymn or, preeminently, in the triumphal Song of the Sea. The Song (Exod. 15:1–18) is worth considering briefly because it provides an instance of narrative at the other end of the spectrum from the terse story of Jael. In twenty-five lines of verse, the poem moves through the whole story of the parting of the sea and the destruction of the Egyptians and onward (in a historical telescoping) through two and a half centuries involving the conquest of the Land and the establishment of the sanctuary in Jerusalem. The line divisions I offer might be contested at a couple of points: lines 13 and 14 and lines 16 and 18, which I have scanned as short lines (two beats per verset) could also be read as long lines (four beats per verset), 13 and 14 making one line and 16–18 another, triadic line, but this formal change would not substantively affect the analysis I shall propose. In any case, the division of the poem into three more or less equal strophes is clear for reasons I shall indicate in my comments, and so I have marked the ends of the strophes by a typographical break.

1 Let me sing to the Lord, Who   Horse and rider He flung into the
    surged, oh surged!   sea.

2	My strength and power is the Lord,	and He became my saving.
3	This is my Lord, let me extol Him,	my father's God, let me exalt Him.
4	The Lord is a warrior,	the Lord is His name.
5	Pharaoh's chariots and his host	He hurled into the sea.
6	And his picked officers	were drowned in the Sea of Reeds.
7	The depths covered them,	they went down to the deep like a stone.
8	Your right hand, Lord, is mighty in power,	Your right hand, Lord, smashed the enemy.
9	In Your great surging You destroyed Your foes,	You sent forth Your wrath, You consumed them like straw.
10	In the blast of Your nostrils the waters piled high,	stood up like a wall the floods,
	the depths froze in the heart of the sea.	
11	The enemy said:	I'll pursue, overtake,
	I'll divide the spoil.	
12	I'll have my fill of them,	unsheathe my sword,
	my hand shall seize them.	
13	You blew Your blast—	the sea covered them.
14	They sank like lead	in the mighty waters.
15	Who is like You among the gods, O Lord,	who like You, mighty in holiness,
	awesome in praise, working wonders?	
16	You stretched out Your hand—	the earth swallowed them.
17	You led in Your kindness	the people You redeemed.
18	You guided them in Your strength	to Your holy abode.
19	Peoples heard and quailed,	shuddering seized the dwellers of Philistia.
20	Then the chieftains of Edom panicked,	the leaders of Moab were seized with trembling.
21	All the dwellers of Canaan were dismayed,	fear and terror seized them.
22	Through the greatness of Your arm	they became like stone.
23	Until Your people passed, O Lord,	until the people passed whom You took up.
24	You brought them, planted them in the mount of Your inheritance.	A firm place for Your dwelling You made, O Lord.
	A sanctuary, God, Your hands made firm.	
25	The Lord shall reign	forever and ever.

The strophic division of the poem, a rare instance in biblical poetry, has long been recognized by scholarship because of the clear indications in the language of the poem.[7] In each strophe the line before the last, or before the penultimate line, includes a nearly identical simile: "like a

51

stone," "like lead," "like a stone." Each strophe then ends with a line celebrating God's power, and these end lines form a progression: first God's power in battle, then His might over all imagined divine beings for whom men have made claims, and finally, in a kind of *envoi*, the affirmation of His eternal sovereignty. The first strophe begins with God's "surging" (the meaning is "to triumph," but I have adopted the literal sense to retain the clear suggestion in the Hebrew of a rising tide of water), and that word begins the first line of the middle strophe as well, though it is absent at the beginning of the last strophe, perhaps because the scene of action is no longer the sea. (It might be noted, however, that a transitional continuity with the sea triumph is maintained by the stretching out of the hand at the beginning of the third strophe, the very action God had commanded Moses to perform in order to part the waters of the sea.) The first two strophes end similarly, with an image of the watery depths; the last strophe ends with an antithetical image of God's firmly or solidly founding (*konen, makhon*) a mountain abode for Himself in the Land of Israel. Within this symmetrical strophic structure, narrative momentum is developed in a particularly interesting way.

The poem begins by signaling in the first line that it is not an independent narrative but a narrative ancillary to the previously told story, and whose purpose is as much to celebrate as to narrate. Thus, the whole "plot" is already transmitted in lapidary fashion in the second verset, "Horse and rider He flung into the sea," and the subsequent telling of the tale is similarly allusive, giving first a general and elliptical account of the victory in the initial strophe, then (once more, in accord with the logic of focusing) proceeding to a more detailed rendering of the same action in the second strophe, where we get images of God's breath (that is, the wind) blowing back the water into solid columns, and dialogue that dramatizes the overweening enemy's deluded hopes of plunder and slaughter. The allied movement we have seen elsewhere in narrative verse of intensification and incremental repetition is prominent throughout this poem. One might even say that the second verset of the opening line "generates" everything in the first two strophes: the initial flinging of horse and rider becomes a drowning, a descent, a sinking of Pharaoh's chariots, his army, his choice captains, and the initial sea becomes the depths, the floods, wind-blown into walls and then back to an engulfing tide.

In this crescendo movement there is, of course, a good deal of interlinear parallelism; one particular use to which it is put—this is again a common procedure in biblical verse—is to serve as compensation for lack of semantic parallelism within the line (compare lines 5–6, 16–19). Even where there is such compensatory interlinear parallelism, one notes a tendency of the poet to forge sequential links between the parallel utterances that go on from line to line. Thus, the relation between versets in line 13, "You blew Your blast— / the sea covered them," is one of cause and effect, before and after, whereas in the next line, "They sank like lead / in the mighty waters," it is a relation between main clause and an adverbial modifier of spatial location; but the semantic parallelism between the two lines also involves temporal sequence: both depict the drowning of the Egyptians, but the wind-blown tidal wave of line 13 clearly precedes the sinking like lead in the mighty waters of the next line. Again, the pursuers' words (lines 11–12), conveyed in a nervous, two-beat triadic rhythm of urgent movement, are a clear instance of parallel acts that are also sequenced acts: pursue, overtake, divide, spoil; have my fill of them, unsheathe my sword, seize them. (In the second series, one might perhaps have expected "have my fill" at the end, but I shall not tamper with the word order of the received text in order to preserve the perfect consistency of a thesis.)

The beginning of the third strophe offers a bolder use of temporally sequenced near-synonyms because the time span involved is more than two centuries. You stretched out Your hand, You led, You guided, the poet says almost in one breath, but the three acts are, respectively, the destruction of the Egyptian host, the forty years of wandering in the wilderness, and the entry into the Land, including the ultimate fulfillment in the conquest of Jerusalem ("Your holy abode"). This telescoping effect is strikingly reinforced in the Hebrew by a phonetic assimilation of these three leading verbs involving alliteration, assonance, and rhyme—*natita, nahita, neihalta.*

The third strophe has troubled some commentators because of its patently anachronistic character: having nothing directly to do with the miraculous victory at the Reed Sea, it might even seem somehow tacked on. The theological-historical point, however, embodied in the narrative art of these verses is precisely to project out of the stunning experience at the Reed Sea a larger pattern of God's powerful—one might say "heroic"—acts in history. I would suggest that a purposeful transition is brilliantly effected at the very beginning of the last strophe with the phrase "the earth swallowed them." This obviously refers to the drowning of the Egyptians, a meaning reinforced, as I have noted, by God's repeating Moses' gesture of stretching out his hand over the sea, and also by the term *'eretz*, which sometimes refers to the underworld rather than to the earth and so makes the substitution of "earth" for "sea" less problematic. But being swallowed up by the earth is reminiscent as well of the punishment of Korah's rebellious crew in one of the most memorable of the Wilderness stories and may also point forward, metaphorically rather than literally, to the fate of the Canaanites. In any case, whereas the first and second strophes begin and end with evocations of the sea, the last stanza begins by prominently introducing the word 'eretz—"earth," "underworld," and, most important for the end of the strophe and of the poem, "land." One might think of this transition as the application on a larger structural scale of the technique of overlap we have seen used between versets and between lines. God the destroyer of the Egyptians at the Reed Sea becomes in a single, scarcely perceptible step the guide of His people through the wilderness and into the Land, and He Who strikes with terror their enemies who would block their entrance into their promised inheritance.

All this happens so fast that there is a kind of illusion of simultaneity (or, perhaps, a kind of fiction of simultaneity), which the poet clearly exploits. It is as if the peoples of Canaan, having heard the rumors of the awesome destruction of the Egyptians, become instantly panic-stricken, long before the actual arrival of the Israelites. But the poet and his audience were perfectly aware that, by the received account, the gradual process of the conquest of the Land did not begin till forty years after the events at the Reed Sea, and the real meaning of this exercise of poetic license is to reproduce in the narrative sweep of the poem a strong and recurrent rhythm of God's action in history: just as He devastated the Egyptians, made them sink like a stone in the watery deep, His mighty presence makes the hostile nations of Canaan turn to stone with fear while He guides His people in and firmly founds His sanctuary far above the engulfing flood.

The Hebrew Bible does offer rare glimpses of another kind of narrative poetry, not theophanic, not the representation in image and action of mounting intensities, but a narrative report of character, gesture, speech, and act that seems more closely akin to the nuanced fictional imagination of the prose tales. Not surprisingly, one finds these glimpses particularly in biblical texts that belong to the ancient Near Eastern category of Wisdom literature, with its freedom from national perspectives and its often secular emphases. Because biblical poetry does remain, after all, fundamentally nonnarrative, most of these manifestations of a nontheo-logical, nonhistorical narrative impulse are brief intimations, on the scale, say, of the passage from Job we looked at as an instance of another sort of narrativity in verse. But there is one complete, relatively extended narrative of this kind, Proverbs 7, which can provide an appropriate conclusion to our consideration of verse narration because it illustrates so vividly another possibility that ancient Hebrew verse might have realized or perhaps, indeed, did realize in a larger body of texts that have not come down to us. In this instance, the line numbers happily coincide with the traditional verse numbers. Although there are no strophic divisions in the poem, lines 1–5 clearly constitute a formal exordium before the narrative proper, as lines 24–27 are a formal conclusion, pointing the moral; and so I have set them apart by typographical breaks:

1	My lad, keep my sayings,	my precepts store up by you.
2	Keep my precepts and live,	my teaching, like the apple of your eye.
3	Bind them on your fingers,	write them on the tablet of your heart.
4	Say to Wisdom, you are my sister,	call Understanding a kinsman.
5	To keep you from a foreign woman,	from an alien woman who talks smoothly.
6	When in the window of my house,	through my lattice I peered,
7	I saw among the fools,	I made out among the lads a witless fellow.
8	Passing through the market, by the corner,	on the way to her house he strides.
9	At twilight, at eventide,	in the dark of night and gloom.
10	And look, a woman to meet him—	whorish attire and devious aims.
11	Bustling and restless,	in her house her steps do not dwell.
12	Now outside, now in the squares,	at every corner she lurks.
13	She seizes him and kisses him,	impudently she speaks:
14	"I had to make peace-sacrifices,	today I fulfilled my vows.
15	So I came out to meet you,	to seek your presence, and I found you.
16	With coverlets I've spread my couch,	dyed cloths of Egyptian linen.
17	I've sprinkled my bed	with myrrh, aloes, and cinnamon.
18	Let's drink our fill of love till dawn,	let us revel in love's delights.
19	For the man is not in his house,	he's gone on a far-off way.
20	The purse of silver he took in his hand,	at the full moon he'll come back to his house."
21	She draws him aside with all her talk,	with her smooth speech she lures him.
22	He goes after her blithely	like an ox coming to the slaughter,

like a fool trotting off to the stocks.[8]

| 23 | Till an arrow splits his liver, | as a bird hurries to the trap, |
| | not knowing it will be fatal. | |

24	And so, lads, listen to me,	hearken to my mouth's sayings.
25	Let your heart swerve not to her ways,	do not stray on her paths.
26	For many are the victims she has felled,	innumerable all she has killed.
27	Through her house are the ways to Sheol,	going down to the chambers of death.

The narrator of this monitory tale is, of course, the mentor who in so many passages in Proverbs, whether narrative or aphoristic, addresses the untutored young man (the "lad" or, more literally, "son") in need of prudential instruction. As a purveyor of conventional wisdom, he speaks, appropriately enough, a kind of verse that is more symmetrically regular and smoother in its use of formulaic phrases than the texts we have so far considered. Most of the lines have a consistent stress pattern of three accents in each verset (with four in just a few lines); there are only two triadic lines, and those at a point where the text is probably corrupt (lines 22–23); and there is a sizable number of lines in which the semantic parallelism reflects a relatively high degree of synonymity or complementarity. The mentor also symmetrically frames his discourse in an envelope structure: five highly formulaic lines at the beginning exhort the young man, as he is exhorted so often elsewhere in Proverbs, to heed the mentor's words, with the fifth line introducing the specific topic of instruction, the perils of the seductress; four equally formulaic lines at the end once more enjoin the young man to hearken to the mentor's advice, now stressing by way of conclusion the lethal effects of the loose woman's blandishments. The frame-verses, moreover, as I shall try to show, are also used to excellent effect to define the thematic field of the narrative and to set up a direct continuity between the concrete images of the story and the thematic implications the narrator wants us to draw.

A distinguishing feature of this text when one compares it with other biblical narratives, whether in prose or in verse, is that the tale is told by a clearly defined persona. The experience-wise mentor is discursive in the frame-verses; then, in the transitional line 6, marked by an introductory subordinate clause, he sets himself up preeminently as a witness to the events he will narrate, peering out from his window and detecting among the "lads" a particularly gullible one about to fall victim to the seductress. Line 6 is a rare instance of retrospective ellipsis, the verb "peered" at the very end of the line doing double duty for both versets. It seems to me quite misguided to emend the line, as some scholars have proposed: the verb is reserved for the end both because of the subordinate clause that carries us into the narrative proper and because the "peering" can thus be withheld climactically, to overlap with "I-saw," the first word (in the Hebrew) of the next line. (A similar use of a retrospective double-duty verb occurs here in line 12, where the climactic revelation of "lurks" is reserved for the end of the line.) Our observer, in other words, is a particularly keen-sighted one: he can pick out of the crowd both the wily woman and her dupe and see exactly what is going on between them, literally and figuratively, even in the growing shadows of evening, which she chooses as the aptest time to meet her lover. The seeming uncertainty, by the way, about the hour between the two halves of line 9 is a lovely instance of the artful use of movement in time and in intensity between versets. It is twilight when she accosts him, but already complete darkness— *'ishon,* the same word used for "apple" of the eye in line 2—is falling, that cover of obscurity under which she will offer him a night of sexual pleasures.

This poem differs in several respects from the theophanic and nationalist texts we have inspected, in regard to the formal strategies it adopts to establish a narrative tempo as well as in its use of such a clear narrative exposition. There is little trace here of a matrix of incremental repetition, and instead of parallelisms of intensification we encounter for the most part parallelisms of specification ("And look, a woman to meet him, / whorish attire and devious aims," "With coverlets I've spread my couch, / dyed cloths of Egyptian linen") and parallelisms of sequential connection ("Passing through the market, by the corner, / on the way to her house he strides," "For the man is not in his house, / he's gone on a far-off way"). The sense of action created by this pattern is not at all the crescendo series of overlapping events we have seen elsewhere but is instead a deployment of vivid thumbnail portraiture (as in lines 10–11) integrated with a rapid syntagmatic movement from one act to the next (note the quick steps from line 8 to line 13), on to the necessary catastrophe (lines 21–23). Although the end is foreseen, there is much less of a feeling of inexorable progression here, more a sense of surprising and arresting revelations as the narrative advances.

The most striking formal feature, however, of this monitory tale directly links its artistry to that of prose narration in the Bible—the fact that the main burden of the story is carried by dialogue, which is at once an instrument of characterization and a vehicle of thematic argument. As in the prose narratives, this centrality of dialogue is even reflected quantitatively: two lines introduce the foolish young man, already hurrying to his ruin; another four lines sketch the wily woman flitting about the streets; then seven lines are devoted to her speech, followed by just three more lines of actual narration to convey the denouement. Significantly, and in consonance with a common device for the selective assignment of direct discourse in the prose narratives, the young man is not allotted any speech, merely hastening after her like an ox to the slaughter.

Is this wily woman who is so wonderfully revealed through her own words what one would call an individual character? If she is compared to figures from the prose narratives like Tamar, Rachel, Rebecca, and Michal the daughter of Saul, the answer would have to be no. A useful analogue would be the peculiar status of characters in English Augustan satirical verse, which, as William Youngren pointed out years ago in an illuminating essay,[9] are quite purposefully a fusion of generality (the embodiments of moral types) and vivid concreteness. The woman here is the general type, seductress, but she also is made to speak and act with a persuasive distinctiveness of presence. In her mouth, the balanced parallel utterances of biblical verse take on a dramatic plausibility, an almost colloquial fluency, that we have not seen in our previous examples—with one divergence from parallelism, line 17, introduced as she proffers, before the actual sexual invitation, the climactic enticement of her having perfumed the destined bed of pleasure.

Her meeting with the young man is not a chance encounter but, apparently, an assignation, for he is already on his way to her house when she accosts him, and she suggests that she has been looking specifically for him. Since her first gesture is to grab him and kiss him, her initial words, "I had to make peace-sacrifices . . . ," already illustrate what the mentor-narrator has just called her impudence. Because this is a kind of freely offered sacrifice where most of the animal is left for the votive's consumption after the burning of the fat and the spilling of the blood, she is telling him that she has a feast prepared for him at home, but the way she chooses to convey this involves making a little parade of her punctilious observance of the cult that is in questionable accord with her transparent posture of sexual solicitation. Offering sacrifices and fulfilling vows (with a wordplay in the Hebrew between *shelamim*, "peace-sacrifices," and *shalem*, "fulfill" or "pay") are close to a formulaic pairing, but here that approximate synonymity gets caught up in the dramatic flow of her speech: it's not just that I've had offerings to make, but this very day—a parallelism of specification—I've fulfilled my vow, so you can count on a hot and piping feast at my place right now. That, in fact (line 15), is precisely why I have come out to meet you, to seek your presence—a parallelism of intensification—and what a delight to have found you!

Having thus declared her eagerness to welcome the young man, the seductress can now move on quickly to the main point—the bed and what is to be done in it. In a strategically effective parallelism of specification (line 16), she first tells him that she has her bed all nicely made up for him, then specifies in the second verset that she is using deluxe imported linens; and this focus on the sheets leads by easy contiguity to the sensual refinement of perfuming the sheets that is recorded in the next line. We might note that she has reached out, as it were, over the length and breadth of the known commercial world to enhance the softness and fragrance of her bed, using fine Egyptian linens from the South and spices from the East, including cinnamon, which might have been brought all the way from India.

The explicit sexual proposition of the next line (line 18) deftly picks up the idea of feasting she used as an overture by adopting a familiar metaphor—compare the Song of Songs—of drinking love's pleasures. Through all this, the young man remains silent, but lines 19–20 invite the inference that she has detected a look of fearful hesitation after her offer of sumptuous sexual delights, for she needs to reassure him that there is nothing to worry about: "For the man is not in his house"—and note how she refers to him impersonally as "the man" (or "the husband")—indeed (parallelism of specification), "he's gone on a far-off way." The specification and heightening, beautifully absorbed into the exigencies of the dramatic occasion, continue into the following line: you see, he's taken along his money bag, so you can rest assured that it's an extended business trip, that he won't be back till the middle of the month. (The full moon is far off. The encounter is probably taking place in the dark of the moon, which would jibe nicely with the reference to a pitch-dark night in 9b.)[10] The invocation of the purse of silver is telling in another direction as well: in the background of the dramatic encounter between seductress and seduced, we get an image of the cuckolded husband, a man of affairs traveling to distant parts to accumulate the wealth his wife lavishes on imported linens and scents. The unfaithful wife, moreover, may have still another bow to string here (besides the one, presumably alluding to venereal disease, mentioned in line 23), which is a design on the young man's money. My husband, she implies, has gone off on the businessman's special without so much as leaving me a credit card, so you will understand, won't you dear, if I ask you to help out with all these expenditures I've had to make?

The last line of the introductory section (line 5) exactly reproduces a line we considered (Prov. 2:16) at the end of chapter 1, with the single, minor substitution of "to keep you" for "to save you." The specifying second verset of the line from Proverbs 2, as we noted, immediately generates a miniature narrative in the following lines. Here, where a narrative is developed on a larger scale, the narrator steps in after "an alien woman who talks smoothly" to set the scene for the action. But the entire action, with the woman's wonderfully calculated smooth talk at the center of it, is really an "unpacking" of the narrative consequences of that initial clause, and this point is underscored, in a kind of frame within the external frame, when the narrator in line 21 sums up the effect of her speech: "She draws him aside with all her talk, / with her smooth speech she lures him."

The connections between frame and story are reinforced by the poem's use of still another prominent device of biblical prose narrative—thematic key-words, or *Leitwörter*. To be sure, we have also encountered *Leitwörter* in very different kinds of poems—the use of "saving" and "rock" in David's victory hymn is one clear instance—but in such texts the repetition of a key-word is chiefly a matter of insistence and emphasis, quite in keeping with the rhetorical strategy of incremental repetition. In Proverbs 7, on the other hand, the *Leitwörter* exhibit the sort of ironic interplay and progressive articulation of meanings one finds in the use of that device in the prose narratives. The most obvious thematic key-word is "sayings," which the mentor introduces in his very first verset and then again in the first line of the concluding frame-verses (line 24), and these sayings of prudent experience are pointedly juxtaposed with the seductress's smooth talk, first mentioned in line 5 with the same Hebrew word, 'amarim, and then illustrated in her speech. More subtly, the poem plays an intricate game with "house" and "way" from the moment narration begins, in line 6, through to the end of the final frame-verses. The narrator sits in the security of his own house looking out on that zone of danger, the streets, where wily women and naïve young men go wandering. The unwitting victim is first seen headed "on the way to her house" (line 8); she, on her part, is not one to let her heels cool in "her house" (line 11), where, of course, a good wife belongs. Her husband (line 19) is not in his own house; on the contrary, he has gone off on a distant way, and only at the full moon will he return "to his house" (line 20). And so she "draws him aside" (line 21), leading him to her house, her bed, his perdition.

What the poet in effect does through all this is to take a stereotypical metaphor for the moral life that is commonplace in both Proverbs and Psalms—going on a way, on a straight path—and give it strong narrative realization. The young man is seen from the first on the way to her house, but since that is not the way on which he should be going, it is presented as an act of being lured aside from the straight path, as the summarizing line 25 makes perfectly clear: "Let your heart not swerve to her ways, / do not stray on her paths." For her house, with its soft, scented couch curtained by the gloom of night, is no house at all but a man-trap dropping down into ruin. The last line of the poem beautifully ties up this whole development by once more invoking both "way" and "house" in its first verset and then carrying us on in a revelatory focusing maneuver from "house" to inner "chambers" and from "ways" to their destination, "death": "Through her house are the ways to Sheol, / going down to the chambers of death."

For all the didactic pressure exerted in the poem, and of course evidenced in the use of thematic key-words, fictional imagination is at work in this narrative, giving concrete definition to an encounter between two drastically different human figures, inventing supple and lively dialogue that not only reveals the character of the speaker but also intimates a whole context of social institutions and relations, material culture, even certain nuances of psychological portraiture of the wife-lover-cuckold triangle. But verse narrative of this sort is obviously untypical in the Bible, which almost everywhere prefers prose to poetry for such complicating play of the fictional imagination. It is far more common to find episodic narrativity rather than actual narrative in biblical verse, as we saw in the briefer examples of narrative movement we examined earlier. Given the fact, however, that in very many lines of poetry the relation between parallel versets involves not consequentiality but some sort of heightening, one often finds that the structure of biblical poems is determined not by any subsurface impulse of narration but rather by a steady progression of image or theme, a sort of mounting semantic pressure, which is to say, a structure of intensification. But, like all things wrought in poetry, that, too, will have to be seen in the details of the poems themselves.

III

Structures of Intensification

THERE IS a certain affinity, let me suggest, between the formal properties of any given prosodic system or poetic genre and the kinds of meaning most readily expressed through that system or genre. I have, of course, triply hedged my bets in this formulation with the evasive "affinity," the qualifying "certain," and the limiting "most readily," but such caution is called for because original poets in most eras often devise ways, whether quietly or ostentatiously, to work successfully against the grain of inherited form. Nevertheless, given form does tend to invite a particular orientation in the poetic ordering of the world. The Shakespearian sonnet can lend itself to love poetry, reflections on life's transience, celebrations of the power of art, and a good deal else, but whatever the topic or mood, a writer using this form can scarcely avoid organizing his statement in a sequence of three equal and balanced blocks, usually with an implied progression from one to the next, and concluding in a pithy summary or witty antithesis embodied in the couplet that follows the three quatrains. The artifice of form, in other words, becomes a particular way of conceiving relations and defining linkages, sequence, and hierarchies in the reality to which the poet addresses himself. A poet who felt moved, let us say, to celebrate the teeming variety and vastness of the human and natural landscape would not get very far with the sonnet form, would need a kind of poetic vehicle that was more expansive, allowing for free-flowing catalogues and effects of asymmetry and improvisation—would need, in short, something like Whitmanesque free verse.

In the case of biblical poetry, the two basic operations of specification and heightening within the parallelistic line lead to an incipiently narrative structure of minute concatenations, on the one hand, and to a climactic structure of thematic intensifications, on the other hand. The astute reader will perceive that in point of poetic fact these two hands are sometimes tightly clasped, especially because, as we have seen, narrative progression in biblical verse often moves up a scale of increasing intensity, and because in practice it is sometimes hard to distinguish between a "focusing" that specifies and implies temporal sequence and one that is chiefly a stepping-up of assertion. There is no special reason to insist on simon-pure categories—one rarely encounters them in literature—but I do think the general distinction between the two different generative principles in biblical poetry is useful. There are, that is, many biblical poems in which any implied events, even metaphoric ones, are secondary while what is primary is a predicament, an image, or a thematic idea that is amplified from verset to verset and from line to line. Poetic form acts in these cases as a kind of magnifying glass, concentrating the rays of meaning to a white-hot point. This means, to translate that static image back into the sequential mode in which the literary text works, that the progression of intensifying thematic particles is brought to a culminating flare-up, or compels resolution by a sharp reversal at the end. This kind of poetic structure lends itself beautifully to the writing of a psalmodic plea for help, a prophetic denunciation, or a Jobian complaint, but not to the aphoristic poise and the sense of cunning interrelation that are at home in the sonnet or to the rhapsodic feeling for the lovely heterogeneity of things that is readily expressed in Whitmanesque verse.

As an initial illustration of the structure of intensification, let us consider a brief and very simple psalm—powerful in its simplicity in a way we may understand better if we try to follow closely the operation of thematic focusing in the text. Psalm 13, in six compact lines, offers a strong model of the supplication—intoned "in straits" or "out of the depths"—that is one of the important genres of psalm.

To the leader, a psalm of David.

1 How long, Lord, will You forget me perpetually,   how long will You hide Your face from me?

2 How long will I cast about schemes in my mind,   grief in my heart all day?

How long will my enemy be over me?

3 Look, answer me, Lord my God,   give light to my eyes, lest I sleep death.

4	Lest my enemy say, "I have him,"	my foes exult when I slip.
5	But I trust in Your kindness,	my heart exults in Your saving might.
6	I will sing to the Lord	for He has requited me.

In discussing narrative verse, I drew attention to the importance of incremental repetition and of ways of advancing meaning that may ultimately be derived from incremental repetition. Psalm 13, like many of the psalms of supplication, uses a very different mode of repetition—anaphora, which is to say, the rhetorically emphatic reiteration of a single word or brief phrase, in itself not a syntactically complete unit. In incremental repetition the restatement, with an addition, of a clause in itself complete as a unit of syntax and meaning often produces an overlap effect where we perceive an action flowing into a related and subsequent action: "Between her legs he kneeled and fell, / where he kneeled, he fell, destroyed." Anaphora, on the other hand, shifts the center of attention from the repeated element to the material that is introduced by the repetition, at once inviting us to see all the new utterances as locked into the same structure of assertion and to look for strong differences or elements of development in the new material. There is, in other words, a productive tension between sameness and difference, reiteration and development, in the use of anaphora.

If we are rigorous about the way poems articulate meanings, we will have to conclude that the repeated word or phrase in anaphora never means exactly the same thing twice, that in each occurrence it takes on a certain coloration from the surrounding semantic material and from its position in the series. This general point about repetition has been nicely formulated by the Russian semiotician Jurij Lotman:

> Strictly speaking, unconditional repetition is impossible in poetry. The repetition of a word in a text, as a rule, does not mean the mechanical repetition of a concept. Most often it points to a more complex, albeit unified, semantic context.
>
> The reader accustomed to the graphic perception of a text sees the repeated outlines of a word on paper and assumes that he is looking at the mere duplication of a concept. In fact he is usually dealing with another, more complex concept, that is related to the given word, but whose complication is by no means quantitative.[1]

Lotman goes on to offer a telling illustration of the principle, an instance of emphatic repetition. When one encounters a line of verse like "Soldier, bid her farewell, bid her farewell," every reader realizes that the second "bid her farewell" could not be identical in meaning with the first. For the soldier is not being urged to say goodbye twice to his girl but, obviously, is being reminded of the poignancy of the leave-taking, the dearness of his beloved, the possibility he may never see her again, the dreadful imminence of the departure, or any combination of such implications. Let me propose that in our psalm the anaphoric series of four times "how long," while clearly informed by what Lotman calls a "unified semantic context," reflects an ascent on a scale of intensity, the note of desperate urgency pitched slightly higher with each repetition. Heightening, as in many other instances, is in part associated with a movement from cause to effect and from general to specific statement, but here without any real development of narrative momentum.

The rising movement is clear, compact, and, as I have suggested, exemplary of the supplication as a form of Hebrew verse. Initially, the speaker complains of being perpetually forgotten (or "neglected") by God; in the parallel verset this plight of neglect is imagined more personally and concretely—in a way, more terribly—as God's hiding His face from the supplicant. The second, triadic line translates the general condition of abandonment into the inward experience of the speaker, who flounders devising futile schemes and, what is more, is in the constant grip of grief—because, as we finally learn in the third verset, his enemy is winning out against him. It is worth noting that this last "how long" in the anaphoric series ("How long will my enemy be over me?") not only introduces a specification barely hinted at in the preceding statements but also has a virtual causal force absent in the previous occurrences of the self-same syllables (that is, How long is my distress to continue?—for this is the reason for it). It thus nicely illustrates how verbatim repetition in a poetic text is not to be equated with total identity of meaning.

At this climactic point of desperation (at the end of line 3), the speaker breaks away from the anaphora and pronounces three imperative verbs— the only such verbs in the poem—addressed to God: "*Look, answer* me, Lord my God, / *give light* to my eyes, / lest I sleep death." The looking, which is heightened in the second verset into giving light to the eyes— presumably the effect of God's gaze—is obviously a prayer for the reversal of that awful hiding of the divine face invoked in line 1. The third verset, a subordinate clause, is linked to the second verset by an association of thematic and causal antithesis: either You make my eyes shine by turning toward me at once or they will close forever in the sleep of death. At this point, the poet complements the initial anaphora of "how long," which stressed his persisting anguish, with an anaphoric insistence on "lest," which stresses the critical precariousness of his present condition. The "lest" at the beginning of line 4 unfolds the meaning of its counterpart in the last verset of line 3: "lest I sleep death"—which is to say, lest my enemy, who has long had the upper hand over me, be granted his final triumph (to cry out *yekholtiv*, "I have him" or, more literally, "I have prevailed over him"). This picture of defeat is then emphatically rounded out in the second verset of line 4, with the representation of the foes exulting as they behold the speaker tottering, about to topple.

The general complaint, then, of being forgotten by God with which the poem began has been brought to a painfully vivid culmination in which the speaker imagines his own death both as a subjective state—sleeping the sleep of death, where God's gaze will never be able to light up his eyes—and as a dramatic scene—going down for the last time, with his enemies crowing in triumph. This is the white-hot point to which the magnifying glass of the structure of intensification has concentrated the assertions of desperate need. At the moment of the imaginative enactment of death, the speaker swings away sharply into a concluding affirmation of faith, introduced by a strongly contrastive "but I," *va'ani* (in the Hebrew, all the previous occurrences of "I" and "me" are by way of suffixes and prefixes in declined or conjugated forms, and this is the sole instance of the pronoun proper). He trusts in God's kindness, or faithfulness (*ḥesed*), and, what is more, his heart exults in God's deliverance, in a precise antithetical response to the enemies who were imagined exulting over his death. The poem that began in a cry of distress to a neglectful God ends (line 6) in a song of praise to God, Whose deliverance of those who trust in Him is already considered an accomplished fact.

Structurally, the countermovement of the last two lines functions differently from the concluding couplet of a Shakespearian sonnet, which reflects a tendency of the speaker to stand back contemplatively from his own preceding assertions and, even when an antithesis to them is proffered, to tie up the meanings of the poem with a certain sense of neat resolution. In the psalm, there is less resolution than surprising emotional reversal impelled by the motor force of faith. In this respect, the uses that later religious tradition made of Psalms are very much in keeping with the spirit of the original poems, even though the psalmist conceived being "saved" in more concrete and literal terms than have most postbiblical readers. (In our text, it is not altogether clear whether the battle imagery is literal or figurative, but in any case the supplicant is complaining of tottering on the brink of death in a world of human action, not of spiritual symbolism.) The speaker, that is, finds himself plunged into a fierce reality where things seem to go from bad to worse to the worst of all. There is no "logical" way out of this predicament—it is an image in miniature of the general biblical predicament of threatened national existence in the dangerous midst of history—as there is no discursive means in verse to imagine anything but its ominous intensification, except for the sudden, unaccountable, paradoxical swing of faith that enables the speaker at the nadir of terror to affirm that God will sustain him, indeed has sustained him. Generically, the supplication has been transformed in a single stroke into a psalm of thanksgiving.[2]

Perhaps the most brilliant elucidation ever written of this psalmodic structure of concluding antithesis is in the Sea Poems of the twelfth-century Hebrew poet Judah Halevi, which are among the most remarkable lyric achievements of the Middle Ages. Halevi, a virtuoso stylist who had profoundly assimilated, along with other antecedent Hebrew texts, the poetic dynamic of Psalms, conjures up in these poems about his voyage to the Land of Israel the roiling chaos of the sea about to engulf him; and, typically, he effects a sharp turn of faith at the end of each poem in affirming his trust in the God Who will pluck him from the wave-tossed plank to which he clings and set him down in the courts of Jerusalem. Transposed into another, more intricately elegant poetic mode, Halevi's Sea Poems perfectly capture the underlying movement of our psalm and of a good many like it. One chief reason for the success of Psalm 13 in giving such a resonant voice to a soul in distress—in its own time and for posterity—is that its spare, compact assertions of critical need, which at first glance may seem merely a series of equivalent statements, in fact generate a rising line of tension, reaching the pitch of ultimate disaster that then triggers the sudden turn and resolution of the believer's trust at the end.

While biblical poets often prefer this strong linear development of the structure of intensification, even for longer poems, there are also many instances of more intricate variations of the structure. Psalm 39 is a particularly instructive text in this regard because it offers three different patterns of thematic development, which are cunningly interwoven.

To the leader, to Jeduthun, a psalm of David.
1   I said: let me keep my way from   let me keep a muzzle on my mouth, offending with my tongue,
             as long as the wicked is before me.

2 I was mute, in stillness,   I was dumb, cut off from good,
    and my pain was stirred.
3 My heart was hot within me, in my thoughts a flame burned,
    I spoke with my tongue.
4 Let me know, Lord, my end, and what is the measure of my
              days,
    that I may know how fleeting I am.
5 Bare handbreadths You made my existence is nothing to You,
  my days,
    mere breath each man stands.*
6 In but shadow man walks about, mere breath his bustlings,
    he stores up, knowing not who will gather.
7 And so what can I expect, O My hope is in You.
  God?
8 From all my transgressions make me not the scorn of the fool.
  deliver me,
9 I was mute, did not open my for Yours was the doing.
  mouth,
10 Take away from me Your from Your blows I perish.
  plague,
11 In chastisement for sin You melting like a moth what he
  afflict a man,   treasures.
    Mere breath are all men. Selah.
12 Hear my prayer, O Lord, give ear to my cry,
    to my tears be not silent.
13 For I am an alien with You, a resident like all my forefathers.
14 Look away from me so I may before I go off and am not.
  recover,*

This, too, is a psalm of supplication, but the speaker's definition of his own plight and of his relation to God is manifestly more complicated than what we encountered in Psalm 13. He, too, is in great straits, but except for the rather oblique reference to the presence of the wicked at the end of the first line, this situation of acute distress is not spelled out in the poem until lines 8–11, and considerable space is first devoted to an introspective meditation on the transience of human life. Moreover, here there is no sharp turning point of faith after the cry of anguish. The speaker introduces the idea that God is his only hope almost as a logical conclusion of desperation, at the exact middle of the poem (line 7). But then he must try to argue God into having compassion on him, using language and ideas strikingly reminiscent of Job as he has just used language reminiscent of Ecclesiastes in lines 5–6 (whether these are anticipations or echoes of Job and Ecclesiastes there is no way of knowing) and ending on a disquieting note in an evocation of his own imminent extinction. The supplicant of Psalm 13 wants God to turn toward him; the supplicant of Psalm 39 wants Him to have mercy and turn away.

In order to follow these complications of meaning more clearly, we will have to attend to the formal articulations of the poem. It is worth noting at the outset that triadic lines are not merely interspersed, as in other texts we have examined, but actually predominate here. The first six lines of the poem are all triadic, the first dyadic line occurring only when the speaker arrives at the crucial statement that God is his sole hope (line 7), and two more triads appear in the second half of the poem. In most of the triadic lines, moreover, there is an element of imbalance in the semantic parallelism, and one suspects that is precisely why the triads are used. This imbalance is especially clear in the first three lines (in my schematic paraphrase, I will indicate the three versets as *a, b,* and *c*):

1 *(a)* resolution to keep silent; *(b)* more concretely worded resolution to keep silent; *(c)* presence of the wicked

2 *(a)* report of having been silent; *(b)* amplified report of having been silent; *(c)* confession of pain

3 *(a)* report of heated thoughts; *(b)* more metaphorically vivid report of heated thoughts; *(c)* report of the fact of speech

In each of these three lines the third verset stands in some relation of tension to the two preceding versets, retrospectively casting a new light on them, and in the case of line 3 also following consequentially from them in a way that involves an element of surprise. In Psalm 13 the speaker's world is desperate but stable: the movement of intensification focuses in and in from being forgotten by God to the image of the supplicant's death, and then is displaced by the concluding affirmation of trust. In Psalm 39, on the other hand, the speaker flounders in a world of radical ambiguities where the antithetical values of speech and silence, existence and extinction, perhaps even innocence and transgression, have been brought dangerously close together. I do not want to propose, in the manner of one fashionable school of contemporary criticism, that we should uncover in the text a covert or unwitting reversal of its own hierarchical oppositions; or more specifically, that silence is affirmed and then abandoned in consequence of the poet's intuition that all speech is a lie masquerading as truth because of the inevitably arbitrary junction between signifier and signified, language and reality. On the contrary, the ancient Hebrew literary imagination reverts again and again to a bedrock assumption about the efficacy of speech, cosmogonically demonstrated by the Lord (in Genesis 1) Who is emulated by man. In our poem, the speaker's final plea that God hear his cry presupposes the efficacy of speech, the truth-telling power with which language has been used to expose the supplicant's plight. The rapid swings between oppositions in the poem are dictated not by an epistemological quandary but by a psychological dialectic in the speaker. Let me try to explain how this dialectic movement unfolds by tracing the three thematic patterns that together constitute the poem's complex structure of intensification.

The speaker begins by saying that he had intended—the initial 'amarti can mean either "say" or "think"—to keep his mouth shut, and this because of a very specific circumstance: he is within earshot of the malicious, and if he audibly complains he will become a target for their gibes, a point made explicit in line 8. The actual exposition of the speaker's particular predicament is postponed until the middle of the poem (lines 8–11), which has the effect of blurring his special fate of suffering—line 10 indicates that the specific affliction is physical illness—into the general vulnerability of the human condition evoked in lines 4–6. At the beginning there is an indication, in the last verset of line 2, that he is in pain, but this might be construed in immediate context as the pain of pent-up complaints. Similarly, the speaker begins by professing a desire to avoid "offending" (or "sinning," haṭʾo) but in immediate context this seems to refer merely to an offense in the realm of public relations in giving the wicked something to crow about. The first two lines present a clear development of intensification of the theme of silence—from a resolution not to offend by speech, to muzzling the mouth, to preserving (in a chain of three consecutive synonyms) absolute muteness. The realized focal point of silence produces inward fire, a state of acute distress that compels a reversal of the initial resolution and issues in speech. But the content of the speech is something of a surprise. Instead of the formulaic "How long, O Lord" that we might expect, and that might play into the hands of the malicious eavesdropper, the speaker undertakes a meditation on the transience of human life, asking God to give him the profound inner knowledge of his own brief span. This meditation on transience is a second movement of intensification in the poem, beginning with the general "my end," moving on to the "measure of my days," to the speaker's "fleeting" nature, then from "handbreadths" to mere "nothing," to empty "breath" (hevel, the reiterated key-word in Ecclesiastes traditionally rendered as "vanity"). The center of this intensifying movement is nicely defined by a shrewd piece of wordplay: in the last verset of line 4, the speaker wants to understand how "fleeting," *ḥadel*, he is; in the middle verset of line 5, his "existence," *ḥeled*, is as nothing in the eyes of God.

Once the transience theme has been brought to its white-hot point—man is nothing, he can hang on to nothing, can truly know only his own nothingness—the climax compels a reversal, as we have seen elsewhere, and the speaker affirms his hope in God. This in turn leads him to admit to having sinned and to speak of the suffering that has visited him because of it (lines 8–11). The sin-suffering conjunction, however, is less confession than simple admission, and, unlike the themes of silence and transience, it is not developed in a pattern of intensification. The reason for this difference is clear: suffering-because-of-sin is what the speaker begs to be rescued from, not anything he wants to conjure up as an intensifying process; he does, however, want to put heavy stress both on his quandary as a person who needs at once to be silent and to cry out and on the sobering perspective of man's terrible transience. The poet nicely subsumes the whole sin-suffering segment under the two more salient themes by paradoxically reaffirming silence at the beginning of the segment (line 9, first verset) and by reintroducing the theme of transience at the end of the segment (the last word of line 10, the last two versets of line 11). By now it would appear also that silence means something different from what might have been supposed at the beginning: "I was mute, did not open my mouth"—that is, I did not give the "fool" (of the preceding line) a chance to deride me: I did not complain about Your justice, only asked to understand the ephemerality of my own existence, a condition that might be taken as grounds (the next line) for Your withdrawing the terrible weight of Your hand from the melting mortal stuff of which I am made.

The last three lines of the poem begin with what momentarily looks like the formulaic conclusion of a supplication—"Hear my prayer . . . , give ear to my cry"—but the third verset of the triadic line once more introduces an unexpected element: "to my tears be not silent." The poet's third synonym for "complaint" is a metonymy, "tears," which, unlike the two others, is mute, while God is asked not to listen or give ear or look but to be not silent—in perfect thematic counterpoint to the speaker himself, who emphatically pledged silence yet, under the sharp cutting edge of suffering, had no recourse except speech.

Having thus resumed the theme of silence and speech, the poet returns to the theme of transience in the last two lines, bringing it to a strategically telling culmination. The power of line 13 is more evident in the Hebrew than in translation because the line turns on what is known in biblical scholarship as a "breakup pattern." That is, two words that are ordinarily a bound collocation, or more specifically a hendiadys (two words to indicate one concept, like "hue and cry" in English) are broken up and made into parallel terms in the two versets of a line of poetry. In this case, the hendiadys *ger vetoshav*, "resident alien," is split into *ger* in the first verset and *toshav* in the second, the effect being to defamiliarize the common idiom and bring to the fore the sense of temporary, tolerated presence of someone who doesn't really belong. "Like all my forefathers" reinforces this implication by placing the speaker in a rapidly moving chain of generations while aptly connecting his own transience with that of all humanity, in keeping with the generalizing perspective of lines 5–6. The poet then concludes, on a very Jobian note, by begging God to turn away from him while he still has his paltry moment to live. The last word of the poem, *'eyneni*, refers to the speaker's death not as a metaphoric idea (to sleep the sleep of death) or as a dramatic scene (my enemies exult as I fall) but as a flat fact of extinction—"I am not," like the "nothing," *'ayin*, to which he compared his existence before God, the two words in the Hebrew being ultimately the same word, *'eyneni* a declined form of *'ayin*. The final term of intensification, then, in the vision of human transience falls into place with the last word of the poem: what had been a strong metaphor ("mere breath") or simile ("My existence is *as* nothing before You") now becomes an unqualified statement in the first person singular of a fact about to be accomplished. The "I said" that was the first word of the poem terminates, in an ultimate convergence of the theme of silence and the theme of transience, in the irrevocable canceling-out of the sayer.

As with the other texts we are considering in this connection, my intention is not to offer an exhaustive analysis of the poem but to indicate certain underlying possibilities of poetic structure manifested in the poem. The impulse of semantic intensification, as we observe it working from verset to verset and from line to line, would lead us to expect a continuous linear development to a climax, or to a climax and reversal. Though that pattern is in fact extremely common in biblical poetry, Psalm 39 illustrates another possibility: two different lines of intensification are prominent in the poem; each is deployed intermittently, being interrupted and resumed; each qualifies and complicates the other; and the meaning of both patterns is not fully realized until they are brought together at the end. Obviously, I do not mean to suggest that the Hebrew poets consciously manipulated patterns of intensification as poets elsewhere have consciously manipulated rhyme patterns. The orientation toward a stepping-up of meaning was, for reasons I have tried to make clear, built into the poetic system. It was in all likelihood quite knowingly perceived on the level of the line and in relatively brief sequences of lines. In regard to larger structural units, I would guess that the tendency to work one's way up a scale of intensity was intuited as a natural way to proceed from line to poem rather than explicitly recognized as a "device." In any event, given the prevalence of this particular mode of moving forward in a biblical poem, it is understandable that a poet might well choose to interarticulate two or more patterns of intensification if his aim was to express something more than usually ambiguous, more multifaceted, more contradictory, more fraught with dialectic tension, or whatever the case might be.

The complementary opposite to this strategy of complication is the way structures of intensification are typically used in the prophetic books. Because the prophets are so frequently concerned with delineating an inexorable process of retribution working itself out in history, ineluctable for its destined victims, staggering the imagination in its extremity, prophetic poems are often built on a single rising line of intensity, or a zooming-in of focus from the process of retribution to its human objects. This movement is easy enough to imagine, simply on the basis of our reading of Psalm 13 and of sundry strategies of intensification within single lines, so two brief illustrations should suffice. Both texts are from the Book of Amos; the second is a complete prophetic poem; the first is part of a longer prophecy of doom. The first text (Amos 8:9–10) is preceded by the words "And it shall come to pass on that day, says the Lord God," which is a prose formula of introduction, and so I have not set them out below with the lines of verse:

1 I shall make the sun set at noon,   and bring darkness to earth on a bright day.
2 I shall turn your festivals into mourning,   all your songs to dirge.
3 I shall wrap every waist with sackcloth,   make every head shaven.
4 I shall set her like the mourning for an only son,   and her end as a bitter day.

The rapid swing inward from the process of retribution to its appointed victims is powerfully clear. The turning of light into darkness of the first line at once anticipates all the dire reversals of the subsequent lines and encompasses them. The movement from circumference to human center already begins between the versets of the initial line: first the cosmic catastrophe (or, depending on your viewpoint, hyperbole) of the noonday sun setting, then its effect on the realm of human habitation, darkness over the earth. Line 2 moves from the world to human institutions, first turning festivals into mourning, then, in a characteristic focusing procedure (substituting synecdoches for the general activities with which they are associated), turning song into dirge. Line 3 moves in from institutions to each individual person who has suddenly been given cause to mourn. Dressing in sackcloth and shaving the head are both ancient Near Eastern mourning practices, but the latter may be more shocking to the sensibilities, both because it is an act performed on the body, not just a change of garment, and because it is a pagan custom actually forbidden by Mosaic law. (This last point illustrates how the conservatism of poetic formulation, sometimes reflecting no-longer-current practices or beliefs, might be exploited for expressive effect.) The final line focuses in from the outward practices of mourning to the inward pain of bereavement: it is not an ordinary loss she—I would assume, the common prophetic personification in the feminine of Israel, though some take this as a reference to the Land—will feel but the sharp pain of losing an only son. The concluding verset, "and her end as a bitter day," then summarizes the whole process of retribution, with a near-rhyming reference back to the "bright day" at the end of line 1 (*yom'or*, which here becomes *yom mar*, "bitter day"), now projecting the intensification of suffering forward on a temporal axis: not only will she mourn bitterly but there will be no period of gradual consolation after this bereavement, for her ultimate end will be bitter as well.

In the second passage from Amos (9:1–4), the formal logic of focusing in and in is made thematically explicit, as it is in related passages—no matter where you flee, you cannot escape Me—in Psalm 139 and in Job. This poem, too, has a prose introduction, in this case a brief piece of narrative report, "I saw God standing on the altar and He said":

1	Smite the capital,	let the pedestals shake.
2	Split all their heads open,*	their last by the sword I'll kill.
3	No fleer of them will flee,	no survivor escape.
4	If they make off to Sheol,	from there My hand will take them.
5	If they ascend to heaven,	from there I'll bring them down.
6	If they hide on the summit of Carmel,	from there I'll search them out and take them.
7	If they're concealed from My eyes on the floor of the sea,	from there I will summon the Serpent to bite them.

| 8 | If they go in captivity before their enemies, | from there I will summon the sword to kill them. |
| 9 | I shall set My eye on them | for evil and not for good. |

Here the process of decimation begins with the sanctuary at Beth El and immediately moves on to the people who worship there, the syntactically obscure first verset of line 2 perhaps serving as a punning marker of transition if, as I would venture to guess, "heads" refers both to the tops of the pillars and to the people (that is, either to "leaders" or to "heads" of bodies). The reference to people, in any case, would seem to be primary, and, like the use of eclipse imagery at the beginning of our previous example, the complementary parallelism of this line constitutes a kind of thematic "table of contents" for the rest of the poem: head and tail, beginning and end, I will kill all of them. After a final introductory line (line 3) of synonymous parallelism (fleer/survivor), the poem proceeds to a series of concrete pictures of the desperate fugitives' futile efforts to escape, almost as though they were trying vainly to run away from the inexorable focus of the very poetic structure in which they are caught. From this point to the end of the poem, semantic parallelism within the line is set aside (unless, that is, one chooses to regroup them as very long lines), to be compensated by a uniform pronounced pattern of interlinear parallelism.

As in Psalm 13, the movement of increasing emphasis is reinforced by the use of anaphora, the repetition of "from there" confirming the fact of God's ineluctable presence in all conceivable corners of creation. Here, too, the meaning of the repeated term is colored by its changing contexts: "there" is heaven and hell ("Sheol"), mountaintop and sea bottom, and finally, in a shift from the cosmos to a concrete historical situation, the captive bands of Israelites trudging into exile; similarly, the taking for destruction is first by the sword, then by God's own hand, then—as the fugitive seeks ultimate shelter in the floor of the sea—by the mythological agency of the Serpent, and, at the historically realistic conclusion of the series, once more by the sword. The second verset of line 8 is both the climax of the process and the closing of a formal envelope structure, echoing as it does the second verset of line 2 ("by the sword . . . kill," "summon the sword to kill them"). The last line of the poem, then, "I shall set My eye on them / for evil and not for good," stands after the process of intensification, summarizing its meaning: as the terrific to-and-fro sweep of the language has shown, when God sets His gaze on you, there is nowhere in the world to hide, and for the smug Israelite perverters of every value of justice and equity whom Amos has been denouncing, this will be no friendly gaze.

This text vividly illustrates why the Hebrew prophets so often chose to cast their urgent message in verse. It was not just for the memorability of poetic language or for the sense that poetry was a medium of elevated and perhaps solemn discourse but also because this poetic vehicle of parallelistic verse offered a particularly effective way of imaginatively realizing inevitability, of making powerfully manifest to the listener the idea that consequences he might choose not to contemplate could happen, would happen, would happen without fail.

In several ways the most profound development of the structure of intensification occurs in what is arguably the greatest achievement of all biblical poetry, the Book of Job. When we move from the prose frame-story in Chapters 1 and 2 to the beginning of the poetic argument in Chapter 3, we are plunged precipitously into a world of what must be called abysmal intensities. It is only through the most brilliant use of a system of poetic intensifications that the poet is able to take the full emotional measure and to intimate the full moral implications of Job's outrageous fate. The extraordinary poem that constitutes Chapter 3 is not merely a dramatically forceful way of beginning Job's complaint. More significantly, it establishes the terms, literally and figuratively, for the poetry Job will speak throughout; and, as I shall try to show in my next chapter, when God finally answers Job out of the whirlwind, the force of His response will be closely bound with a shift introduced by His speech in the terms of the poetic argument and the defining lines of poetic structure. What I am suggesting is that the exploration of the problem of theodicy in the Book of Job and the "answer" it proposes cannot be separated from the poetic vehicle of the book, and that one misses the real intent by reading the text, as has too often been done, as a paraphrasable philosophic argument merely embellished or made more arresting by poetic devices. For the moment, however, it will suffice to see how the poetry unfolds step by step in Job's first speech (Job 3:3–26):

1 Perish the day I was born,   the night that said, "A man has been conceived."

2 That day, let it be darkness,   let God above not seek it out,
        let no brightness shine on it.

3 Let darkness and deep gloom   let a pall dwell over it,
    claim it,
            let what darkens the day cast terror on it.

4	That night, let blackness seize it,	let it not join with the days of the year,
	let it not come into the number of months.	
5	That night, let it be desolate,	let no sound of joy come into it.
6	Let the doomers of day curse it,	those destined to undo Leviathan.
7	Let its twilight stars stay dark,	let it hope for light and have none,
	let it see not the eyelids of dawn.	
8	For not blocking her belly's doors,	to hide suffering from my eyes.
9	Why did I not die from the womb,	out from the belly expire?
10	Why were there knees to receive me,	or breasts for me to suck?
11	For now would I lie, be at peace,	I would sleep and find rest,
12	With kings and counselors of the earth,	who build ruins for themselves,
13	Or with nobles who have gold,	who fill their houses with silver.
14	Or like a buried stillborn, I would be not,	like infants who never saw light.
15	There the wicked cease to trouble,	there the exhausted rest.
16	Prisoners are utterly tranquil,	no longer hear the taskmaster's voice.
17	Small and great are there,	the slave free of his master.
18	Why does He give to the sufferer light,	and life to the bitter of soul,
19	Who wait for death and it comes not,	who dig for it more than for treasure,
20	Who rejoice to exultation,	and are glad to find a grave,
21	To a man whose way is hidden,	whom God has hedged about?
22	In place of my bread my groaning comes,	my roars pour out like water.
23	For I feared a fear—it befell me,	and that which I dreaded came on me.
24	I was not quiet, was not at peace,	did not rest, and trouble came.

Because the author of Job is one of those very rare poets, like Shakespeare, who combine awesome expressive power with dazzling stylistic virtuosity, the translation dilutes the original even more than for other biblical poems. The original has a muscular compactness that is extremely difficult to reproduce while finding honest equivalents for the Hebrew words in a Western language,[3] and it makes repeated and sometimes highly significant use of sound-play and wordplay. Let me offer a transliteration of just the first line, which begins the poem with a strong alliterative pattern: *yóvad yom iváled bó / vehaláylah 'amár hórah gáver;* and let me just mention the rhymed antithesis of *'ananáh* ("pall," in line 3) and *renanáh* ("sound of joy," in line 5), and the weighted sequencing of *qéver,* "grave," and *géver,* "man," at the very end of line 20 and the very beginning of line 21. Nevertheless, since the development of the poem depends more on an intensification of semantic materials than on an elaboration of phonetic and syntactic patterns (however much the latter are tied in with meaning), much of the poetic movement is still perceptible in English, especially if the translation preserves (as mine, whatever its defects, has done) the same lexical equivalents for recurring words in the Hebrew.

The poem begins with an obvious and, so it momentarily seems, quite conventional complementary parallelism of day and night (there are abundant lines of biblical verse in which "day" appears in the first verset and "night" in the second). But this conventional pairing undergoes a startling development, both within the line and in what follows. If, as we have seen elsewhere, intensification between versets is often allied with temporal sequence, here Job, who wants to cancel out his own existence, goes *backward* in time, first cursing the day he was born, then, nine months previous, even the night he was conceived. This line is one of the most striking instances in biblical poetry of how the second verset in a line with a double-duty verb is emphatically not a "ballast variant" of the first. Since the initial verb, "perish," governs both clauses, the poet has the space in the second verset to invent a miniature dramatic scene, and one quite flagrantly founded on a fantastic hyperbole: that at the moment of conjugal consummation, the night or perhaps even the future father himself cried out in triumph, "A male [in the translation above, "man," *géver,* the same word that begins line 21] has been conceived." The "day" and "night" of the first and second versets, which are introduced as complementary terms on a scale of intensity defined by the difference between blotting out birth and blotting out conception, are then split into binary oppositions, and the interplay between those oppositions constitutes the entire first section of the poem, to the end of line 8.

This section might be described as a kind of "conjugation" of the semantic poles of light and darkness in the grammatical mode of imprecation, which means, of course, that every flicker of light invoked is wished into darkness, swallowed up by darkness, or canceled into nonbeing by the chain of "not's" and "none's" that runs down the poem. Let me stress that these lines reflect not a mere piling on of images of darkness engulfing light but rather as so often elsewhere in biblical poetry, a rising line of intensity in the articulation of such images.

The rising line is generally evident between versets, as for example in line 3, where in the first verset darkness and gloom merely "claim" (or, in another construal of the Hebrew verb, "besmirch") the day, and by the third verset "cast terror" over it. But the rising movement is still clearer from line to line. First Job wants the day of his birth to be totally swathed in darkness (lines 2–3); then he asks that the night of conception also be seized by blackness and desolation (lines 4–5), thus raising the inherent darkness of the night, one might say, to the second power, and that the fatal night be expunged from the very calendar. (By now, a sequence of day, night, months, and year has been worked into the poem, all to support Job's wish that he had never been brought into the cycle of time.) The "sound of joy" at the end of line 5 that is to be canceled out not only echoes the sound of the Hebrew for "pall" in line 3 but also takes us back to the second verset of line 1, where a joyous announcement of the conception of a male was made.

Having brought the scale of curses to this pitch, Job steps up his statement still further by invoking, in line 6, mythological and cosmogonic imagery: a mere human hex is not enough, and so those cosmic agents designated to disable the primordial sea beast Leviathan must be enlisted to curse the moment that saw Job into the world, and, implicitly, the initial movement backward in time now reaches across aeons to the world's beginnings. "Doomers of day," which I'm afraid I have made sound rather Anglo-Saxon in my translation, is a terrific piece of compressed wit in the Hebrew because "doomers" or "cursers," 'orerei, puns on 'or, "light," and so introduces a spectral echo of the thing being blotted out in the word indicating the agents of obliteration. Finally, line 7, which is the last moment in the series, conjures up an image of literally hopeless longing for light in a world where the first twilight star will never show, the dawn never begin to glimmer. This climax then leads to a summary and interim conclusion in line 8, which bracket the seven preceding lines: may all these curses fall on that day and night for not blocking up the womb in which I was to lie (an image that picks up the preceding images of being totally enveloped in darkness), for not hiding suffering (or "trouble") from my eyes. A newborn child sees light (compare line 14), but by this point Job has established a virtual equation between light or life and anguish, so the substitution of "suffering" for "light" at the end of the segment has a brilliantly concise recapitulative function.

Now, all along I have been speaking of "structures" of intensification, as a concession to common critical usage and for want of a better metaphor, but structure suggests an image of static form extended in space, like a building, and I want to correct that implication by reminding readers that what we think of approximately as structure in literature is, by the serial nature of the medium, dynamic movement unfolding sequentially. If we try to imagine this for a moment not in terms of the finished product we experience in our reading but rather as the process the poet initiates in his making of the poem, we might well speak of a generative principle of intensification. The thematic-imagistic terms of "day" and "night," "light" and "darkness," are introduced, set in sharp opposition, and then the possibilities of that opposition are strongly developed from image to image and from line to line, until the speaker can imagine no more than the concrete picture of his own nonbirth, shut up forever within the dark doors of the womb. The momentum of intensifying this whole opposition, making the darkness more and more overwhelming in relation to the light, is what carries the poem forward step by step and what in some sense generates it, determining what will be said and what will be concluded.

The grimly comforting picture of enclosure in the womb in turn triggers a second major development in the poem, the evocation of the peace of the grave that runs from line 9 to line 21. This represents a transfer of the wish for extinction expressed in the first eight lines from a cosmic to a personal scale and so reflects the movement of specification or focusing that also operates within smaller compass in the poem. The blocked doors of the belly of line 8 lead to a more realistic image of stillbirth in line 9, and only now is the wish for extinction translated into explicit words for death, here repeated with synonymic emphasis ("die" and "expire"). Line 10 is then a further concretization of the birth that Job wishes never had been, moving along a temporal axis: he comes out of the womb, is greeted by knees (either the mother's knees parted in birth or, as some scholars have proposed, the father's knees, on which the newborn may have been placed in a ceremony of legitimation), and then is given the breast. Though womb and tomb are not a rhyme in Hebrew, they are at least an assonance (*réḥem, qéver*), and in any case the archetypal connection between the two would seem to be perfectly evident to the imagination of the poet, who has Job go on from the womb he never wanted to leave to the grave where he would have found lasting rest. Perhaps because rest is intrinsically a condition of stasis, the development of this theme is cumulative rather than crescendo, proceeding through a series of near-synonyms: to lie, be at peace, sleep, rest, be tranquil.

Meanwhile, the catalogue of all those who find repose in the grave has the effect of locating Job's suffering as only one particularly acute instance of the common human condition. Old and young, the mighty and the oppressed, all end up in the grave, and all find respite from the "suffering" (*'amal*) of existence—an idea beautifully summarized in the last line of the catalogue, line 17, "Small and great are there, / the slave free of his master," where all verbs are suppressed ("are" being merely implied in the Hebrew), as befits the place where all actions and disturbances cease.

The picture of earthly existence implied by the catalogue of course confirms Job's vision of life as nothing but trouble. Kings and counselors rebuild ruins in the cycle of creation and destruction that is the life of men—or perhaps, since Hebrew has no "re" prefix, the phrase even suggests, more strikingly, that what they build at the very moment of completion is to be thought of as already turning into ruins. Because of the interlinear parallelism between lines 12 and 13, the houses storing silver and gold stand themselves under the shadow of ruin, an Ecclesiastean image of the futility of all gathering and getting. The catalogue, beginning at the top of the social hierarchy, evokes a world where men are set against men, poor against rich, criminal against law enforcer, slave against master, and where prisons, exhausting labor, and coercion are the characteristic institutions. The third of these six lines introduces the zero-degree instance of existence and hence, from Job's viewpoint, the happiest—the stillborn infant; this both defines the lower limit of the catalogue and pointedly links up with Job's personal wish in lines 11–13 that he had died at birth.

Lines 18–21 sum up the meaning of the catalogue and effect a transition from the general plight of man back to Job's individual case. The smoothness and strength of the transition are reflected in the fact that the four lines, unusual for biblical verse, constitute a single, continuous grammatical sentence. "Why does He give to the sufferer light, / and life to the bitter of soul . . . ?" Here two of the key-words of the poem, *'ameil* and *'or*, "sufferer" and "light," are placed side by side, perhaps even explicitly reminding us of that strategic substitution of *'amal* for *'or* at the very end of the first half of the poem. Now the equation between light and life that underlay the first half of the poem is unambiguously stated, and, appropriately, in the chiastic shape of the line, "light" and "life" are the inside terms, boxed in by "sufferer" and "bitter of soul."

The Art of Biblical Poetry

The sufferers (line 19) waiting for a death that will not come, seeking it more than treasure, invite an ironic glance backward both to the night awaiting a dawn that will never come and to the nobles storing up actual treasure that will not avail them. Line 20, picking up the digging image at the end of the preceding line, focuses the just-stated longing for death in the concrete action of rejoicing over the grave. (This effect is still stronger if one makes a small emendation of *gal* for *gil* in the word I have rendered as "exultation," which would then yield: "Who rejoice over the gravemound [or, pile of ruined stones], / who are glad to find a grave.") Line 21 then slides from the plural to the singular, as Job, in a concluding maneuver of focusing, inserts himself in the general category of the embittered who long for death, and prepares to enunciate three final, summarizing lines in the first person singular.

There are several verbal clues in this line that connect its still rather generalized third-person utterance to Job's predicament as articulated both in the poem and in the frame-story before the poem: "To a man whose way is hidden, / whom God has hedged about." Job calls himself "man," *géver*, the same word he imagined in line 1 being cried out on the night of his conception. (The fondness of biblical writers for this sort of closure of literary units through envelope structures hardly needs to be demonstrated.) He would have wanted trouble to be hidden from his eyes, to remain himself hidden in the darkness of the womb/tomb, but instead his own way has been hidden from him; he is lost in the darkness of life. The Adversary in the frame-story had complained that God showed favoritism by setting up a protective "hedge" around Job and his household (Job 1:10); here the very same idiom is used to suggest entrapment, the setting up of dire obstacles. With its echo of the frame-story, this line is also the first and only time that God is mentioned by name in the poem, as if Job found it almost too painful to refer to or address the resented source of his sufferings (the pronominal presence of God at the beginning of line 18 is indicated in the Hebrew by nothing more than the conjugated form of the verb "to give" in the third person singular).

With the final move of the transition from general to personal effected by line 21, Job now speaks out again in the first person, as he did both at the beginning of the poem (line 1) and at the beginning of the second half of the poem (lines 9–11). The form of these three concluding lines, as we would expect at the end of a large movement of intensification, is powerfully emphatic. In line 22, while "bread" and "water" are complementary terms, "groaning" is stepped up into "roaring" and "comes" into "pours out." The obvious emphasis of the next line is in its heavy insistence on the lexicon of fear: "For I feared a fear—it befell me, / and that which I dreaded came on me." The climactic power of the line, however, is less in its formal configuration than in its location as a psychological revelation just before the end of the poem. From the start, Job had made clear that he was in great anguish, but only now does he reveal that he has been living in a state of dread—dread before the catastrophes, dread that bitter experience has made into a virtual equivalent of life. The final line then completes a strong closural effect by doubling semantic parallelism, each verset internally as well as the line as a whole being built on the bracketing of equivalent terms: "I was not quiet, was not at peace, / did not rest, and trouble came." All these terms, of course, recapitulatively take us back by way of contrast to the tranquillity and repose of the grave evoked in lines 11–17. The last word in the line and the poem in the Hebrew is *rógez*, "trouble," breaking the pattern of the three first-person-singular verbs that preceded it and reminding us of that from which even the wicked cease in the grave (line 15).

And finally, the simple verb "to come" at the end ties up in this image of turbulence a developmental thread that has been running through the poem. "To come" in biblical idiom, depending on both context and the preposition with which it is linked, has a wide variety of meanings. The ones reflected in our poem are: to be included or counted (line 4), to enter (line 5), to substitute or serve as (line 22), to overtake (line 23), and to arrive or simply to come (line 24). In a cunning use of the technique of *Leitwort*, this seemingly innocuous word becomes a sinuous hide-and-seek presence in the poem, first attached to subjects Job tries to control verbally in his curse, then to Job's own groaning, and, climactically, to the dreaded disaster that overtakes him, and to the state of unremitting turbulence that comes to him inwardly in place of the tranquillity for which he yearns. This fine verbal thread, then, is a formal realization of the sense of terrible inexorability upon which Job's complaint is founded.

In everything I have said about this fundamental generative principle of intensification in biblical poetry, I have not intended to claim that this is a feature of poetics entirely unique to ancient Hebrew verse. The fact is that poetry in general involves, necessarily, a linear development of meaning, which means that in one respect it is a linear form of thinking or imagining. "Those images that yet / fresh images beget," Yeats wrote in one of his most famous poems about art and the imagination, and that, approximately, is the way most poems would seem to work: one image suggests a related one, or a further manifestation of the same underlying image; one idea leads to a cognate or consequent one; one pattern of sound, interinvolved with a particular semantic direction, leads to a similar pattern that reinforces some underlying similarity or suggestive antithesis of meaning. Since we tend to expect development of meaning in the specially significant form of discourse that is poetry, it is hardly surprising that poems in many literary traditions will begin with some general notion or image and by stages bring it to a pitch of intensity, or into a sharp focus. Having cited the sonnet at the outset of this discussion as a counterexample to biblical verse, I should add now that one can certainly find sonnets—in English, some of those of Gerard Manley Hopkins come to mind—that evince something like a structure of intensification. There are, however, important differences of degree in the way poets in different traditions may exploit this structure, and differences in what I referred to earlier as the orientation toward reality encouraged by a particular poetic system. Because, as we have abundantly seen, the very prosodic conventions on which the lines of biblical poetry were shaped led poets to a focusing of statement and a heightening of emphasis, they were repeatedly drawn to articulating whole poems and segments within poems as pronounced, often continuous progressions of mounting intensities.

This is, however, a generalization about the system as a whole that needs nuanced qualification. The movement of intensification in Job is by no means identical with that in the Prophets; and, even within a single genre, careful scrutiny may reveal that, for example, Jeremiah and Deutero-Isaiah respectively use the general orientation toward progressive heightening in rather different ways. One should not conclude, moreover, that either intensification or narrative focusing invariably dictates a single rising line of development in the structure of a biblical poem. Particularly in Psalms, one encounters many poems that show elaborate formal patterning that is not at all linear and that serves other expressive purposes than those of intensification and specification. But if we now have some general sense of the distinctive poetics of biblical verse, the time has come to see how the poetry works specifically in some of the major texts, and what links there may be between the various refractions of the biblical vision embodied in these texts and the forms of poetry through which that vision was realized.

IV

Truth and Poetry in the
Book of Job

THE POWER of Job's unflinching argument, in the biblical book that bears his name, has rarely failed to move readers, but the structure of the book has been a perennial puzzle. It begins, as we all recall, with a seemingly naïve tale: Job is an impeccably God-fearing man, happy in his children and in his abundant possessions. Unbeknownst to him, in the celestial assembly the Adversary—despite the translations, not yet a mythological Satan—challenges God to test the disinterestedness of Job's piety by afflicting him. When Job, in rapid succession, has been bereft of all his various flocks and servants and then of all his children, and is stricken from head to foot with itching sores, he refuses his wife's urging that he curse God and die but instead sits down in the dust in mournful resignation.

At this point, the prose of the frame-story switches into altogether remarkable poetry. The poetic Job begins by wishing he had never been born. Then, in three long rounds of debate, he confronts the three friends who have come with all the assurance of conventional wisdom to inform him that his suffering is certain evidence of his having done evil. Job consistently refuses to compromise the honesty of his own life, and in refuting the friends' charges he repeatedly inveighs against God's crushing unfairness. Eventually, the Lord answers Job out of a whirlwind, mainly to show how presumptuous this human critic of divine justice has been. Job concedes; the prose frame-story then clicks shut by restoring to Job health, wealth, and prestige, at the same time symmetrically providing him with another set of children.

This ending has troubled many readers over the centuries. Even if we put aside the closing of the folktale frame, so alien to later sensibilities in its schematic doubling of lost property and its simple replacement of lost lives, the Voice from the Whirlwind (or more properly, Storm) has seemed to some a rather exasperating answer to Job's anguished questions. The common objection to what is clearly intended as a grand climax of the poetic argument runs along the following lines: The Voice's answer is no answer at all but an attempt to overwhelm poor Job by an act of cosmic bullying. Job, in his sense of outrage over undeserved suffering, has been pleading for simple justice. God ignores the issue of justice, not deigning to explain why innocent children should perish, decent men and women writhe in affliction, and instead sarcastically asks Job how good *he* is at hurling lightning bolts, making the sun rise and set, causing rain to fall, fixing limits to the breakers of the sea. The clear implication is that if you can't begin to play in My league, you should not have the nerve to ask questions about the rules of the game.

Some modern commentators have tried to get around such objections by arguing that the very inadequacy of the solution to the problem of theodicy at the end of Job is a testimony to the integrity of the book and to the profundity with which the questions have been raised. There is, in other words, no neat way to reconcile ethical monotheism with the fundamental fact that countless innocents suffer terrible fates through human cruelty, blind circumstance, natural disaster, disease, and genetic mishap. Rather than attempt a pat answer, then, the Job poet was wise enough to imply that there could be no real answer and that the sufferer would have to be content with God's sheer willingness to express His concern for His creatures. This reading of the Voice from the Whirlwind is up to a point plausible, but it may glide too easily over the fact that God's speeches at the end have, after all, a specific content, which is articulated with great care and to the details of which we are presumably meant to attend carefully.

It has also been suggested that the "solution" to Job's dilemma is in the essential act of revelation itself, whatever we think about what is said. That does seem a very biblical idea. Job never doubts God's existence, but, precisely because he assumes in biblical fashion that God must be responsible for everything that happens in the world, he repeatedly wants to know why God now remains hidden, why He does not come out and confront the person on whom He has inflicted such acute suffering. The moment the Voice begins to address Job out of the storm, Job already has his answer: that, despite appearances to the contrary, God cares enough about man to reveal Himself to humankind, to give man some intimation of the order and direction of His creation.[1]

This proposal about the importance of revelation at the end brings us a little closer, I think, to the actual intent of the two climactic divine discourses. What needs to be emphasized, however, considerably more than has been done is the essential role poetry plays in the imaginative realization of revelation. If the poetry of Job—at least when its often problematic text is fully intelligible—looms above all other biblical poetry in virtuosity and sheer expressive power, the culminating poem that God speaks out of the storm soars beyond everything that has preceded it in the book, the poet having wrought a poetic idiom even richer and more awesome than the one he gave Job. Through this pushing of poetic expression toward its own upper limits, the concluding speech helps us see the panorama of creation, as perhaps we could do only through poetry, with the eyes of God.

I realize that this last assertion may sound either hazily mystical or effusively hyperbolic, but what I am referring to is an aspect of the book that seems to have been knowingly designed by the poet and that to a large extent can be grasped, as I shall try to show, through close analytic attention to formal features of the poem. The entire speech from the storm not only is an effectively structured poem in itself but is finely calculated as a climactic development of images, ideas, and themes that appear in different and sometimes antithetical contexts earlier in the poetic argument. In saying this, I do not by any means intend to dismiss the scholarly consensus that there are composite elements in the Book of Job, that it is not all the work of one hand. The most visible "seams" in the book are between the frame-story and the poetic argument, but this evident disjuncture is not really relevant to our concern with the Voice from the Whirlwind, and it makes little difference whether one regards the frame-story as an old folktale incorporated by the poet or (my own preference) as an old tradition artfully reworked by the poet in a consciously archaizing style. Within the poetic argument itself, there is fairly general agreement among scholars that the Hymn to Wisdom, which is Chapter 28, and the Elihu speeches, Chapters 32–37, are interpolations for which the original Job poet was not responsible. I am not inclined to debate either of these judgments, but I should like to observe that the later poet and, in the case of Chapter 28, the editor who chose the poem from the literature of Wisdom psalms available to him were so alive to the culminating function of the Voice from the Whirlwind that they justified the inclusion of the additional material at least in part as anticipations of the concluding poem. In fact, the claim made by some scholars that Chapters 38–41 are themselves an addition to the original text seems to me quite inadmissible precisely because the poetry of this final speech is so intricately and so powerfully a fulfillment of key elements in the body of the poetic argument.

There are, to begin with, occasional and significant adumbrations of the cosmic perspective of God at the end in the speeches of both Job and the Friends. Sometimes, in the case of the Friends, this is simply a matter of getting divine knowledge backward. Thus Eliphaz, in a speech asserting complacent confidence that God invariably destroys the evil man, draws an analogy from the animal kingdom: "Roar of the lion, voice of the cub, / but the king-of-beasts' teeth are broken. // The lion perishes lacking prey, / and its whelps are scattered" (4:10–11). The point, presumably, is that in God's just world even the fiercest of ravening beasts can be disabled, as seemingly powerful evildoers in the human sphere will get their comeuppance. But this is to draw a general moral rule from a rare zoological case, and when God Himself evokes the lion (38:39) along with other beasts of prey, He recognizes unflinchingly that the real principle of the animal kingdom is that the strong devour the weak to sustain their own lives and those of their young. It is that harsher, more unassimilable truth that He chooses to make an integral part of His revelation to Job concerning the providential governance of the world.

More frequently, the Friends, as self-appointed defenders of God's position, touch on certain notions that are actually in consonance with the divine speech at the end, but both the terms in which such notions are cast and the contexts in which they are set turn them into something jejune and superficial. In this regard, the Voice from the Whirlwind is a revelation of the contrast between the jaded half-truths of cliché and the startling, difficult truths exposed when the stylistic and conceptual shell of cliché is broken open. Thus Eliphaz, in one of the Friends' frequent appeals to the antiquity of received wisdom, upbraids Job: "Are you the first man to be born, / were you spawned before the hills? // Have you attended to the council of God, / and taken to yourself all wisdom?" (15:7–8). Eliphaz's heightening of a sarcastic hyperbole from verset to verset (first born man—created before the world itself—a uniquely privileged member of God's cosmogonic council) leads us to a point in some ways similar to God's overwhelming challenge to Job at the beginning of His great speech. But Eliphaz invokes creation in the smoothly formulaic language of poetic tradition, which is quite different from the vertiginous vision of the vastness of creation that God's bolder language will offer. And Eliphaz speaks smugly without suspecting that there might be a chasm between divine knowledge and the conventional knowledge of accepted wisdom. This immediately becomes clear as he goes on to reduce his cosmogonic hyperbole to a mere competition of longevity with Job: "What do you know that we don't know, / or understand that we do not? // There are grayheads and old men among us, / older by far than your father" (15:9–10).

A little earlier, there is a speech of Zophar's that sounds even more like an anticipation of the Voice from the Whirlwind, but again the stylistic and attitudinal differences between human and divine discourse are crucially instructive.

Can you find out the limit of God,   the last reaches of the Almighty
                                       can you find?
With the heights of the heavens   what's deeper than Sheol, how
what can you do,   can you know?
Longer than earth is its measure,   and broader than the sea.
                                                          (11:7–9)

In the biblical way of thinking, all this is unexceptionable, and it would seem to accord perfectly with God's own words in Chapter 38 about the unbridgeable gap between powerful Creator and limited creature. But the very smoothness of the stereotyped language Zophar uses (heights of heaven, depths of Sheol, longer than earth, broader than the sea) is a clue that this is a truth he has come by all too easily. This suspicion is confirmed when he immediately proceeds to move from an affirmation of God's power to the usual pat assertion that the all-knowing Creator detects all evil—by implication, to chastise the evildoers: "If He goes by and confines, or calls together,* who can turn Him back? // For He knows the deceitful, / when He sees iniquity, does He not discern it?" (11:10–11). The actual prospect of God as sole master of the heights of heaven and the depths of hell is a staggering one, as the Voice from the Whirlwind will make awesomely clear. But in Zophar's speech there is too facile a transition from the invocation of that prospect to the time-worn notion that God will never allow crime to pay.

In Job's complaint there are two extended anticipations of the Voice from the Whirlwind, 9:5–10 and 12:7–25. For the sake of economy, I shall cite only the first, and shorter, of these two passages, with brief reference to the second. Job, in the midst of objecting that God is an impossible legal adversary because He is so overpowering, shifts his imagery upward from the arena of law to the cosmos:

Who tears up mountains that know not, Who overturns them in His wrath,
Who shakes earth from its place, so that its pillars quake,
Who orders the sun not to rise, Who seals up the stars,
Who stretched out the heavens alone, and trod on the back of the sea,
Who made the Bear and Orion, Pleiades and the chambers of the south wind,

Who does great things without limit, wonders without number.

Job's cosmic poetry, unlike that of the Friends, has a certain energy of vision, as though it proceeded from some immediate perception of the great things it reports. Most of the images he uses will reappear, more grandly, in God's first discourse in Chapter 38. There, too, God is the sole sovereign of the sun and the stars, the master of the very constellations and of the chambers of the wind mentioned here. There is, nevertheless, a decisive difference in emphasis between the two chapters, which leads me to infer that this and other passages in the poetic argument are in one respect patiently teaching us how to read God's speech when it finally comes. The Creator in Chapter 38 is distinguished by His ability to impose order. The Creator in Job's poem is singled out first of all for His terrific, and perhaps arbitrary, power—tearing up mountains in His wrath, eclipsing the sun, and blotting out the stars. (The speaker, we should remember, is the same Job who had prayed for every glimmer of light to be swallowed by darkness.) If both the present text and Chapter 38 allude indirectly to the Canaanite creation myth, in which the land god conquers the primordial sea beast Yam, what is stressed in Chapter 38 is God's setting limits to the breakers of the sea, His bolting doors against the chaotic rush of the flood, while Job here gives us instead God the mighty combatant, treading on the back of the conquered sea. To be sure, there is also an element of celebration of the Creator in Job's words, at least in the last two lines of the passage quoted, but his general perception of the master of the universe is from the viewpoint of someone who has been devastated by His mastery. This sense is made perfectly clear in the lines that introduce our passage (9:2–3), and the point is even more emphatic in the lines that follow it: "Why, He snatches— who can turn Him back? / Who can tell Him, 'What are You doing?' // God will not turn back His wrath, / beneath Him sink the Sea Beast's allies" (9:12–13).

The analogous passage in Chapter 12 stresses still more boldly the arbitrary way in which God exercises His power. Here, too, God, as in the revelation from the storm at the end, is imagined as the supreme master of nature—a truth that, according to Job, we can learn from the very birds of the heavens and the beasts of the field (*behemot,* a term that in a different acceptation will designate one of the featured attractions of the grand zoological show in the speech from the storm). And like the Lord Who will reveal Himself in the end to Job, God here is imagined above all as the absolute sovereign of light and darkness: "Who lays bare deep things from darkness, / and brings out to light the gloom" (12:22). But this divine monarch as Job conceives Him shows a singular inclination to capricious behavior, befuddling counselors and judges, unmanning kings, humiliating nobles, using His prerogative over light and darkness to draw the leaders of nations into trackless wastes: "They grope in darkness without light, / He makes them stray as though drunk" (12:25). Job's vision of God's power over the world has an authority lacking in the parallel speeches of the Friends, but he sees it as power willfully misused, and that perception will require an answer by the Voice from the Whirlwind.

Somewhat surprisingly, the two extended anticipations of the concluding poem that show the greatest degree of consonance with it occur in the presumably interpolated passages, the Elihu speech and the Hymn to Wisdom. This may seem less puzzling if we remember that in the ancient Near East a "book" remained for a long time a relatively open structure, so that later writers might seek to amplify or highlight the meaning of the original text by introducing materials that reinforced or extended certain of the original emphases. In the case of Elihu, the immediate proximity to God's speech is the most likely explanation of the high degree of consonance with it. That is, Elihu is an irascible, presumptuous blowhard (images of inflation and evacuation cluster at the beginning of his discourse), and as such he is hardly someone to be in any way identified as God's "spokesman." But as he approaches the end of his long harangue—as the poem draws close, in other words, to the eruption of the Voice from the Whirlwind—he begins to weave into his abuse of Job images of God as the mighty sovereign of a vast creation beyond the ken of man. First he conjures up a vision of God Whose years are without number mustering the clouds and causing the rains to fall (37: 26–33). Then, at the very end of his speech, in a clear structural bridge to the divine discourse that directly follows, Elihu asks Job whether he can really grasp God's wondrous management of the natural world, invoking it as evidence of the moral perfection of the Divinity that man cannot fathom:

Give ear to this, Job,	stop and consider the wonders of God.
Do you know what God sets on them,	when He makes His thunderheads glow?
Do you know in the cloud-expanses	the wonders of the Perfect in Knowledge?
Why your clothes are hot	when earth is becalmed from the south?
Can you beat flat the skies with Him,	firm as a molten mirror?
Let us know what to say to Him,	we can make no case from darkness.
Will it be told Him if I speak,	can man say if he is distraught?
Now, one sees not the light,	though bright in the skies,

till a wind comes and clears them.

From the north gold comes,	around God awesome the splendor.
The Almighty—we attain Him not—	justice and great right He will not pervert.*
lofty in power,	
So men fear Him,	no wise man can see Him.

(37:14–24)

Elihu's cosmic poetry does not quite soar like that of the Voice from the Whirlwind (and this passage also involves several textual difficulties), but it is considerably more than the rehearsal of formulas we saw in Eliphaz and Zophar. The various items of his panorama of creation—the power over rain and thunder and the dazzling deployment of sunlight—will in a moment recur, more grandly, in God's speech, and, above all, the final emphasis on man's inability to see the solar brilliance of the all-powerful God points toward the extraordinary exercise of divine sight in which we are privileged to share through the poetry of God's concluding speech.

The Hymn to Wisdom, Chapter 28, is in certain obvious ways cut from different cloth from the rest of the Book of Job. Lexically and stylistically, it sounds more like Proverbs than Job. Its celebration of divine Wisdom does not at all participate in the vehement argument on theodicy into which it is introduced. Structurally, the hymn is divided into three strophes of approximately equal length with the boundaries between them marked by a refrain; such explicit symmetry of form is not observable elsewhere in the poetry of Job. The imagery of precious stones that dominates the middle strophe has very few parallels elsewhere in the book. But all these disparities may have troubled the ancient audience a good deal less than they trouble us, with our notions of literary unity based on the reading of unitary texts produced by single authors who generally could be fully responsible for them from first draft to corrected page proofs. Whatever editor or ancient literary gremlin decided to insert this poem just after the completion of the rounds of debate with the Friends and before Job's final Confession of Innocence (Chapters 29–31) chose the new material with a firm sense of how it could help tune up the proper attentiveness for God's concluding speech. That tuning up is a matter not just of emphasizing the vast scope of God's Wisdom against man's limited understanding but also of poetically defining a *place* where we can begin to imagine the unfathomable workings of the Creator. A whole world of sprawling expanses and inaccessible depths and heights is evoked in the poem—"A path unknown to the hawk, / ungrazed by the falcon's eye" (28:7), unguessed realms of hidden recesses that only God can see or bring to light if He chooses. The thematic stress on sight intimated at the end of the Elihu speeches is prominent here and made powerfully explicit in the concluding strophe. At the same time, specific details of the cosmic imagery that will begin the divine discourse are strategically anticipated (or, to think in the order of the editorial process rather than in the sequential order of the book, are strategically echoed):

And Wisdom, from where does it come,
It is hidden from the eyes of all living,
Perdition and Death say,
"With our ears we but heard its report."

where is the place of understanding?
from the birds of the heavens concealed.

God understands its way,
For He looks to the ends of the earth,
Fixing a weight to the wind,
When He fixed a limit to the rain,
Then he saw and gauged it,
And said to man,

He knows its place.
all beneath heaven He sees,
setting a measure to water,
and a way to the thunderstorm,
set it firm and probed it out.
Look, fear of the Lord is Wisdom,

and to shun evil is understanding.

(28:20–28)

The aphoristic concluding line is distinctly unlike the Voice from the Whirlwind not merely stylistically but also in the neatness of its sense of resolution. (Its formulaic pairing, however, of "wisdom" and "understanding" is quite like the one God invokes in His initial challenge to Job.) In any case, the discrepancy in tone and attitude of the last line was no doubt far less important to whoever was responsible for the text of Job as we have it than the consonance of the hymn's vision of God with the Voice from the Whirlwind—that is, a vision of God as the master of sight, searching out the unknowable ends of the earth.

How are the resources of poetry marshaled in the divine speech to give us an intimation of that omniscient perspective? Some preliminary remarks on the progression of the concluding poem may help indicate where it means to take us. The structure of the poem is expansive and associative (quite unlike the tight organization of Chapter 28), but it also reflects the sequential and focusing strategies of development that are generally characteristic of biblical poetry. After the two brief opening lines in which the Lord challenges Job (38:2–3), the poem leads us through the following movements: cosmogony (38:4–21), meteorology (38:22–38), zoology (38:39–39:30). This sequence is implicitly narrative: first God creates the world, then He sets in motion upon it an intricate interplay of snow and rain and lightning and winds, and in this setting He looks after the baffling variety of wild creatures that live on the earth. God's first discourse is followed at the beginning of Chapter 40 by a brief exchange between a reprimanding Lord and a humbled Job (40:1–5), and then the beginning of the second discourse, which again challenges Job to gird up his loins and see if he can really contend with God (40:6–13). (Scholarship has generally detected a scrambling or duplication of texts in these thirteen verses, but I find that the various conjectural attempts to reassemble the text create more problems than they solve, while the lines as we have them do not substantially affect the larger structure of the poem.) In the second discourse, we continue with the zoological interests that take up the last half of the first discourse. In accordance, however, with the impulse of heightening and focusing that informs so much of biblical poetry, the second discourse is not a rapid poetic catalogue of animals, like the last half of the first discourse, but instead an elaborate depiction of just two exotic beasts, the hippopotamus and the crocodile, who are rendered, moreover, in the heightened and hyperbolic terms of mythology as Behemoth and Leviathan.

These are the broad structural lines of the concluding poem, but in order to understand how it works so remarkably as a "revelation," in both the ordinary and the theological sense of the term, it is important to see in detail how its language and imagery flow directly out of the poetic argument that has preceded. I shall quote in full the first two movements of cosmogony and meteorology, then refer without full citation to the naturalistic zoology before attending to the mythopoeic zoology at the end. Since the verse divisions here correspond precisely to the line division, I shall use the conventional verse numbers, starting with verse 2 of Chapter 38, where the poem proper begins.

2	Who is this darkening counsel	in words without knowledge?
3	Gird up your loins like a man,	I'll ask you, and you may inform Me.
4	Where were you when I founded earth?	Tell, if you know understanding.
5	Who set its measures, do you know?	Or who stretched the line upon it?
6	In what were its bases sunk,	or who laid its cornerstone,
7	When the morning stars sang together,	all the sons of God shouted for joy?
8	Hedged the sea in with doors,	when it gushed forth from the womb,
9	When I made cloud its clothing,	deep mist its swaddling bands,
10	Placed on it breakers as My limit,	set up bolt and doors.
11	I said, "Thus far come, no farther,	here halt the surge of your waves."
12	Did you ever muster the morning,	appoint dawn to its place,
13	To seize the corners of the earth,	that the wicked be shaken from it?
14	It turns like sealing clay	till fixed like [the hues of] a garment.*
15	Their light is withheld from the wicked,	the upraised arm is broken.
16	Have you come to the depths of the sea,	at the ends of the deep walked about?
17	Have the gates of death been shown you,	the gates of gloom have you seen?
18	Can you take in the breadth of the earth?	Tell, if you know it all.
19	Where is the way light dwells,	and darkness, where is its place,
20	That you may take it to its home,	understand the paths to its house?
21	You know, for you were then born,	the number of your days is great.
22	Have you come into the storehouse of snows,	the storehouse of hail have you seen,
23	Which I set aside for time of strife,	the day of war and battle?
24	By what way is the west wind² spread,	the east wind whipped across earth?

25	Who cut the torrent a channel,	a way for the thunderstorm?
26	To rain upon land without man,	wilderness without human soul,
27	To sate the wild wasteland,	and make the grass sprout there?
28	Does the rain have a father,	or who sired the drops of dew?
29	From whose belly did the ice come forth,	to the frost of heaven who gave birth?
30	Like stone water congeals,	the face of the deep locks hard.
31	Can you tie bands to the Pleiades,	or loose Orion's reins?
32	Can you bring out Mazarot in season,	conduct the Bear with its cubs?
33	Do you know the laws of the heavens,	can you fix their rule on earth?
34	Can you lift your voice to the cloud,	and the water-spate covers you?
35	Can you order the lightning to go,	make it say, "Here I am"?
36	Who put wisdom in the hidden parts,*	who gave the mind understanding?
37	Who told the heavens in wisdom,	the bottles of the heavens who tipped down?
38	When dust melts to a mass,	and clods clump together.

At the very beginning of the poetic argument, we entered the world of Job's inner torment through the great death-wish poem that takes up all of Chapter 3. These first thirty-seven lines of God's response to Job constitute a brilliantly pointed reversal, in structure, image, and theme, of that initial poem of Job's. Perhaps the best way to sense the special weight of the disputation over theodicy is to observe that it is cast in the form of a clash between two modes of poetry, one kind spoken by man and, however memorable, appropriate to the limitations of his creaturely condition, the other the kind of verse a poet of genius could persuasively imagine God speaking. The poem of Chapter 3, as we had occasion to see in detail, advanced through a process of focusing in and in—or, to shift metaphors, a relentless drilling inward toward the unbearable core of Job's suffering, which he imagined could be blotted out by extinction alone. The external world—dawn and sunlight and starry night—exists in these lines only to be canceled. Job's first poem is a powerful, evocative, authentic expression of man's essential, virtually ineluctable egotism: the anguished speaker has seen, so he feels, all too much, and he wants now to see nothing at all, to be enveloped in the blackness of the womb/tomb, enclosed by dark doors that will remain shut forever.

In direct contrast to all this withdrawal inward and turning out of lights, God's poem is a demonstration of the energizing power of panoramic vision. Instead of the death wish, it affirms from line to line the splendor and vastness of life, beginning with a cluster of arresting images of the world's creation and going on to God's sustaining of the world in the forces of nature and in the variety of the animal kingdom. Instead of a constant focusing inward toward darkness, this poem progresses through a grand sweeping movement that carries us over the length and breadth of the created world, from sea to sky to the unimaginable recesses where snow and winds are stored, to the lonely wastes and craggy heights where only the grass or the wildest of animals lives. In Job's initial poem, various elements of the larger world were introduced only as reflectors or rhetorical tokens of his suffering. When the world is seen here through God's eyes, each item is evoked for its own sake, each existing thing having its own intrinsic and often strange beauty. In Chapter 3, Job wanted to reduce time to nothing and contract space to the small, dark compass of the locked womb. God's poem by contrast moves through aeons from creation to the inanimate forces of nature to the teeming life on earth and, spatially, in a series of metonymic links, from the uninhabited wasteland (verse 26) to the mountain habitat of the lion and the gazelle (the end of Chapter 38 and the beginning of Chapter 39) and the steppes where the wild ass roams.

This general turning of Job's first affirmation of death into an affirmation of life is minutely worked out in the language and imagery of the poem that God speaks. Job's initial poem, we recall, began by setting out the binary opposition between day and night, light and darkness, and then proceeded through an intensifying series of wishes that the light be swallowed up by darkness. The opening verset of God's speech summons Job as someone *"darkening* counsel,'' and the emphatic and repeated play with images of light and darkness in the subsequent lines makes it clear that this initial characterization of Job is a direct critique of his first speech and all that follows from it. (The allusion here to the poem in Chapter 3 is reinforced by the term God uses at the beginning of the second line in addressing Job, *géver,* "man," which also occurs at the beginning of Job's first poem—"the night that said, 'A man has been conceived.' " It is as though God were implying: you called yourself man, *géver,* now gird up your loins like a man and see if you can face the truth.) Job, the Voice from the Whirlwind suggests, has gotten things entirely skewed in regard to the basic ontological constituents of light and darkness. The two in fact exist in a delicate and powerful dialectic beyond the ken of man, and the balance between them is part of the unfathomable beauty of creation. This point is intimated in many of the first thirty-seven lines of the poem and made explicit in verses 19–20: "Where is the way light dwells, / and darkness, where is its place, // That you may take it to its home, / understand the paths to its house?"

Job in Chapter 3 prayed for cloud and darkness to envelop the day he was born. Cloud and deep mist reappear here in a startlingly new context, as the matinal blanket over the primordial seas, as the swaddling bands of creation (verse 9). Job wanted "gloom" (*tzalmável*) to cover his existence; here that term appears as part of a large cosmic picture not to be perceived with mere human eyes: "Have the gates of death been shown you, / the gates of gloom have you seen?" (verse 17). In the one explicitly moral point of theodicy made by the Voice from the Whirlwind (verses 12–15), the diurnal rhythm of light succeeding darkness is taken as both emblem and instrument of God's ferreting out of evildoers—an idea not present to the "Ecclesiastean" vision of Chapter 3, where evil and oppression are merely part of the anguished and futile cyclical movement of life. It is not surprising that this particular passage should be terse and a little cryptic, for whatever God means to suggest about bringing wrongdoing to light, He is not invoking the simple moral calculus used so unquestioningly by the Friends. Job in the ascending spirals of his pain-driven rhetoric sought to summon all forms of darkness to eclipse forever the sun and moon and stars. In response God asks him whether he has any notion of what it means in amplitude and moral power to be able to muster the dawn (verse 12) and set the constellations in their regular motion (verses 31–33).

Perhaps the finest illustration of this nice match of meaning and imagery between the two poems is the beautiful counterbalance between the most haunting of Job's lines wishing for darkness and the most exquisite of God's lines affirming light. Job, one recalls, tried to conjure up an eternal starless night: "Let its twilight stars stay dark, / let it hope for light and have none, / let it not see the eyelids of the dawn" (3:9). God, near the beginning of His first discourse, evokes the moment when creation was completed in an image that has become justly famous in its own right but that is also, it should be observed, a counterimage to 3:9: "When the morning stars sang together, / all the sons of God shouted for joy" (verse 7). That is, instead of a night with no twilight stars, with no glimmer of dawn, the morning stars of creation exult. The emphasis in this line on song and shouts of joy also takes us back to the poem of Chapter 3, which began with a triumphant cry on the night of conception—a cry Job wanted to wish away—and proceeded to a prayer that no joyous exclamation come into that night (3:7). Finally, the vestigially mythological "sons of God"—with the semantic breadth in Hebrew of "son," this implies not biological filiation but something like "celestial company"—takes us back beyond Chapter 3 to the frame-story. There, of course, it was the Adversary who was the prominent and sinister member of "the sons of God." The discordant note he represented has been expunged here in this heavenly chorus of creation. What I am pointing to is not one of those contradictions of sources on which biblical scholarship has too often thrived but a culminating moment in which the vision of the poet transcends the limited terms of the folktale he has chosen to use.

There is a second set of key images in the first movement of God's speech that harks back to Job's initial poem, namely, the imagery of physical generation and birth. Since this imagery, unlike light and darkness, which are literal substances of creation, is imposed metaphorically by the poet as a way of shaping the material, it provides even clearer evidence of how the poem in Chapter 38 was purposefully articulated as a grand reversal of the poem in Chapter 3. Job's first speech begins with birth and conception and circles back on the belly or womb where he would like to be enclosed, where he imagines the fate of the dead fetus as the happiest of human lots. Against those doors of the belly (3:10) that Job wanted shut on him forever, the Voice from the Whirlwind invokes a cosmic womb and cosmic doors to a very different purpose: "[He] hedged in the sea with doors, / when it gushed forth from the womb" (verse 8). This figuration of setting limits to the primal sea as closing doors on a gushing womb produces a high tension of meaning absent from Job's unequivocal death wish. The doors are closed and bolted (verse 10) so that the flood will not engulf the earth, but nevertheless the waves surge, the womb of all things pulsates, something is born—a sense made clear in the incipiently narrative development of the womb image into the next line (verse 9), where in a metaphor unique in biblical poetry the primordial mists over the surface of the deep are called swaddling bands.

One might note that in the anticipations of this passage in Job's speech there are allusions to the Canaanite cosmogonic myth of a triumph by force over an archaic sea monster, while in God's own words that martial story is set aside, or at the very least left in the distant background, so that the cosmogony can be rendered instead in terms of procreation. What we are invited to imagine in this fashion is creation not as the laying low of a foe but as the damming up and channeling of powers nevertheless allowed to remain active. (The only clear allusion in the poem to God's doing battle, verse 23, is projected forward in time to an indefinite, perhaps vaguely apocalyptic future.) The poet uses a rather unexpected verb, "to hedge in," in order to characterize this activity of holding back the womb of the sea, and that is a double allusion, to God's protective "hedging round" of Job mentioned in the frame-story and to Job's bitter complaint toward the end of his first poem of having been "hedged in" by God. The verb, in its various conjugations, is nowhere else in the Bible used for the closing of doors but generally suggests a shading or sheltering act, as with a wing or canopy. One usage that might throw some light on our line from Job is this verse in Psalms (139:13): "For You planted conscience within me, / You sheltered me [or, hedged me around, or, wove me] in my mother's belly." The Creator, that is, at the end of Job, is actively blocking off, bolting in, the surge of the sea, but the word carries after it a long train of associations having to do with protection and nurture, so that the negative sense of the verb in Chapter 3 is in a way combined with the positive sense in which the frame-story uses it. What results is a virtual oxymoron, expressing a paradoxical feeling that God's creation involves a necessary holding in check of destructive forces and a sustaining of those same forces because they are also forces of life. One sees in a single compact phrase how the terms of God's poetry—which is to say, ultimately, His imagination of the world—transcend the terms of Job's poetry and that of the Friends.

When the poem moves on—as I have suggested, in an implicitly narrative movement—from cosmogony to meteorology, birth imagery is once more introduced. First Job is challenged sarcastically, "You know, for you were then born" (verse 21), which, in addition to the ultimate allusion to the beginning of the poem in Chapter 3, sounds quite like Eliphaz's words to Job in Chapter 15. The crucial difference is that instead of being a rhetorical ploy in a petty contest of supposed longevity, this address is set against a background of cosmic uterine pulsations and leads into a thick cluster of birth images a few lines down (verses 28–29), so that we quickly grasp the ontological contrast between Job, a man born of woman in time, and the principle of generation infinitely larger than man that informs nature. The two lines below that articulate this principle richly develop the implications of the birth imagery in a characteristically biblical fashion:

| Does the rain have a father, | or who sired the drops of dew? |
| From whose belly did the ice come forth, | to the frost of heaven who gave birth? |

In each of these two lines we are carried forward from agent (father) or agency (belly) to the active process of procreation (sired, gave birth—in the Hebrew, two different conjugations of the same verb). Between the first line and the second, what amounts to a biological focusing of the birth image is carried out as we go from the father, the inseminator who is the proximate cause of birth, to the mother, in whose body the actual birth is enacted. The interlinear parallelism of this couplet also plays brilliantly with the two opposed states of water, first liquid and falling or condensing, then frozen. In the first line, the flaunted inapplicability of the birth imagery is a result of multiplicity: How could one imagine anyone fathering the countless millions of raindrops or dewdrops? In the second line, the incongruity—which is to say, the chasm between man's small world and God's vast world—is a more shocking one (still another intensifying development) as the poet's language forces us to imagine the unimaginable, great hunks of ice coming out of the womb. Figurative language is used here to show the limits of figuration itself, which, in the argumentative thrust of the poem, means the limits of the human imagination. The immediately following line (verse 30) is a focusing development of this ice imagery: "Like stone water congeals, / the face of the deep locks hard." The tension of opposites that is at the heart of God's vision of the world is strongly felt here: fluid and stone-hard solid, white-frozen surface and watery depths. Having reached this point, the poet lays aside birth imagery, and after three lines devoted to the stars concludes the whole meteorological segment with a focusing development of the phenomena of natural precipitation we just observed in verses 28–30, which themselves capped a whole sequence on snow and rain that began with verse 22. There remains, of course, an implicit connection between fructification or birth and rain, as anyone living in the Near Eastern climate and topography would be readily aware, and as verse 27 reminds us quite naturalistically and verse 28 by a sort of riddling paradox (no one is the father of the rain, but the rain is the father of life). In any case, the concluding four lines of our segment—putting aside verse 36, whose meaning is uncertain—offer an image of downpour on parched land that is, at least by implication, a final turn of the screw in the poetic rejoinder to Chapter 3. In Job's initial poem the only water anywhere in evidence is the saltwater of tears (3:24), and clouds are mentioned only as a means to cover up the light. It is surely appropriate that God should now challenge Job to make lightning leap from the thickness of the cloud and that in His cosmic realm, as against Job's rhetorical realm, the meaning of clouds is not darkness but a source of water to renew the earth with life.

The rest of God's speech—the second half of the first discourse and virtually all of the second discourse—is then devoted to a poetic panorama of the animal life that covers the earth. The sequence of beasts, like the movement of the poem through space via metonymic links, is loosely associative but also instructive: lion, raven, mountain goat and gazelle, wild ass, wild ox, ostrich, war horse, hawk and eagle. The first two and the last two creatures in the sequence are beasts of prey whose native fierceness in effect frames the wildness of the whole catalogue. The sequence begins, that is, with an image of the lion crouching in ambush for its prey (38:39–40), determined to sate its keen appetite; and the sequence closes with this striking evocation of the eagle seeking food for its brood: "From there [the mountain crag] he spies out food, / from afar his eyes discern. // His fledglings gulp blood; / wherever the slain are, there is he" (39:29–30). This concluding poem in Job is probably one of the most unsentimental poetic treatments of the animal world in the Western literary tradition and, at least at first thought, a little surprising coming from the mouth of the Lord. But the violence and, even more, the peculiar beauty of violence are precisely the point of God's visionary rejoinder to Job. The animal realm is a nonmoral realm, but the sharp paradoxes it embodies make us see the inadequacy of any merely human moral calculus—not only that of the Friends, learned by rote, but even Job's, spoken out of the integrity of suffering. In the animal kingdom, the tender care for one's young may well mean their gulping the blood of freshly slain creatures. It is a daily rite of sustaining life that defies all moralizing anthropomorphic interpretation. And yet, the series of rhetorical questions to Job suggests, God's providence looks after each of these strange, fierce, inaccessible creatures. There is an underlying continuity between this representation of the animal world and the picture of inanimate nature in 38:2–38, with its sense of terrific power abiding in the natural world, fructification and destruction as alternative aspects of the same, imponderable forces.

That continuity is reinforced by the carryover of images of procreation from the cosmogonic and meteorological sections of the poem to the zoological section. In the two former instances, as we just saw, the language of parturition and progeny was first metaphoric and then both metaphoric and heavily ironic; among the animals, it becomes quite literal. The raven at the beginning of this section (38:41) and the eagle at the end are seen striving to fulfill the needs of their young. Immediately after the raven, the birth process and early growth of the mountain goat and gazelle are given detailed attention:

Do you know the time when the mountain goat gives birth,   do you mark the birth pangs of the gazelles?

Do you number the months till they come to term,   do you know the time when they give birth?

They couch, they push out their young,   in the throes of labor.

Their offspring batten, grow large in the wild,   go off and do not return.

(39:1–4)

The emphasis on time here in conjunction with the evocation of birth brings us back in still another strong antithesis to Job's wish in Chapter 3 that he could wipe out his birth. There, one recalls, he cursed the night of his conception by saying, "Let it not come into the number of months" (3:6). Here, in God's poem, that same phrase (with the minor morphological shift in the Hebrew of "number" from noun to verb) recurs as an instance of how time becomes a medium of fruition under the watchful gaze of the divine maker of natural order. Reproduction and nurturing are the very essence of a constantly self-renewing creation as the poet imagines it. But even the universal principle of generation is not free from uncanny contradiction, as the strange case of the ostrich (39:13–18) suggests. That peculiar bird, at least according to the ornithological lore on which the poet drew, abandons her eggs in the dirt, unmindful of the danger that they may be trampled underfoot by wild beasts, "For God deprived her of wisdom, / gave her no share of understanding" (39:17). Nature for the Job poet is not a Newtonian clock operating with automatic mechanisms. The impulse to reproduce and nurture life depends upon God's imbuing each of His creatures with the instinct or "wisdom" to carry it out properly. If the universal provider of life chooses in any case to withhold His understanding—as Job himself is said to lack wisdom and understanding—things can go awry.

In both structure and thematic assertion, Chapters 38–41 are a great diastolic movement, responding to the systolic movement of Chapter 3. The poetics of suffering in Chapter 3 seeks to contract the whole world to a point of extinction, and it generates a chain of images of enclosure and restriction. The poetics of providential vision in the speech from the storm conjures up horizon after expanding horizon, each populated with a new form of life. Thus, in the second segment of the zoological panorama (38:5–12, though in fact cued by 38:4), we see a parade of animals moving outward into the wild, far beyond the yokes and reins of man: first the young of the mountain goats and gazelles, heading out into the open, then the onager and the wild ox that will never be led into a furrow. In Chapter 3, only in the grave did prisoners "no longer hear the taskmaster's voice" (3:18), and only there was "the slave free of his master" (3:19). But this, God's rejoinder implies, is a civilization-bound, hobbled perception of reality, for nature abounds in images of freedom: "Who set the wild ass free, / who undid the bonds of the onager, // Whose home I made in the steppes, / his dwelling-place the salt land? // He scoffs at the bustle of the city, / the shouts of the taskmaster he does not hear" (39:5–7).

The way in which these various antitheses between Chapter 3 and Chapters 38–39 are elaborately pointed may suggest why some of the subsequent major movements in Job's poetic argument are not also alluded to here. In part, the reason might have been a problem of technical feasibility: it is manageable enough to reverse the key-terms and images and themes of one rich poem at the beginning in another poem at the end, but it might have become unwieldy to introduce into the conclusion allusions to a whole series of intervening poems. More substantively, however, God chooses for His response to Job the arena of creation, not the court of justice, the latter being the most insistent recurrent metaphor in Job's argument after Chapter 3. And it is, moreover, a creation that barely reflects the presence of man, a creation where human concepts of justice have no purchase. We are accustomed to think of the radicalism of the challenge to God in the Book of Job, but it should be recognized that, against the norms of biblical literature, God's response is no less radical than the challenge. Elsewhere in the Bible, man is the crown of creation, little lower than the angels, expressly fashioned to rule over nature. Perhaps that is why there is so little descriptive nature poetry in the Bible: the natural world is of scant interest in itself; it engages a poet's imagination only insofar as it reflects man's place in the scheme of things or serves his purposes. But in the uniquely vivid descriptive poetry of Job 38–41, the natural world is valuable for itself, and man, far from standing at its center, is present only by implication, peripherally and impotently, in this welter of fathomless forces and untamable beasts.[3]

Truth and Poetry in the Book of Job

The most elaborately described as well as the most arresting member of the bestiary in the first discourse is the war-horse. Few readers of the poem would want to give up these splendid lines, though some have wondered what this evocation of the snorting stallion has to do with Job's predicament. Indeed, some have suspected that the vignette of the war-horse, like the clearly related portraits of the hippopotamus and the crocodile in the next two chapters, is really a sort of descriptive set piece which the poet brought in because he knew he could do it so well. It seems to me on the contrary that all three beasts are intrinsically connected with the vision of creation that is God's response to Job's questioning. The stallion enters the poem through a verbal clue: if the foolish ostrich only had wisdom, we are told, it would soar into the sky and "scoff at the horse and its rider" (39:18). This moves us directly into a consideration of the horse, which occupies the penultimate position in the first bestiary, before the concluding image of the eagle that will bring us back in an envelope structure to the initial picture of wild creatures caring for their young:

Do you give the horse his might, do you clothe his neck with a mane?
Do you make him shake like locusts, his majestic snorting—terror?
He churns up the valley, exults in power, goes out toward the weapons.
He scoffs at fear, is undismayed, turns not back from the sword.
Arrows by the quiverful rattle past him, the flash of spear and lance.
With clamor and clatter he swallows up ground, swerves not at the trumpet's blast.
As the trumpet sounds, he says, "Aha!" From afar he sniffs battle,
the roaring of captains, their shouts.

(39:19–25)

The passage is a rich interweave of heightening maneuvers and narrative developments between versets and between lines, as the war-horse itself is the vivid climactic image of the story the poet has to tell about the animal kingdom—before, that is, Behemoth and Leviathan, who, as we shall see, are a climax beyond the climax. In other words, we perceive the stallion narratively, first snorting and pawing the ground, then dashing into the thick of battle; and we see, for example, his whole body aquiver in a first verset, then a startling focus in the second verset on his nostrils snorting terror. The stallion is a concrete embodiment of contradictions held in high tension, in keeping with the whole vision of nature that has preceded. Though fiercer than the onager and the wild ox, he allows his great power to be subjected to the uses of man; yet, as he is described, he gives the virtual impression of joining in battle of his own free will, for his own pleasure. It would be naïve to conclude from these lines that the poet was interested in promoting martial virtues, but the evoked scene of mayhem does convey a sense that a terrible beauty is born and an awesome energy made manifest in the heat of war. These qualities are continuous with the ravening lion who began the bestiary and with the meteorological poetry before it in which lightning leapt from the cloud and the Lord stored up cosmic weapons in the treasure-houses of snow and hail.

To be sure, the whole zoological section of the poem is meant to tell Job that God's tender mercies are over all His creatures, but tonally and imagistically this revelation comes in a great storm rather than in a still, small voice, for the providence portrayed is over a world that defies comfortable moral categorizings. The most crucial respect in which such defiance makes itself felt is in the immense, imponderable play of power that is seen to inform creation. The world is a constant cycle of life renewing and nurturing life, but it is also a constant clash of warring forces. This is neither an easy nor a direct answer to the question of why the good man should suffer, but the imposing vision of a harmonious order to which violence is nevertheless intrinsic and where destruction is part of creation is meant to confront Job with the limits of his moral imagination, a moral imagination far more honest but only somewhat less conventional than that of the Friends. The strange and wonderful description of the hippopotamus and the crocodile, which after the introductory verses of challenge (40:7–14) takes up all of the second discourse, then makes those limits even more sharply evident by elaborating these two climactically focused images of the poem's vision of nature.

There has been a certain amount of quite unnecessary confusion among commentators as to whether the subject of the second discourse is in fact zoology or mythology. Many have argued that the two beasts in question are nothing more than the hippopotamus and the crocodile. Others, like Marvin Pope in his philologically scrupulous treatment of Job,[4] have claimed that both are mythological monsters. "Leviathan" in fact appears in Chapter 3 as a mythological entity, and the word is clearly cognate with the Ugaritic *Lotan*, a kind of sea dragon. The argument for mythology is shakier for Behemoth because there is no extrabiblical evidence of the term as a mythological designation, and all the other occurrences within the Bible would seem to be as a generic term for perfectly naturalistic grass-eating beasts of the field, including an earlier use of the term in Job itself (12:7).

The either/or rigidity of the debate over Behemoth and Leviathan quickly dissolves if we note that these two culminating images of the speech from the storm reflect the distinctive poetic logic for the development of meanings that we have been observing on both small scale and large in biblical poetry. The movement from literal to figurative, from verisimilar to hyperbolic, from general assertion to focused concrete image, is precisely the movement that carries us from the catalogue of beasts to Behemoth and Leviathan. The war-horse, who is the most striking item in the general catalogue and the one also given the most attention quantitatively (seven lines), is a way station in the rising line of semantic intensity that terminates in Behemoth and Leviathan. The stallion is a familiar creature but already uncanny in the beauty of power he represents. From this point, the poet moves on to two exotic animals whose habitat is the banks of the Nile—that is, far removed from the actual experience of the Israelite audience and even farther from that of the fictional auditor Job, whose homeland is presumably somewhere to the east of Israel. The listener, that is, may have actually glimpsed a war-horse or a lion or mountain goat, but the hippopotamus and crocodile are beyond his geographical reach and cultural ken, and he would most likely have heard of them through travelers' yarns and the fabulation of folklore. The hippopotamus is given ten lines of vivid description that place him on the border between the natural and the supernatural. Not a single detail is mythological, but everything is rendered with hyperbolic intensity, concluding in the strong assertion that no hook can hold him (in fact, the Egyptians used hooked poles to hunt the hippopotamus). The evocation of the crocodile is then accorded thirty-three lines, and it involves a marvelous fusion of precise observation, hyperbole, and mythological heightening of the real reptile, and thus becomes a beautifully appropriate climax to the whole poem.

To put this question in historical perspective, the very distinction we as moderns make between mythology and zoology would not have been so clear-cut for the ancient imagination. The Job poet and his audience, after all, lived in an era before zoos, and exotic beasts like the ones described in Chapters 40–41 were not part of an easily accessible and observable reality. The borderlines, then, between fabled report, immemorial myth, and natural history would tend to blur, and the poet creatively exploits this blur in his climactic evocation of the two amphibious beasts that are at once part of the natural world and beyond it.

What is stressed in the description of the hippopotamus is the para-doxical union of pacific nature—he is a herbivore, seen peacefully resting in the shade of lotuses on the riverbank—and terrific power, against which no human sword could prevail. (Thus, whether hippopotami could actually be captured is not important, for the poet needs to drive home the point that this awesome beast is both literally and figuratively beyond man's grasp.) And with strategic effectiveness, the notion of muscular power—bones like bronze, limbs like iron rods—is combined with a striking emphasis on sexual potency, thus extending the images of generation and birth of the first discourse:

Look, his power is in his loins,	his potency in the muscles of his belly.
He makes his member⁵ stand like a cedar,	the sinews of his testicles knit together.

(40:16–17)

Biblical poetry in general, certainly when measured by the standard of Greek epic verse, is not very visual, or rather is visual only in momentary flashes and sudden climactic developments. But the description of the crocodile is exceptionally striking in its sustained visual force, in keeping with its role as the culmination of this long, impressive demonstration of God's searching vision contrasted to man's purblind view. I shall translate the last twenty-two lines of the poem, which follow the initial assertion that Leviathan, like Behemoth, is impervious to every hook and snare and every scheme of being subjected to domestication. The line numbers reflect verse numbers in the Hebrew text of Chapter 41, beginning with verse 5:

5	Who can uncover his outer garb,	come into his double mail?
6	Who can pry open the doors of his face,	all around his teeth is terror.
7	His back is rows of shields,	closed in a tight seal,
8	One touching the next,	no breath could come between them.
9	Each cleaves to the next,	locked together, they will not part.
10	His sneezes flash light,	his eyes are like the eyelids of the dawn.
11	Firebrands leap from his mouth,	fiery sparks fly off.
12	From his nostrils smoke comes forth,	like a boiling pot on brushwood.
13	His breath kindles coals,	flame comes out of his mouth.
14	Strength dwells in his neck,	before him violence dances.
15	The folds of his flesh cling together,	hard-cast, he will not totter.
16	His heart is cast hard as stone,	cast hard as the nether millstone.

17	When he rears, the gods quail,	when he crashes down, they cringe.
18	No sword that reached him could stand,	neither spear, nor dart, nor lance.
19	Iron he deems as straw,	and bronze as rotten wood.
20	No arrow can make him flee,	against him, slingstones turn straw.
21	Missiles* are deemed mere straw,	he mocks the javelin's clatter.
22	His underside jagged shards,	he spreads a harrow over mud.
23	He makes the deep seethe like a caldron,	he turns sea to an ointment pan.
24	Behind him glistens a wake,	he makes the depths seem hoary.
25	He has no match on earth,	made as he is without fear.
26	All that is lofty he sees,	he is king over all proud beasts.

The power of the crocodile is suggested both through a heightening of the descriptive terms and through a certain narrative movement. First we get the real beast's awesome teeth and impenetrable armor of scales, then a mythologizing depiction of him breathing smoke and fire and sneezing sparks of light. This representation, moreover, of the fire-breathing beast is strangely reminiscent of the description of the God of battles in 2 Sam. 22 and elsewhere in biblical poetry.[6] At the same time, the series of challenging interrogatives that has controlled the rhetoric of the divine discourse from the beginning of Chapter 38 glides into declaratives, starting in verse 7, as the poem moves toward closure.[7]

As elsewhere, the poet works with an exquisite sense of the descriptive needs at hand and of the structural continuities of the poem and the book. The peculiar emphasis on fire and light in the representation of the crocodile takes us back to the cosmic imagery of light in God's first discourse, to the lightning leaping from the cloud, and beyond that to Job's initial poem. In fact, the remarkable and celebrated phrase "eyelids of the dawn,"[8] which Job in Chapter 3 wanted never to be seen again, recurs here to characterize the light flashing from the crocodile's eyes. This makes us draw a pointed connection and at the same time shows how the poet's figurative language dares to situate rare beauty in the midst of power and terror and strangeness. The implicit narrative development of the description takes us from a vision of the head, armor plate, and body of the beast (verses 13–24), to a picture of him rearing up and crashing down, brushing off all assailants, and then churning out of our field of vision, leaving behind a foaming wake that, like his mouth and eyes, shines (verses 25–32). If the language of sea (*yam*) and deep (*tehom, metzulah*) rather than of river water predominates in this final segment, that is in part because of the associations of the mythic Lotan with those terms and that habitat, but also because this vocabulary carries us back to the cosmogonic beginning of God's speech (see in particular 38:16). Job's merely human vision could not penetrate the secrets of the deep, and now at the end we have before our mind's eye the magnificent, ungraspable beast who lives in the deep, who is master of all creatures of land and sea, who from his own, quite unimaginable perspective "sees" all that is lofty. Leviathan is nature mythologized, for that is the poet's way of conveying the truly uncanny, the truly inscrutable, in nature; but he remains part of nature, for if he did not it would make little sense for the poem to conclude, "he is king over all proud beasts."[9]

By now, I would hope it has become clear what on earth descriptions of a hippopotamus and a crocodile are doing at the end of the Book of Job. Obviously, there can be no direct answer to Job's question as to why, having been a decent and God-fearing man, he should have lost all his sons and daughters, his wealth, and his health. Job's poetry was an instrument for probing, against the stream of the Friends' platitudes, the depths of his own understandable sense of outrage over what befell him. God's poetry enables Job to glimpse beyond his human plight an immense world of power and beauty and awesome warring forces. This world is permeated with God's ordering concern, but as the vividness of the verse makes clear, it presents to the human eye a welter of contradictions, dizzying variety, energies and entities that man cannot take in. Job surely does not have the sort of answer he expected, but he has a strong answer of another kind. Now at the end he will no longer presume to want to judge the Creator, having been brought through God's tremendous poetry to realize that creation can perhaps be sensed but not encompassed by the mind—like that final image of the crocodile already whipping away from our field of vision, leaving behind only a shining wake for us to see. If Job in his first response to the Lord (40:2, 4–5) merely confessed that he could not hope to contend with God and would henceforth hold his peace, in his second response (42:2–6), after the conclusion of the second divine speech, he humbly admits that he has been presumptuous, has in fact "obscured counsel" about things he did not understand. Referring more specifically to the impact of God's visionary poem, he announces that he has been vouchsafed a gift of sight—the glimpse of an ungraspable creation surging with the power of its Creator: "By what the ear hears I had heard You, / but now my eyes have seen You."

V

Forms of Faith

in Psalms

O<small>F ALL</small> the books of the Bible in which poetry plays a role, Psalms is the one set of texts whose poetic status has been most strongly felt throughout the generations, regardless of the vagaries of translation, typographical arrangement of verses, and notions about biblical literary form. This unwavering perception that the psalms were formal poems— even in ages, for example, when most readers imagined that the prophets spoke nothing but emphatic figurative prose—was no doubt reinforced by the musical indications in the texts themselves. Many of the psalms, that is, are explicitly presented as liturgical songs to be intoned to the accompaniment of the lyre, the ten-stringed instrument, cymbals, drums, and whatever else was once used to fill the temple courts with melody. The name of the book in Western languages, from the Greek *psalmos,* a song sung to a plucked instrument, stresses this musical character, as does the full Hebrew title, *mizmorei tehillim,* "songs of praise." It is symptomatic of the general response to these poems that so many poets in Renaissance England, though equally innocent of Hebrew and of an understanding of biblical poetic structure, should have tried their hand at producing metrical English versions of Psalms. In whatever way biblical versification was thought to work, it was almost universally assumed that the psalms exhibited the rhythmic regularity, the symmetries, the cadenced repetitions, of artful poems.

A countervailing assumption, however, has also enjoyed a great deal of currency down to our own times: that if the Book of Psalms is poetry, it is quintessentially a "poetry of the heart," a spontaneous outpouring of feeling expressed with directness and simplicity, almost without the intervention of artifice, its poignancy and universal appeal deriving from this very lack of conscious artifice. An extreme but by no means uncharacteristic instance of this view is an effusion by the Israeli *littérateur*, Yeshurun Keshet, written in 1954: "In the Book of Psalms everything is said in a primary fashion, without any 'literariness.' What characterizes the poetic expression of Psalms is that the poet allows objects and nature to speak for themselves without explaining them to us as modern poets often do. . . ."[1] This statement strikes me as fundamentally misconceived in imagining that any kind of literary expression can really escape "literariness," but one of course sees the features of Psalms that the writer has in mind. Whereas in Job, for example, one encounters daring leaps of invention in the imagery or, in the Prophets, intricate elaborations of rhetorical figures, the psalms do generally stick to something more "primary"—which does not mean something less literary but, on the contrary, a greater reliance on the conventional, the familiar, in imagery, in the sequence of ideas, in the structure of the poem. Such a reliance on the conventional is perfectly understandable. For a text that is to be chanted by pilgrims in procession on their way up the temple mount, or recited by a supplicant at the altar or by someone recovered from grave illness offering a thanksgiving sacrifice, you don't want a lot of fancy footwork in the imagery and syntax; you want, in fact, an eloquent rehearsal of traditional materials and even traditional ways of ordering those materials in a certain sequence.

This conventionality of the psalms, linked as it is in so many instances to the liturgical function of the poems, has led to a pronounced stress on typologies in studies of the psalms, beginning with the form-critical categories proposed by the German scholar Hermann Gunkel early in our century.[2] I will not attempt to review or refine any of these typologies here, but I would like to observe that, though such classifications have a certain usefulness in making clearer the various genres of psalms, they tend to miss an essential point about literary convention in their search for the general formulas that define a genre. Convention gives writers of both verse and prose a solid framework in which to construct their own discourse, but good writers always exert a subtle pressure on convention, in certain ways remaking it as they build within it.

Our own post-Romantic predisposition to originality in literature may lead to a certain perplexity about how to think of a collection where in any given genre a dozen or more poems seem to be saying the same thing, often with more or less the same metaphors and sometimes even with some of the same phrasing. What I think we need to be more attuned to as readers is the nuanced individual character—"originality" in fact may not be the relevant concept—of different poems reflecting the same genre and even many of the same formulaic devices. There are abundant instances in later poetic tradition, as in Arabic and Hebrew poetry of medieval Spain, Petrarchan love poetry, much English Augustan verse, where the power of the individual poem is meant to be felt precisely in such a fine recasting of the conventional, and that is what we ought to be able to discern more minutely in the psalms.

Let me state the question about the form of Psalms in the most basic fashion: apart from the obvious utility of versification for texts that in many instances were actually sung, what difference does it make to the content of the psalms that they are poems? At this point I must confess allegiance, repeatedly confirmed by my own experience as a reader, to a notion about the language of poetry that was central to the American New Critics a generation ago and that more recently has been corroborated from a very different perspective by the Soviet literary semioticians: that poetry, working through a system of complex linkages of sound, image, word, rhythm, syntax, theme, idea, is an instrument for conveying densely patterned meanings, and sometimes contradictory meanings, that are not readily conveyable through other kinds of discourse. To be sure, in any given text, some of the proposed linkages may turn out to be a product of the interpreter's ingenuity, and a poem may exhibit real disjunctures or inconsistencies where we look for intricate unities. Nevertheless, it need not be an act of "idolatry of the text" to claim, on the evidence of countless poems ancient and modern, that poetry is a way of using language strongly oriented toward the creation of minute, multiple, heterogeneous, and semantically fruitful interconnections in the text. As Jurij Lotman has put it, invoking contemporary notions of computer science, if we understood better how a poem achieved the astonishing degree of "information storage" that it does, our understanding of cybernetics in general might well be advanced.[3]

The psalms are of course poems written out of deep and often passionate faith. What I am proposing is that the poetic medium made it possible to articulate the emotional freight, the moral consequences, the altered perception of the world that flowed from this monotheistic belief, in compact verbal structures that could in some instances seem simplicity itself. Psalms, at least in the guise of cultic hymns, were a common poetic genre throughout the ancient Near East, but as the form was adopted by Hebrew poets, it often became an instrument for expressing in a collective voice (whether first person plural or singular) a distinctive, sometimes radically new, sense of time, space, history, creation, and the character of individual destiny. In keeping with this complex expressive purpose, many psalms, on scrutiny, prove to have a finely tensile semantic weave that one would not expect from the seeming conventionality of the language.

An instructive case in point is the very first psalm in the traditional collection. The ancient editors must have felt, with considerable justice, that this was a characteristic psalm and thus fitting to set at the beginning of the collection, perhaps as a kind of introduction to the rest. The very formula with which it begins, "Happy the man," occurs in a whole series of psalms, as do its praise of God's teaching (*torah*) and its assured sense that the wicked will be requited with evil, the righteous with success. This poem has been described as a Wisdom psalm, that is, a psalm spelling out the practical consequences of the good and the evil life respectively. It works entirely in the third person as a series of factual assertions—there is no distraught or exultant "I" here addressing God. There is in fact not much that seems "poetic" about Psalm 1 and certainly nothing that looks original. The only figurative language occurs in the middle three of the poem's seven lines, and the agricultural similes that are invoked could scarcely be more conventional—fruit-bearing trees over against wind-driven chaff. In what, then, does the poem's power reside, and in what way might it be, for all its simplicity and conventionality, more than the versification of an ancient monotheistic moral cliché? In the translation that follows, the numeration is of poetic lines because there is one more line than there are verses in the traditional division. Also, perhaps a little eccentrically, I have set out the initial phrase as an introductory formula or virtual title before the first line, since otherwise line 1 would begin with an impossibly long rhythmic unit.

Happy the man:

1 Who has walked not in the council of the wicked,   nor on the way of sinners has stood,

nor in the session of fools has sat.

2 Rather, in the Lord's teaching his delight,   His teaching he murmurs day and night.

3 He shall be like a tree planted by streams of water,   that gives its fruit in season,

4 Whose leaf does not wither	and all it puts forth, prospers.
5 Not so the wicked:	rather, like the chaff the wind blows.
6 Thus the wicked will not stand up in judgment,	nor sinners in the council of the righteous.
7 For the Lord embraces the way of the righteous,	and the way of the wicked is lost.

To begin with, we might note that this poem, which insists on a neat contrast between the wicked and the righteous, is fashioned with a tight logical structure of antithesis. In a manner rather uncharacteristic of biblical poetic style, the psalmist takes pains to place explicit indicators of logical transition at the head of four different versets: rather—not so—rather—thus (*ki-'im, l'o-ken, ki-'im, 'al-ken*). Reality is thus made to yield an exact moral calculus: there are things the just man will not do; indeed, there is something antithetical he does instead; the fate of the wicked is the contrary of the fate of the just; and there is a consequential generalizing summary ("thus") to be drawn from what has been asserted. The assertion itself, of course, is precisely what seems most dubious to the author of Job. The force of the poetic formulation of this idea of neatly retributive justice is that the language of the poem makes it seem built into the very structure of reality or, at any rate, is strongly felt by the speaker to be built into the structure of things, and as a result the didactic movement from "not so" to "thus" is in the poem something more than preaching insistence. Perhaps the best way to see this is to look closely at the use of verbs, which are important in regard to their denotation, sequence, and grammatical voice, and the way they support and define the images in lines 3–5.

The first line, and, emphatically, the only triadic one in the poem, defines the righteous man negatively (and thus simultaneously introduces his antithesis, the wicked) in a narrative sequence from one verset to the next of three verbs: walk, stand, sit. If he actually performed these actions, he would be on the constant move, headed toward the destination (third verset) of being ensconced in an assembly of fools (or of the insolent, the Hebrew *letz* embracing both these meanings). When in the first verset of line 2 the righteous man is characterized by what he actually does do, he initially is given no verb, then, in the second verset, a verb of contemplative activity or conning a text (the Hebrew *hagah* can mean both "to murmur" or "recite" and "to meditate on"). The image that describes him is then introduced (line 3) not with an active verb but with a past participle that denotes the opposite of movement—"planted."

It is from this firmly anchored location that the tree—not the man, verbal activity being displaced from the referent to the vehicle of the simile—can put forth fruit and grow unwithering leaves. The last verset of line 4 in the original is a kind of punning summation of the simile because the verbs there (Hebrew having no equivalent of "it") evidently refer to the tree but could as well refer to the man. When the wicked are finally introduced for direct characterization, in line 5, they are not the subject but rather the object of a verb, and one that denotes unstable motion, a scattering action.[4] The righteous man stands still—indeed, his righteousness may depend on his ability to stand still and reflect upon true things. The wicked are in constant motion, restless, without direction, carried hither and thither by forces over which they exert no control. This contrast is even reinforced quantitatively within the limits of the compact poem. At the poem's figurative center, lines 3–5, the rooted substantiality of the righteous is accorded two lines, four versets, while the fleeting insubstantiality of the wicked is given one line, and really only one verset.

The last two lines of the poem close it in the envelope structure (the end formally echoing the beginning) of which biblical writers in all genres are so fond. The poem began with sinners and the wicked; it ends with those same agents of wrongdoing, into whose midst, however, the righteous—mentioned explicitly as such for the first time—are now introduced in a neat chiastic pattern: wicked and sinners—righteous—righteous—wicked. The poem began by invoking evil councils and assemblies; it concludes by mentioning proper councils and legal sessions, in which the wicked cannot hope to prevail, or cannot presume to join. The movement attached through verbs to the wicked proceeds from being windblown to the negative not standing up (a different verb from "stand" in line 1) to being lost. But the syntax of the final line articulates this contrast between the just and the unjust with a further complication of meaning. The first verset of line 7 is the only point in the poem in which God appears as a grammatical subject: God "knows" (a verb implying special intimacy, as in its frequent sexual sense; hence my translation, "embraces") the way of the righteous. The second verset is then made pointedly to swerve from syntactic parallelism while it pursues an antithesis: and the way of the wicked is lost (or perishes). The very "way" of evildoers on which at the beginning of the poem the fortunate man did not stand is here at the end seen to lead nowhere, or to perdition. The wicked themselves are not even accorded the dignity of being a proper grammatical subject of an active verb: windblown like chaff, whatever way they go on is trackless, directionless, doomed.

The effectiveness of the whole poem surely has a good deal to do, as many readers have recognized, with the archetypal simplicity of the contrasted images of tree and chaff. But the study in movement and stillness that underlies both the figurative and the nonfigurative lines gives the pious assertions a certain depth of perception. We may even wonder whether this evocation of impotent kinesis over against fruitful stasis may be conceived in terms of moral psychology—as, for example, precisely that contrast is conceived by Jane Austen in *Mansfield Park*— and not merely as a matter of reward and punishment. That is, the essence of wrongdoing is to miss the mark (that is etymologically what the Hebrew word for "sinners" means), to pursue foolish or unattainable objects of desire that will lead only to frustration, while the man whose delight is in the Lord's teaching knows the art of sitting still in the right place, of finding fulfillment within the limits of law and of his own human condition.

The morally symbolic use of agricultural imagery in Psalm 1 points to a general feature of the collection: there is no real nature poetry in Psalms, because there is in the psalmist's view no independent realm of nature, but there is creation poetry, which is to say, evocations of the natural world as the embodiment of the Creator's ordering power and quickening presence. The justly celebrated Psalm 8 is a luminous instance of how poetic structure was made to yield a picture of the world that eloquently integrated underlying elements of Israelite belief. The poem might be described as a kind of summarizing paraphrase of the account of creation in Genesis 1, more or less following the same order of things created and stressing, as does Genesis 1, man's God-given dominion over the created world. The difference in form, however, between the two texts is crucial, and instructive. Genesis 1, being narrative, reports creation as a sequence of acts—indeed, as a kind of regulated procession moving from the dividing of light and darkness and the making of heaven, earth, and sea to God's rest on the seventh day after the creation of the animal kingdom and of man. It is all forward movement, from origins through time to a fulfillment. Psalm 8 assumes as a background this narrative process, but takes it up after its completion, and like many lyric poems it is the complex realization of one moment of perception: the speaker looking around at the created world and marveling at it, and at man's place in it. All literary texts are of course serial, unrolling in

time like the scrolls on which they were once written. A narrative may
to some extent qualify this temporal thrust by inviting us through its
deployment of repetition and analogy to shuttle mentally back and forth
along the text continuum as we read. It is the short lyric poem, however,
that has the greatest potential for neutralizing the temporal movement
inherent in verbal artworks. Within a small compass, through the use of
intricate and closely clustered devices of linkage and repetition, it can
create the illusion of actual simultaneity, offering to the mind's eye a
single panorama with multiple elements held nicely together. Let us see
how this is done in Psalm 8.

For the leader on the *gittit*, a psalm of David.

1 O Lord, our master,   how majestic Your name in all the earth.

2 You, whose splendor was told[5] over the heavens,   from the mouth of babes and sucklings.

3 You have founded strength because of Your foes,   to put an end to enemy and avenger.

4 When I see Your heavens, the work of Your fingers,   the moon and stars You established,

5 What is man that You should note him,   human creature, that You pay him heed?

6 You have set him little less than the angels,   with honor and glory You have crowned him.

7 You have made him rule over the work of Your hands,   all, You have placed at his feet.

8 Sheep and oxen, all of them,   and beasts of the field as well.

9 Bird of the heavens and fish of the sea,   what passes over the paths of the seas.

10 O Lord, our master,   how majestic Your name in all the earth.

Let me hasten to say that what I have laid out as lines 2 and 3 (I will
explain in a moment the reasons for my lineation) is not very intelligible
in the Hebrew text that has been passed down to us. Though "from the
mouth of babes and sucklings" has become a proverbial phrase, it is far
from clear what these infants are doing in our poem, and the relevance
to the context of the following line about foes and avengers is equally
obscure. Even so, something can be discerned about the place of these
initial utterances in the structure of the poem, and our concern is that
structure, not the solution of the textual crux at the beginning.

Psalm 8 gives us the extreme instance of envelope structure—the
repetition in a refrain of the first line as the last. That, of course, is a

common ending device in many bodies of poetry, but it is used only occasionally in biblical verse. The appropriateness of a refrain for our poem is clear enough. A perfect circle is closed: the majesty of God, affirmed at the beginning, is restated verbatim at the end, but with the sense accrued through the intervening eight lines of what concretely it means for His name to be majestic throughout the earth. The Hebrew says specifically "all" the earth, thus framing the whole poem with two symmetrical "all's", and that monosyllable, a mere grammatical particle, becomes the chief thematic key-word of the psalm. His dominion is over all, heaven and earth, angels and men and creatures of the field and air and sea, and He places "all" at the feet of man.

After this resounding formula of introduction and address to God in line 1, we may be able, tentatively, to rescue a few fragments from the enigma of lines 2–3. The heavens telling God's glory (as in Psalm 19) is intelligible enough, and leads directly to the assertion of line 4 about the awe-inspiring sight of heaven and moon and stars. "Heavens" in the first verset of line 2 also links up with "earth" at the end of line 1, thus recalling the creation story and reinforcing the idea of allness, "heaven and earth" being good biblical idiom for "all of creation.". I have made a hesitant guess that "from the mouth of babes . . ." is a parallel verset to the one in which the heavens tell God's splendor because it would also seem to be an indication of praise—that is, Your magnificence is borne witness to by the whole range of creation, from the beauty of the heavens to the prattle of infants. Any construal of the following line is bound to be conjectural. I would propose that the notion of laying low enemies and "founding" something strong, in the context of a creation story, looks like an elliptic allusion to the mythic imagery of cosmogony often borrowed from the Canaanite tradition, in which God, like Baal, is said to have subdued a primordial sea beast in order to secure the world on dry land.[6] If my guess is right, this would also introduce the sea at the beginning of the poem to make a cosmogonic triptych with heaven and earth. At any rate, "founded" at the beginning of line 3 would seem to be linked with "established" at the end of line 4, both pointing to the completed work of solid creation, whose perfection the speaker now beholds.

The only verb in the poem attached to a human action is "see" at the beginning of line 4. The speaker, having begun with a cosmic perspective and a perhaps not yet personal address to God in the first three lines, now introduces himself explicitly into the frame of the poem, and we are invited to stand with him, an individual human being looking up at the splendor of the night sky and marveling over man's place in the intricate scheme of things. This sequence of six lines before the final refrain constitutes a special adaptation of the focusing impulse of biblical verse, being a vertical metonymic descent down the scale of creation. First the speaker beholds the heavens, then, in the second verset, according to a pattern we have seen elsewhere, what is contained within them—the moon and the stars. The heavens are "the work of Your fingers," apparently as an elegant variant of the standard locution, "the work of Your hands" (line 7), but especially since this particular construct form appears only here in the whole Bible, we may well be expected to hear in it the indication of especially delicate work as the speaker scans the exquisite tracery of the night sky. After the focusing between versets of line 4, we move from heaven to man, who is a little lower than the heavens and the celestial beings (´elohim), and below him to the rest of God's handiwork, "all" that is "at his feet" (the Hebrew says literally "under his feet," thus reinforcing the downward vertical movement in the picture of the cosmic hierarchy). The famous cry of amazement over God's singling out of man (line 5) is a particularly striking instance of the intuition of counterpoint that often guided biblical poets in their occasional use of static semantic parallelism. In every other line of the poem, there is dynamic movement between the versets: specification, focusing, heightening, or sequentiality. Here, by contrast, at the exact thematic center and in the fifth of the poem's ten lines, semantic movement is slowed to allow for the strong, stately emphasis of virtual synonymity, noun for noun and verb for verb in the same syntactical order: "What is man that You should note him, / human creature, that You pay him heed?"

God has set this human creature only a little lower than the divine, and that means (parallelism of specification and sequentiality) crowning him with honor and glory, quite like the attributes He Himself possesses (lines 1 and 2). The next line (7) then specifies the meaning of this coronation as man's having been given dominion over earthly things, and thus makes a transition in the vertical scheme from heaven through man to the world below. The last two lines before the refrain, with their inventory of living creatures loosely recalling Genesis 1 (though the terms are different from those in Genesis), go on to specify what is contained within the "all," the "work of Your hands" referred to in line 7. In apt concision, the four versets invoke both domestic and wild animals and all three spheres of terrestrial life—field and air and sea. The last of these versets focuses "fish of the sea" by replacing it with a kenning—indeed, one that sounds vaguely Anglo-Saxon—"what passes over the paths of the sea." Interestingly, it is the only active verb in the poem attached to a created thing. God acts on all realms of creation; man beholds the various realms; but until this penultimate movement the created things themselves have been merely listed as objects of God's attention and that of his surrogate, man. Now, in the final detail of the catalogue of creation, we see an image of movement, a nice intimation in this panoramic view of the chain of being of that teeming vitality, surging through the most inaccessible reaches of the created world, over which man has been appointed to rule.

The God of biblical faith, however, as has often been noted, is not a God of the cosmos alone but also a God of history. A good many psalms—including those referring explicitly to the Judean king and classified as "royal psalms"—are responses to the most urgent pressures of the historical moment, whether as pleas to God to save His king and people at a time of national danger or as celebrations of some recent or remembered military victory. Poems of this sort abound in the premono-theistic world, where every nation was presumed to have its own particular god of battles whose intercession was solicited in time of military need. Even in monotheistic guise, this may seem one of the less edifying forms of worship (one recalls Voltaire's bitter mockery at the beginning of *Candide*, when he has both sides simultaneously celebrate Te Deum over the smoking battlefield for having been vouchsafed the grace to slaughter thousands of the enemy). But the strongest of what we may call the political psalms are neither as narrow nor as crudely pragmatic as modern preconceptions might lead us to expect. Most fundamentally, the composers of the political psalms were confronted with expressing in poetic form a paradox at the heart of biblical religion: the universalistic belief in a single God of all the earth Who had chosen as the medium of His relations with humanity the particularism of a compact with one people. This paradox had a major geographical corollary. The psalms having been made for use in and around the temple cult in Jerusalem, how was the Israelite to imagine this capital city of a nation-state, first conquered by David for strategic and political reasons, as the "city of our God," the God who was master of all the nations of the world? The poetic medium, I would suggest, with its extraordinary capacity for interlocking disparate elements and establishing intricate progressions of images and ideas, provided a uniquely apt instrument for the expression of such meanings held in high tension. Here is Psalm 48, which would seem to be a song sung by—or perhaps

to—pilgrims as they made their way up the steep ascent to the ramparts
of Jerusalem.

A song, a psalm of the Korahites.

1	Great is the Lord and much acclaimed	in the city of our God, His holy mount.
2	Lovely in heights, joy to all the earth,	Mount Zion, peak of Zaphon,

town of the great King.

3	God through its bastions	has become known as a stronghold.
4	For, look, the kings assembled,	advanced together.
5	They saw, indeed were dismayed,	were panicked, were shaken.
6	Trembling seized them there,	shaking, like a woman in labor.
7	With an easterly wind	You smashed the Tarshish ships.
8	Just as we heard	now we see.
9	In the city of the Lord of hosts,	in the city of our God,

may God keep it firm-founded forever. Selah.

10	We have glimpsed, God, Your steadfastness	in the midst of Your temple.
11	Your name, God, like Your acclaim,	is to the ends of the earth.

Your right hand is filled with justice.

12	Let Mount Zion rejoice,	let the daughters[7] of Judea exult

because of Your judgments.

13	Go round Zion, encircle it,	count its towers.
14	Take note of its ramparts,	scale[8] its bastions,
15	So you may recount	to the last generation:
16	That this is God, our God, forever.	He will lead us evermore.*

The first two lines of the poem lock together the particularist and
universalist poles of the psalmist's vision. God's greatness is acclaimed
in—and perhaps the particle also means "through," as in line 3—the
one city in the world that is uniquely His, but the high-bastioned city
itself, viewed from below as the celebrants climb up to it, is a "joy to all
the earth." This sense of Jerusalem's looming importance is enhanced by
the mythological designation "peak of Zaphon." In Canaanite tradition,
Mount Zaphon (elsewhere, the term means "north") was the abode of
the gods; so Mount Zion is imagined here, if we may mix mythologies,
as a kind of Olympus. If I am right in assuming that this whole triadic
line is built on a heightening movement from verset to verset, the
reference to the great King at the end would be to God, not to the
reigning Davidic monarch, thus culminating a rising pitch of assertion in
the following fashion: (a) lofty Jerusalem is a joy to all the world; (b)

Mount Zion is a veritable dwelling-place of the gods; *(c)* in fact, it is the chosen capital of the world's King. Line 3, in an assertion that dares to come to the brink of redundancy, nicely summarizes what has preceded and leads into the narrative of lines 4–11: one has only to look up at the impregnable citadels of Jerusalem to realize concretely how in historical fact God has become a stronghold for His people.

The speaker now launches into the story of a spectacular defeat inflicted on an alliance that at some point in the near or distant past had set out to invade Israel by sea. As the poem moves forward on this narrative momentum, it switches freely from semantic parallelism involving sequentiality (lines 4–5) and focusing (line 6) to lines that abandon semantic parallelism in following a narrative thread (lines 7, 10, 11). The precise historical reference is probably unrecoverable, but the language used to render the naval victory vividly shows how the poet locates Jerusalem in historical time and space.

Clearly, there is a pointed antithesis between the "great King" of line 2 who becomes known (*nod'a*) and the conspiring kings of line 5 who assemble, or join forces (*no'adu*). Perhaps, as some scholars have proposed, "Tarshish ships" refers not to the port of embarcation but to a particular kind of low-keeled, oar-propelled warship. Be that as it may, the invasion fleet would have had to come somewhere from the west, on the Mediterranean, and Tarshish is a far-off port (one recalls, it is the destination of the fleeing Jonah) that educated guesses have placed anywhere from Tarsus in Cilicia to somewhere on the Iberian Peninsula. In other words, as our gaze now swivels around from the ramparts of Jerusalem to look down over the coastal plain and to the Great Sea beyond it, and as we move at the same time from present to past, we are invited to imagine hostile forces assembling from the ends of the known earth to attack the Land of Israel.

The link between Mount Zion and an attempted invasion by sea may at first seem a little tenuous, depending merely on the implicit notion that the capital city would have been the invaders' ultimate goal. The juxtaposition, however, of Mount Zion and the sea makes perfect sense as soon as one realizes that the whole description of the overturning of the enemy fleet by an easterly gale is a phrase-for-phrase allusion to the Song of the Sea (compare lines 6–7 with Exodus 15:14–16). Moses' victory song, we should remember, concludes in a third strophe that counterpoints the firm-founded sanctuary God will build in Israel's future Land with the engulfing sea that destroys Israel's enemies. Our psalm starts from the other end of the geographical perspective, that is, from what constitutes the concluding verses of the poem in Exodus 15—the solid mountain sanctuary established for Israel, from whose rocky heights one can see that all God's enemies by contrast tread on, perish in, unstable water. When we move back, in lines 8–9, from the story of the defeat by storm to "the city of our God," the allusion to Exodus 15 is continued, for the poet's prayer for the city is that it be forever "firm-founded" (konen, the very verb that dominated the concluding lines of the Song of the Sea).[9] Thus, through the poetic perception of a particular routing of a sea-borne foe as a reenactment of the triumph at the Reed Sea, facts of geography—the mountainous eminence of Jerusalem over against the watery expanses of the Mediterranean—are turned into a symbolic pairing that concretely depicts God's dominion over all the earth and the power of His presence in history. And as the spatial imagery of the poem takes us from Jerusalem to the far reaches of the known world, the temporal indications unite the present with the relatively recent past (the sea victory) and the distant past (Moses' victory) as well as with the indefinite future ("forever," "to the last [or, a future] generation," "evermore"). Thus, the towering ramparts of the fortress-city become a nexus for all imagined time and space.

As the psalm comes back, beginning with line 10, to town and temple, this paradox of the God of all the earth Who has chosen a local place and habitation is flaunted: God's "steadfastness," or "loving care" (ḥesed), can be discerned within "the midst of [His] temple," while His acclaim (compare the first versets of lines 1 and 2) reaches "to the ends of the earth." The return to the location of Zion is marked by two triadic lines (11–12), as was the conclusion of the poem's opening (line 2). The interlinear parallelism between the two triads here breaks up and matches the two terms of a set formula, justice and judgment (tzedeq umishpat). The first of these terms can also mean "victory" or "bounty," and the poet is clearly playing on the multiple meanings of the word in invoking the idea of the just God Who grants security to His people in the face of His enemies. The four concluding lines of the poem then revert, in a loose envelope structure, to the perspective with which the poem began of the spiritual tourist approaching the city from below. Those who came to the city are invited to take in its entire imposing circumference, to "count" its towers deployed in space so that they may "recount" God's greatness for all future time (the pun is in the Hebrew sifru, tesapru, two different conjugations of the same verb). All this adroit juggling of time and space around the idea of Jerusalem will hardly allay the doubts of the modern reader who may be nervous about such mixtures of politics and faith, but with even a grudging suspension of disbelief we can see how the poem's finely regulated sequencing of images and actions is a strong translation of the monotheistic belief in a world-embracing God Who chooses a place, and takes sides, in the large sweep of history.

The personal and penitential psalms, in any case, are the ones that continue to speak most unambiguously to a wide range of readers, even with all the transformations that the faith of Jews and Christians has undergone since biblical times. In these religious poems without a strong national context, one does not generally see a poetic redefinition of space, because geography and geopolitics are not at issue, but some of them strikingly refashion time as the imagination stretches to gauge the abyss between man's creaturely temporality and the eternality of the Creator. The fleetingness of human life is of course a perception by no means limited to monotheistic or religious poetry, either in ancient literature or later, but the biblical poets deepened this recurrent human perception in a distinctive way by rendering the ephemerality and incompleteness of the life of man against the background of God's eternity. And since poetry—especially, for reasons we have seen, biblical poetry—often works out meanings through an interplay of polarities, the brevity of human existence could also provide a certain imaginative access through contrast to the inconceivable timelessness of God. In the *Iliad*, the consciousness of life's brief span is the occasion for asserting a code of heroic action. In the Bible, where it is set against the consciousness of God's eternality, it becomes the occasion for a new kind of inwardness, one element of which is a recognition of the tenuousness, the dependence, the impotence of man's existence.

Perhaps the most remarkable expression of these juxtaposed times, man's and God's, is Psalm 90. Since the poem is composed of four segments, which are successive stages in a rhetorical structure though not formally marked strophes like those in Exodus 15 and Job 28, I have indicated the transitions by typographical breaks. The segments may be described as follows: (1) proem, addressing God and invoking His eternality (lines 1–3); (2) characterization of human transience, referring to man in the third person (lines 4–7); (3) confession of ephemeral man's sinfulness, in the first person plural (lines 8–13); (4) prayer of the ephemeral creature for wisdom and for God's grace (lines 14–19).

A prayer of Moses, the man of God.

1 Lord, You have been our dwelling   in every generation.
2 Before mountains were born,   before You spawned earth and world,

3	From eternity to eternity	You are God.
4	You bring man back to dust,	You say, "Turn back, humankind."
5	For a thousand years in your eyes	are like yesterday gone,
	like a watch in the night.	
6	You engulf them with sleep,*	in the morn they're like changing grass,
7	In the morn it sprouts and changes,	by evening it withers and dries.
8	For we are consumed in Your wrath,	in Your anger we are destroyed.
9	You set our transgressions before You,	our hidden faults in the light of Your face.
10	All our days slip by in Your fury,	we consume our years like a sigh.
11	The days of our years but seventy years,	or if in great strength, eighty years—
12	Their pride is trouble and grief,	for swiftly cut down, we fly off.*
13	Who can know the power of Your wrath?	As the fear of You is Your fury.
14	To count our days truly, teach us,	that we may get a heart of wisdom.
15	Turn back, Lord! How long?	Have pity on Your servants.
16	Sate us in the morn with Your kindness,	let us sing and rejoice all our days.
17	Give us joy as the days You afflicted us,	the years we saw evil.
18	Let Your deeds be seen by Your servants,	Your glory by their children.
19	Be the favor of the Lord our God on us,	the work of our hands firmly found for us,
	the work of our hands, firmly found!	

In respect to genre, this poem is a collective penitential supplication. The community has apparently been suffering some unspecified ill or ills for a considerable length of time (God's reiterated "wrath" or, more concretely, the affliction and years of evil referred to in line 17), whether through famine or plague or military defeat or a combination of such disasters. The recurrent formula of the psalms of supplication, "O Lord! How long?" is introduced in line 15, at the beginning of the plea to God for a change of heart (*hinaḥem*, rendered here as "take pity") with which the poem concludes. But whereas most supplications typically use poetic structures of intensification to express the unbearableness of the speaker's anguish, sometimes with allusions to an actual political or medical context for the entreaty, the poet here transforms the occasion of supplication into a haunting meditation on human transience. The proem, framed by a large chiasm ("Lord, You . . . You are God"), invokes the beginnings of the world through the birth imagery (line 2) that is conventional in biblical cosmogonic verse. Such imagery has a special point here, because the language of biological reproduction, focused on the world itself, simultaneously points forward to man born of woman in passing time and underscores the contrast with the Creator, Whose existence is "from eternity to eternity."

After the proem, the penitential note is first struck when the speaker imagines God urging men to "turn back," that is, to repent, with the actual agency of this urging a deed not an utterance—that is, God's having "brought man back" (the same verb) to dust (or, as some translators render it, to contrition) through suffering. Whatever the precise nature of this suffering, it has served to remind the speaker of the painful mortality of humankind, and that is the burden of the rest of the poem, the "turning back" God urged thus already embodied in the chastened self-knowledge of the poetic discourse.

Line 5, triadic for emphasis in its function as initiator of the meditation on human transience, is one of the most exquisite uses of interverset focusing in the Bible, as we glide swiftly from a thousand years in God's eyes to yesterday that has just passed to a brief watch in the night. This is time viewed from God's end of the telescope, but the last term takes us down into the world of human existence, and in a beautiful interlinear overlap, "watch in the night" carries us on, by both contiguity and contrast, to man engulfed by sleep (the syntactically problematic Hebrew literally says: "You engulf them. They are sleep."). That is, a thousand years for God are a fleeting moment of wakefulness in the dark of eternity, while man's whole existence is little more than fluid, fitful sleep. Against the focusing development used to intimate God's time, man's time is represented through a narrative movement, strictly limited to a twenty-four-hour framework that, by implication, recurs cyclically for each new individual: from night (line 6a) to morning (6b–7a) to evening (7b).

As the speaker switches into the first person plural and proceeds to the confession proper (lines 8–13), he implicitly continues the imagery of withering and drying up in the special emphasis he gives to God's wrath. The term I have rendered as "anger" (*ḥeimah*) clearly suggests heat (like the English term "incensed"), and the parallel pair "wrath"/

"anger" in line 8 is actually the breakup of a biblical idiom, ḥamat-ʾaf, which means literally the "hot breath of the nostrils." The whole confession is bracketed by an internal envelope structure (line 8: wrath/anger—line 13: wrath/fury), and the unit is defined by an underlying image of insubstantial, combustible humanity being burned up in the hot blast of God's wrath. This effect is reinforced by the likening of man's life (line 10) to a "sigh" (or, perhaps, "murmur," the noun implying a low muttered syllable, the same root that is used at the beginning of Psalm 1)—an ineffectual breath of sound in contrast to God's consuming blast. The units of time introduced here move progressively in the opposite direction from the units of time linked to God in line 5, advancing from small to large, from "days" (line 10a) to "years" (10b), to a compound, "days of our years" (11a), but never getting beyond seventy or eighty, not even as far as the thousand that is a brief passing interval for God.

The petition, then, for the wisdom "to count our days truly" with which the final prayer begins (line 14) carries the accumulated weight of meaning of the poem. God, who urged man to turn back, is now implored to respond by Himself turning back to man. In keeping with this upbeat of hopeful prayer, the temporal terminology already invoked is taken up once more, but in a vision of fulfillment in time instead of vanishing in time: "Sate us *in the morn* with Your kindness, / let us sing and rejoice *all our days*. // Give us joy *as the days* You afflicted us, / *the years* we saw evil." The narrative progression from morning to days and from days to years looks beyond the futile cycle of transience to imagine life as a forward movement from smaller to greater in joy. Significantly, the sole temporal terms from the previous parts of the poem not repeated here are the ones symbolically associated with fitful sleep and death—"evening" and "night." In this perspective, "their children" in the second verset of line 18 is not merely a convenient counterpart in the parallelism to "Your servants" in the first verset, for at the penultimate moment of the poem, what it does is to project the fragile human community into the future. As an objective fact of biological existence, we wither and die like grass, in what is no more than a moment under the aspect of eternity. But granted God's kindness, His sustaining care (ḥesed), we can be gladdened in the days of our years, as can be our children after us.

The final line of the poem, concluding the prayer for divine favor, introduces the closural emphasis of a triad in order to repeat a climactic phrase: "the work of our hands firmly found for us, / the work of our hands firmly found." We have encountered in other poems this verb *konen,* elsewhere used in the Bible to characterize the solid foundations of houses and temples. The special force of the reiteration of this verb at the end of Psalm 90 must be felt as a reversal of the imagery of withering grass, sighs, things burnt up by God's wrath, and (if the received text for line 6a is correct) humanity flooded or engulfed by sleep. With God's blessing, there is something solid, lasting, well-founded in human endeavor. Each of our lives is fleeting—and the greatness of the poem is that it never loses hold of this painful truth, even in the hopeful piety of the conclusion—but the works we perform, out of a proper awareness of our vulnerable mortality, can have substance, are our human means of continuity and renewal from one generation to the next.

The multifaceted sense of time's permutations that is made possible through the structure of the poem is altogether remarkable. By means of a subtle sequence of fairly simple, and for the most part conventional, images, the verbal deployment of basic units of time, backward and forward and forward again, the poet is able to realize imaginatively in rapid succession three very different perceptions of time—from the divine perspective of eternity, from man's vanishing vantage point of the moment, and, reversing that view, from the perspective of a community that can see in the uses it makes of its moments a prospect of happy persistence.

If the poetic medium of Psalms is an instrument for reconstructing time and space and the order of history and society in the light of faith, the optative mood of the prayers and the celebratory note of some of the songs of thanksgiving lead at points to a strikingly utopian vision. Though the psalms, that is, are uttered out of the real dangers and fears and doubts of a historical or existential here and now, they also sometimes project, like the last lines of Psalm 90, an image of what life must be like sheltered by God from the wasting winds of mischance, when human performance and divine expectation are in perfect accord. We have considered examples of the monotheistic reconstitution through poetry of history, geography, and time; it may be instructive to observe an analogous transformation of the social order. Psalm 72, which was selected by the ancient editors to conclude the Second Book of Psalms, is a royal psalm and thus by definition a political one, apparently bestowing blessings of earthly power and justice on a real king in the Davidic line—just possibly Solomon himself, if the superscription of the poem is original to it rather than the addition of a later redactor who thought of Solomon because of the poem's emphasis on wise judgment.

In any case, real historical events of the sort alluded to in Psalm 48 do not appear here. The harmonious vision of a perfectly just and compassionate king whose name will be eternally blessed is the projection forward out of history of an ideal, and as such it has much in common with the messianic visions of the prophets, as in Isaiah 11 and Amos 9: 13–15. But if both prophet and psalmist use poetry to approach this utopian bourn, poetic structure in the psalms tends to be more elaborately defined and more formally delimited than what one typically finds in the Prophets, and it is worth seeing how such structure lends itself to the psalms' particular recension of biblical utopianism. In what follows, I omit the last three verses of Psalm 72, which clearly belong to the editorial formula of conclusion to Book Two of Psalms, and not to the poem itself.

For Solomon.

1. God, Your judgments to the king grant,   and Your justice to a king's son.
2. May he rule Your people justly,   Your lowly ones, with judgment.
3. May the mountains bear peace to the people,   the hills, through justice.
4. May he champion the lowly of the people,   deliver the needy,

and crush the oppressor.

5. May they fear You while the sun lasts,   as long as the moon, age after age.
6. May he descend like rain on new-mown grass,   a downpour of showers on earth,
7. May the righteous man flower in his days,   abounding peace till the moon's no more.
8. May he rule from sea to sea,   from the River to the ends of the earth.
9. Before him desert-dwellers will kneel,   his enemies will lick the dust.
10. Kings of Tarshish and the isles will pay tribute,   kings of Sheba and Saba bring gifts.
11. All kings bow down to him,   and nations serve him.
12. For he saves the needy crying out,   the poor, who have no helper.
13. He pities the poor and the needy,   the lives of the needy he rescues.
14. From fraud and havoc he redeems their lives,   their blood is dear in his eyes.
15. Long live, and give him Sheban gold,   and prayers always said for his sake,

all day long be he blessed.

16. Let there be rich* grain in the land,   on the mountaintops.

130

17 Let his fruit rustle like Lebanon,   let them sprout from the towns*
                                             like the grass of the land.
18 Let his name be forever.   As long as the sun, let his name
                                             go on,
19 Let men through him be blessed,   all nations call him happy.

Taking advantage of the ambiguity of Hebrew verb tenses, the poem manages at once to be prayer, prophecy, portrait, and benediction. Strictly speaking, there are only two tenses in biblical Hebrew, the perfect and the imperfect. The latter, which is employed throughout Psalm 72, can be used for future actions, or habitually repeated actions, or as a jussive or optative, for actions the speaker wishes would happen, and the force of the verbs in our poem seems to overlap all these possibilities. The prayer of the first two lines that God grant the king a sound sense of justice quickly glides, after a brief glance at nature (line 3), to which we shall return, into a series of optatives attached to the king. The optatives, however, become almost at once a predictive portrait of the utopian monarch, with the point of transition perhaps marked by line 5, which might easily be rendered as a simple future: "They will fear You while the sun lasts, / as long as the moon, age after age." Although nuances of tense and mood in biblical Hebrew are admittedly hard to distinguish from where we stand, the stress here on what will go on and on sounds a shade or two firmer than the mere hopefulness of an optative. The positiveness of assertion actually begins to build in the previous line where the subject of the imperfect verb "bear" is not a conscious agent, capable of doubt and divagation, but the mountains and the hills.

What, in fact, do the hills and mountains have to do with the reign of a perfectly just king? Elsewhere in Psalms the lofty mountains and the subterranean sea are used as images, or cosmic gauges, of God's world-embracing justice: "Your justice is like the vast mountains, / Your judgments the great abyss, / man and beast You rescue, Lord" (Ps. 36: 7). Our poem begins with the same formulaic pairing, "judgment"/ "justice," chiastically repeated to produce a double emphasis: "Your judgments"—"Your justice"—"justly"—"with judgment." (The verbs in lines 2 and 4 rendered as "rule" and "champion" both also mean to judge, the latter a cognate of "judgment" in lines 1 and 2.) Once there is justice, the natural world, as though sympathetically influenced, confers its blessing of "peace" or "well-being" (shalom) on man, and, conversely, the reign of justice perfectly implemented has the perdurable solidity of the timeless natural landscape. Nature having been thus introduced in the third line of the poem, the language of the psalm continually intimates a double relation between the order of justice and the order of nature as cause and effect and as symbolic correspondence.

Eternal continuance is indicated here not by the usual abstract adverb, "forever," but by the striking celestial images "while the sun lasts," "as long as the moon," as though to concretize the speaker's sense that the reign of justice will persist along with the everlasting presences of nature made at the beginning of creation. The ideal king is then rendered metaphorically (line 6) as a fructifying force of nature, rain on new-mown grass, an image that leads narratively to the blossoming of the righteous and the abundance of endless peace in the next line. The agricultural imagery will return just before the end of the poem (lines 16–17), as both literal statement and metaphor. Though the Hebrew text seems problematic at this point, two related assertions can be made out: the land will be dense with grain and fruit (16–17a), and people will flourish like the vegetable world (17b).

One important effect of the agricultural imagery is to help transform the notion of power in the portrait of empire (lines 8–11) that these images surround. The ideal king will rule from sea to sea, but even the verb of dominion, *yerd*, is qualified by its punning echo of *yered*, the verb describing the ruler's "descent" like rain on grass. The kings of all the earth, from Sheba and Saba in the south to westward Tarshish and the islands of the Mediterranean, do in fact prostrate themselves before the just monarch, but there is no indication in the poem of how he has managed to seize power over them. Indeed, the only verb of aggression he governs is "to crush" in line 4, an activity directed against the oppressors of the poor, and continued in the king's compassionate acts of rescue in the progressively heightened four versets of lines 13–14. The poem tactfully implies, without explicitly stating, a causal link between the beneficent effect of the just king indicated in lines 6–7 and the subsequent vision of imperial dominion. It is as though all the rulers of the earth will spontaneously subject themselves to this king, lay tribute at his feet, because of his perfect justice. The correspondence between justice and nature first indicated in line 3 is matched here by a correspondence between justice and history. If the fear of God inspired by the just king and (at the end of the poem) his name, repeatedly invoked in blessing, will go on as long as the sun and moon, then endlessness in time is somehow correlated with endlessness in space, and his just dominion will span the known limits of the world, "from the River to the ends of the earth."

To say that time and space are "somehow" correlated is of course a bit evasive, but that is an unavoidable symptom of the clumsiness of paraphrase. A poem of this sort is surely not an effort at serious historical explanation, and like any utopian statement it is accountable to history only as a projection, from the scant historical grounds for hope, of how history might be transformed. What would the world look like, the psalmist implicitly asks, if we imagine a ruler governing not by coercion but by compassion and unswerving equity, who did not exploit the weak but championed them? The biblical writers may well have understood intuitively that such projections might be as spiritually indispensable as the most unblinking reports of the savagery that occurs in history, and with which the biblical record abounds. Although points of real geography are invoked, everything comes together not in the intersection of Sheba and Tarshish at Jerusalem but in the poetic structure where a king's defense of the helpless becomes rain over the land, the land itself burgeons with beauty, all the earth takes his name for a blessing, in a lovely verbal intimation of social and political harmony denied us by ordinary experience but which, in the momentum of the poem, goes on till the moon's no more.

The instances we have examined of poetic form used to reshape the world in the light of belief are meant to suggest some major possibilities, but they are hardly a comprehensive survey of Psalms. There are ten or more distinguishable genres (as analysts ever since Gunkel have recognized) represented in the 150 psalms of the traditional collection, and the variousness of many of these invites further division into subcategories. But if it is impracticable within the scope of a chapter to offer illustrative readings for all the discrete genres of psalms, it may be useful to conclude our sampling with a text that embodies an emphasis shared by many poems of different genres in the collection. A "psalm," *mizmor,* is an act of singing or chanting, a way of using language, with or without actual musical accompaniment, rhythmically and regularly, to implore, to admonish, to reflect—and, above all, to celebrate (hence the Hebrew title, *mizmorei tehillim,* "songs of praise"). Many of the psalms devote special attention to the activity of song or utterance enacted in them, making it their virtual subject, "foregrounding" the act of speech, as the Prague Structuralists would have put it. Psalm 30 is a characteristic poem in this regard. It is a psalm of thanksgiving that succinctly rehearses the conventions of the genre: the speaker having been saved from some mortal danger, probably physical illness, imagines that he has descended into the underworld and has been miraculously brought back by God. Like many psalms belonging to this and other genres, the entire poem is formally framed by the self-conscious marking of the language of praise.

A psalm, song for the dedication of the house, of David.

1	I will exalt You, God, for You drew me up,	and You did not rejoice my enemies.
2	O Lord, my God,	I cried out to You, and You healed me.
3	Lord, You raised me from Sheol,	gave me life among those gone down[10] to the Pit.
4	Sing to the Lord, you faithful,	and praise His holy name.
5	But a moment in His wrath—	life, in His pleasure.
6	At evening one lies down weeping;	in the morning—shouts of joy.
7	And I thought when I was carefree:	"I'll never be overthrown."
8	Lord, in Your pleasure	You made me strong as a mountain.
9	You hid Your face,	and I was dismayed.
10	To You, O Lord, I called,	to my Lord I pleaded:
11	"What's to be gained by my going down deathward?	Will dust praise You, declare Your truth?
12	Hear, O Lord, and pity me,	Lord, become my helper!"
13	You have turned my dirge to dancing,	undone my sackcloth, decked me with joy,
14	So that glory be sung You, never-stilled.	O Lord, my God, forever I'll praise You.

This is the most consecutively narrative of any of the psalms we have considered, and in keeping with that impulse, there is a good deal of narrative movement between versets (see especially the sequence from line 5 to line 9), with semantic parallelism at two or three points entirely abandoned to follow the curve of narrated events. Line 1 simultaneously sets out the purpose of the whole poem ("to exalt") and encapsulates the story of the speaker's rescue from the Pit, using a verb that elsewhere serves for the drawing of water from a well. But the expanded summary of the story in lines 2–3 includes a new and essential moment of the plot: the crying out before the healing. For this is a poem that celebrates not only God's saving power but the efficacy of speech—both speech to God in prayer and praise of God in thanksgiving. There is, then, a submerged logical link between the summarizing account of the effect of prayer in lines 2–3 and the exhortation to sing and praise in line 4. Interestingly, as the speaker turns here from God to the congregation, he gives us the first line constructed on relatively balanced synonymity, without narrative movement or focusing, as though to underscore the thematically central assertion of song.

Lines 5–6, still addressed to the congregation, are a kind of aphoristic generalization on the recurrent human context of the speaker's particular experience: God's wrath, inflicting anguish, passes in a moment, and afterward there is lasting gladness. The reference to "shouts of joy" (*rinah*, which can also mean "song") keeps in the foreground the act of chanting praise that is the articulated form of the psalm and its message.

A more detailed narration of the speaker's rescue from the doors of death then follows (lines 7–13). There is a brief piece of direct speech quoted, for the length of one verset, to indicate the speaker's time of foolish complacency ("I'll never be overthrown."). Then four versets are devoted to a quotation of the plea the speaker addressed to God in his distress. The language of his appeal to God takes us right back to the thematic foreground of language: there is no point in God's allowing him to die, because lifeless dust cannot praise Him, cannot report to others His "truth" (or "faithful performance"), one instance of which would be now to save the supplicant.

It is perhaps not so surprising to find in a poem that the whole argument is tilted along the bias of the poem's medium, language. It is through language that God must be approached, must be reminded that, since His greatness needs language in order to be made known to men, He cannot dispense with the living user of language for the consummation of that end. God responds appropriately, by transforming a particular kind of poem, a "dirge," that presumably would have been recited by others over the departed speaker, into a dance. In the rhythmic movement of the joyous dance, the speaker, one infers, can himself continue to utter song, as the last line of the poem makes clear by bracketing in parallelism the thematic key-words "sing" and "praise," to which is added the climactic emphasis of *l'o yidom*, "will not be still"—the essential condition of active articulation that distinguishes all of us above the Pit from those who have gone down into it.

The foregrounding of language in this and a good many other psalms is, I think, a special case that illustrates a general rule. The ancient Hebrew poets are surely not to be thought of as precursors to Mallarmé, and there is no apotheosis of the artifice of language in their work. God exists before and beyond language, and is by no means the product or the captive of the poets' medium. But God manifests Himself to man in part through language, and necessarily His deeds are made known by any one man to others, and perhaps also by any one man to himself, chiefly through the mediation of language. Psalms, more than any other group of biblical poems, brings to the fore this consciousness of the linguistic medium of religious experience. These ancient makers of devotional and celebratory poems were keenly aware that poetry is the most complex ordering of language, and perhaps also the most demanding. Within the formal limits of a poem the poet can take advantage of the emphatic repetitions dictated by the particular prosodic system, the symmetries and antitheses and internal echoes intensified by a closed verbal structure, the fine intertwinings of sound and image and reported act, the modulated shifts in grammatical voice and object of address, to give coherence and authority to his perceptions of the world. The psalmist's delight in the suppleness and serendipities of poetic form is not a distraction from the spiritual seriousness of the poems but his chief means of realizing his spiritual vision, and it is one source of the power these poems continue to have not only to excite our imaginations but also to engage our lives.

VI

Prophecy and Poetry

WHY DID the Hebrew prophets cast their urgent messages in verse? In point of fact, sometimes they did not, and we may get a preliminary bearing on this question by first reminding ourselves of the many passages, long and short, in Jeremiah, Ezekiel, and the late Minor Prophets that were written in prose. Some of these prose prophecies make use of loosely parallel semantic-syntactic structures that distantly recall the background of poetry, but without the compactness, the strong rhythmic character, and the regularity of semantic matching and development that are observable in biblical verse. One cannot plausibly attribute this uneven drift toward prose to changing literary preferences in the decades around and following the destruction of the First Commonwealth in 586 B.C.E., since, after all, one of the most brilliant of prophetic poets was the anonymous figure of the Babylonian exile that scholarship calls Deutero-Isaiah, and the sublime poetry of Job was probably a still later product of this same general period after the destruction. I don't think we can confidently explain in all instances why a prophet made the crossover into prose, and in a good many cases the move may have been dictated chiefly by individual sensibility and gifts of expression. If there are more general reasons, they must be sought not primarily in chronology but in considerations of genre and discursive situation; these, in turn, may begin to suggest why the more prevalent medium of poetry was so well suited to the characteristic prophetic purposes.

One common type of prophecy for which prose seems to have been preferred is the oracular vision, like those that take up a good part of Zechariah, or like the vision of the seething caldron at the beginning of Jeremiah (1:13–19). In such visions, the prophet is shown, whether by

God or by an angel, an enigmatic picture, and the burden of the prophecy is an explanation of the envisioned enigma: " 'What do you see?' And I said, 'A seething caldron turned away from the north.' And the Lord said to me, 'From the north the evil will open up against all the inhabitants of the land' " (Jer. 1:13–14). As this particular prophecy proceeds, it exhibits enough loosely symmetrical utterances to have encouraged some modern scholars to attempt to scan it as verse, but it lacks the rhythmic regularity of matching statements that we will encounter in prophetic poetry proper. Perhaps prose was felt to be more appropriate here because of the expository nature of the prophecy. The oracular picture itself does the main work of forcefully arresting our attention, and then the argument is carried out by an unpacking of the meaning of the picture. Equally important, the discursive exchange is entirely between God and the prophet: no one else is addressed. One assumes that Jeremiah conveyed this prophecy to his Judean contemporaries, but only by allowing them to "overhear" what was initially a transaction between him and the Lord, not by turning to them in direct formal address. The latter discursive stance, let me suggest, would have been more suitably realized through poetry, for reasons that I hope will become clearer as we proceed.

Beyond the special case of oracular visions, prose would appear to have been the preferred vehicle in most situations where the vector of speech was God to prophet rather than God through prophet to the people. Often, this means a high quotient of narrative or instructional content in the Lord's message to the prophet. Let us look quickly at one extended example before we turn to the dominant counterinstance of poetry:

The word of the Lord came to Jeremiah after the king burned the scroll with the words Baruch had written at Jeremiah's dictation: "Take for yourself another scroll, and write on it the same words that were on the first scroll which was burned by Jehoiakim king of Judea. And concerning Jehoiakim king of Judea, you shall say—'Thus said the Lord. You burned this scroll, saying, Why did you write in it saying, The king of Babylon will surely come and destroy this land and blot out from it man and beast? Therefore, thus said the Lord concerning Jehoiakim king of Judea. No one of his line will sit on the throne of David, and his carcass will be exposed to heat by day and cold by night. And I will punish him and his seed and his servants for their iniquity, and also the inhabitants of Jerusalem and the men of Judea—all the evil of which I spoke to them but they would not listen.' " (Jer. 36:27–31)

God's words to Jeremiah here are continuous with the immediately preceding narrative that reported how the king had the scroll containing the offensive words burned, section by section. That consideration of a narrative burden in itself makes the prose form of the message appropriate. But it is also important to note that the message Jeremiah receives is peculiarly a transaction between him and the Lord, despite the inclusion of a prophecy of doom for the house of Jehoiakim and the kingdom of Judea. To begin with, Jeremiah is given practical instructions: seeing that the king has burned your scroll, you must get to work and produce another one identical to the first. He is then enjoined to deliver still another prophecy of impending disaster to and about Jehoiakim and his followers, but the vocative aspect of the prophecy is stressed less than the notion that it is soon to be fulfilled and that the prophet must and will persist in announcing it. From a certain point of view, Jeremiah's new marching orders here are a kind of personal vindication, as though God were saying: the king has tried to destroy your words, but I will send you back to him and very soon prove their terrible truth. The triangular complications of the relation between prophet and God and king are aptly conveyed through a quadruple embedding of direct discourse that would be extremely difficult to work out in biblical verse. That is, God's words to Jeremiah are quoted (everything after the first colon in the passage), and within that frame there is a prospective quotation of the words Jeremiah is to pronounce to Jehoiakim ("Thus said the Lord . . ."), and within that inner frame we have a quotation of Jehoiakim's angry words to Jeremiah at the time of the book burning, and, finally, those words of the king include a quotation from the words Jeremiah wrote in the scroll ("the king of Babylonia will surely come . . ."). This odd Chinese-box construction nicely conveys the sense of a message about the sending and receipt of messages, about how people try to ignore, appropriate, or destroy the discourse of others, and about the inexorable persistence of prophetic discourse because of its divine source. This, too, would suggest that a large part of the business under way here is between God and prophet, with the embedded prophecy of doom against Jehoiakim and his subjects devised for oblique transmission. Jeremiah is, of course, instructed to confront Jehoiakim, but in its form the prophecy is a prospective summarizing report of such a confrontation, not an enactment or full-fledged transcription of it, and for this, prose is the proper vehicle.

What essentially distinguishes prophetic verse from other kinds of biblical poetry is its powerfully vocative character. There are, to be sure, prominent elements of direct address in other poetic genres, but these differ fundamentally not only in tone and purpose but also in discursive situation. Thus, the enraptured lovers' dialogues in the Song of Songs are addresses from one lyric fictional personage to another; and the moral exhortations in Proverbs directed from the mentor to the inexperienced young man are similarly a communication from one fictional construct to another. Psalms, or at any rate a large part of it, constitutes an instructive complementary antithesis to prophetic poetry. The psalm is typically cast in the form of direct address, but because the vocative is invariably from man to God, the one addressed is really not an object of rhetorical manipulation. The speaker may try to remind God of His promises to Israel, of human transience, of the speaker's desperate plight, and by so doing to plead for divine mercy, but the more prominent processes of change effected by speech are in the speaker himself, who through the act of poetry probes his own nature or comes to see more clearly the world around him or the pattern of history or the moral character of man.

Prophetic poetry, in contrast to all these cases, is devised as a form of direct address to a historically real audience. Amos the Tekoite speaks to a real assemblage of Israelites in Beth El during the reign of Jeroboam, son of Joash, beginning two years before the great earthquake. His poetry is addressed not to a hypothetical Israelite in need of reproof but to his actual northern contemporaries, who might well rise up against him as he speaks or, as Chapter 7 intimates, send him packing to the Judean farm from which he came.

Is the verse form, then, of prophetic speech no more than a means of making a public address more emphatic and—both literally and figuratively—more memorable? Parallelistic verse obviously did perform that function for the prophets, but its uses were rather more complicated than this notion of a simple rhetorical aid would suggest. What needs to be stressed at the outset about the special situation of prophetic discourse is that in the vast majority of instances it is not, in formal terms, the prophet who is speaking but God Who is speaking through the prophet's quotation. Indeed, one plausible etymology that has been proposed for the term *navi*, "prophet," is "spokesman." There is no necessity to plunge into the shadowy realm of conjecture about the nature of prophecy as a psychological phenomenon—that is, about whether the prophets of ancient Israel actually thought they heard God speaking to them in lines of poetry that they then reported or whether they framed the lines of poetry as a "translation" of the message they felt they had received from the Lord. Scholarly efforts, moreover, to discriminate analytically between a kernel that is the Lord's direct message and an elaboration of the message by the prophet strike me as still another exercise in futility. The important point for our purposes is that, with very few exceptions, prophetic poetry is formally presented, usually with an introductory formula like "thus said the Lord," as divine discourse. This means that, formally, prophetic poetry is represented speech rather than historical speech.

At this point, we have to make allowance for a paradoxical feature of our subject. I have said that the prophets addressed themselves to real historical audiences. In regard to audience, and in regard to the concrete effect they sought to work on the audience, they were using natural language to a purpose not fundamentally different from that, say, of a present-day political leader who addresses his constituents in the hope of persuading them to support a particular policy they might otherwise be inclined to oppose. But one way of understanding why prophetic poetry invites a wealth of interpretation that would not seem appropriate for political speeches or mere oral exhortation is to note that the speaker's use of language is, as Barbara Herrnstein Smith has described poetic language in general, "fictive" rather than natural.[1] God's speech, that is, in the mouth of the prophets bears an important formal resemblance to the divine discourse at the end of the poetic argument in Job. In both, for all the spiritual urgency of the message, an implied element of "as if" is involved: If we could actually hear God talking, making His will manifest in words of the Hebrew language, what would He sound like? Since poetry is our best human model of intricately rich communication, not only solemn, weighty, and forceful but also densely woven with complex internal connections, meanings, and implications, it makes sense that divine speech should be represented as poetry. Such speech is directed to the concrete situation of a historical audience, but the form of the speech exhibits the historical indeterminacy of the language of poetry, which helps explain why these discourses have touched the lives of millions of readers far removed in time, space, and political predicament from the small groups of ancient Hebrews against whom Hosea, Isaiah, Jeremiah, and their confreres originally inveighed.

What are the principal modes of prophetic poetry? The overarching purpose is reproof (and not, I would contend, prediction), and this general aim is realized through three related poetic strategies: (1) direct accusation; (2) satire; (3) the monitory evocation of impending disaster. It is in the first of these three categories that the sheer vocative force of prophetic poetry plays the largest role. Such poetry is a kind of terrific verbal buttonholing of the listener, directly calling him the names he has earned through his actions, reminding him of all that he has perpetrated. A good deal more, however, is involved than mere invective, as we shall see in a moment from an example. Accusation obviously shades into satire, but in the latter mode there is more latitude for sarcasm and irony, for the depiction of practices, attitudes, institutions, paraphernalia, to which the target of the satire is attached and from which the satirist expects to see him forcibly severed. The punitive consequences of moral depravity or cultic disloyalty are a second stage or even a kind of grim coda in the poetry of accusation and satire, while they become the main subject in the monitory evocation of disaster. In this third category of prophetic castigation, the special momentum of narrativity of biblical verse is used, as we saw in the awesome description of the Day of the Lord in Joel 2,[2] to convey a sense of inexorable process. Beyond these dominant aims of reproof, the prophets use poetry on occasion to wrestle with the painful weight of their own vocation (Jeremiah 20:7–13, the poem in which the prophet speaks of the word of the Lord as "fire shut up in my bones," is an impressive instance) and, more centrally, to conjure up the vision of a radiant restoration that will follow the cataclysm.[3] Finally, the prophets occasionally adapt to their purposes a nonprophetic poetic genre, such as elegy, parable, supplication, thanksgiving psalm.

In the poetry of reproof, direct accusation is obviously the primary mode, satire and monitory evocation being alternative or supplementary strategies of attack that are derived from the basic situation of the prophet's unflinching confrontation with his audience. The poem with which the first chapter of Isaiah begins (Is. 1:2–9) can tell us a good deal about the complexity of the mode of accusation.

1   Listen, heavens,   give ear, earth—
              for the Lord has spoken.
2   Sons have I raised and reared up,   and they rebelled against Me.
3   The ox knows his owner,   the ass his master's crib.
4   Israel does not know,   My people does not grasp.
5   Ah, sinful folk,   people laden with crime,
6   Seed of evildoers,   sons depraved!
7   They've forsaken the Lord,   despised the Holy One of Israel,
              they have dropped away.
8   Why need you be beaten more,   continue to offend?
9   Every head is ailing,   every heart is sick.
10 From head to foot   there is no sound spot.

11 Wound and welt and running sore—   neither pressed nor bound
                  nor soothed with oil.
12 Your land's a desolation,   your cities burned with fire.
13 Your soil before your eyes   strangers devour,
        a desolation as by strangers overthrown.
14 And the daughter of Zion is left like   like a hut in a cucumber field,
    a shelter in a vineyard,
                 like a city besieged.
15 Had not the Lord of Hosts   left us a bare remnant.
16 We should be like Sodom,   resemble Gomorrah.

The poem begins with a familiar opening formula in biblical poetry, the invocation of heaven and earth as witnesses to the speaker's words, using the formulaic pairing of "listen" (*shamo'a*) and "give ear" (*ha'azen*). Indeed, this convention of beginning poems with heaven and earth is so strong that it occurs even when they are not addressed as witnesses (see, for example, the beginning of Psalm 8), and if only one of the two terms occurs at the beginning of the poem, the complementary second term often crops up within a few lines, as though there were a hiatus waiting to be filled (see, for example, Psalm 104, which starts with "heaven," verse 2, and duly moves on to "earth" in verse 5). Here as elsewhere, it should be stressed that what is formulaic need not be mechanical. This is a particularly abrupt version of the listen/give-ear beginning, which I would scan as a triadic line with the minimal allotment of two beats per verset. Even with a different scansion, the introductory formula in Hebrew still takes only six bisyllabic words and a particle before plunging into the prophecy proper, very much in keeping with the speaker's sense of urgency. The "earth" (*'eretz*) of the opening is picked up by "land" (also *'eretz* in Hebrew) at the beginning of line 12, which then engenders soil, field, and the whole picture of agricultural life invoked both literally and in the metaphors of the concluding lines of the poem. The speaker addresses heaven, whence God's message issues, and the eternal, encompassing earth, but the latter leads by pun, metonymy, and through a series of concentric circles—another instance of the focusing logic of biblical poetry—to the land that is devastated because of the iniquity of its inhabitants.

The approach to the audience in the poem is defined by a careful progression of modes of address. The initial vocative is directed to heaven and earth, presumably by the prophet. Then, when the quotation of divine speech begins, in line 2, God first speaks of Israel in the third person (through to the end of line 7), addressing Himself to heaven and earth, or perhaps by implication to any sensible human audience that will recognize the outrageous character of the behavior described. The triadic line 7 marks the end of a segment; the third verset, "they have dropped away," is not an anticlimactic scribal interpolation, as some commentators have proposed, but rather a recapitulation that ties up the segment. A new segment clearly begins with the switch to second person plural at the beginning of line 8 (in the Hebrew the verbal and pronominal forms for plural and singular in all persons are distinct), and the rest of the poem until the last two lines is a direct address to the Judean audience. The rhetorical strategy is in one respect like that of Nathan's use of the parable of the poor man's ewe (2 Samuel 12) in order to make David face his own guilt. First we are given the parabolic illustration of the ox and ass, then a denunciation of Israel that, because it is in the third person, might be construed by a complacent listener as referring to "the others," then a direct accusation, the equivalent of Nathan's climactic accusation of David, "You are the man!" Prophetic poetry is thus very often constructed as a *rhetoric of entrapment*, whether in the sequence of a few lines or on the larger scale of a whole prophecy.

Figurative language plays an important role in this rhetoric. Although it is of course difficult to generalize from one poem to the whole corpus of prophetic poetry, the patterns observable here are fairly typical. One figure, or a cluster of closely related figures, tends to govern a sequence of several lines. *Leitwörter*, key-words, are insisted on as a way of driving home the thematic emphasis of the poem. (Elsewhere in prophetic poetry, there is also a good deal of anaphora and sometimes even refrain-like devices.) A concentration of nearly synonymous words is deployed over a whole passage, with a particularly rich lexicon of designations for sin and its metaphorical equivalents (sickness, defilement) and for destruction (burning, overthrowing, and, elsewhere, smashing, shattering, rending, and so forth). It may be useful to observe how this procedure of thematic intensification works in our initial poem from Isaiah.

God's first word is "sons," a pointed metaphorical translation of "My people" (line 4). (The same reiterated sons-people pair is used to define the thematic movement of Moses' valedictory song, Deuteronomy 32.) Very frequently elsewhere, "Israel" occurs formulaically in parallelism after "Jacob"; here the poet chooses to begin line 4 with "Israel" and then pair it with the more thematically pointed "My people"—that is, a dumb animal knows where its benefits come from, to whom it belongs, but not these sons, My people. In the Hebrew, this point is sharpened through wordplay: *hitbonan*, the verb that means to "perceive" or "grasp," flaunts a false but poetically apt etymology of *banim*, "sons," so that line 4b contains a shadow meaning of "My people did not act as sons." The "sons" of line 2 are then pilloried as the evil seed, the depraved sons of line 6, and the filial metaphor continues implicitly into lines 8–11, where the imagery of beating suggests a child who has not been spared the rod but who nevertheless perversely persists in being spoiled. Lines 12–16 pick up the theme of sons by way of antithesis— instead of to the loving care of a father, the people are abandoned to the ruthlessness of strangers.

Presumably, what Isaiah is referring to in the second half of the poem is Assyrian incursions that should have been construed as harbingers of still greater retribution to come and thus led Israel to change its ways but that instead have been ignored. The Hebrew verbs seem to indicate a destruction that has already occurred, which might make it, as has often been suggested, a reference to Sennacherib's campaign against Judea in 701 B.C.E., in which he destroyed the major fortress-city of Lachish, devastated the countryside, but was unable to take Jerusalem. The figurative elaboration of this historical situation makes it powerfully vivid to the imagination and also defines it as an egregious instance of the folly of all such persistence in self-destructive behavior. Lines 8–11 do this entirely through metaphor in the image—whose historical referent may not yet be entirely clear to those addressed—of the beaten and bloody sons who invite more beatings. Lines 12–16 relate to the metaphor of the preceding four lines as tenor to vehicle. Now the concrete referent of the beatings becomes perfectly clear: "Your land's a desolation, / your cities burned with fire . . ." Lines 14–15 then elaborate this literal picture of devastation with metaphors connected metonymically to the actual landscape. First, in a spatially focusing parallelism, we were carried from land to cities to soil; now personified Zion resembles a solitary "hut in a cucumber field," "a shelter in a vineyard." The third member of this triadic line, "like a city besieged," follows a common tendency of triadic lines to swerve from strict parallelism in the third verset. In so doing, it brilliantly creates a small envelope structure by bringing the vehicle of the metaphor in contact with the tenor. That is, the sequence of lines begins with "cities burned with fire" and it now closes with "like a city besieged," a statement that is both simile and literal utterance. Lines 15– 16 constitute a kind of concluding couplet, marked by still another shift in grammatical person, into the first person plural. Now the speaker— either the prophet, identifying himself with the people, or simply one of the people—says that were it not for God's forbearance, we would have already utterly perished. The Sodom and Gomorrah pairing of the last line is of course a proverbial biblical image of total devastation, and it was already present by intimation at the end of line 13 in "strangers overthrown" because "overthrow" (*mahapekhah*) is frequently linked as a formula with Sodom. Sodom and Gomorrah are also in two senses the antitype of Israel/My people at the beginning of the poem—because they were consigned to total destruction and because they were societies irredeemably pervaded by moral corruption. Isaiah will pick up this second meaning of Sodom and Gomorrah as he begins the immediately subsequent poem[4] with a formula of address that harks back to line 1 of the poem we have been considering: "Listen to the word of the Lord, / captains of Sodom, // Give ear to the teaching of our Lord, / people of Gomorrah" (1:10).

What I would like to suggest about the effect of the language of poetry in this and most other biblical prophecies is that it tends to lift the utterances to a second power of signification, aligning statements that are addressed to a concrete historical situation with an archetypal horizon. The Judean contemporaries of Isaiah the son of Amoz become the archetypes Sodom and Gomorrah in respect to both their collective destiny and their moral character. If one considers, as the metaphors of the poem require one to consider, how God has treated them as beloved sons, then their exploitation of the poor and the helpless in their midst (1:23 and elsewhere), in flagrant violation of God's commands, becomes a paradigmatic instance of treachery, of man's daunting capacity for self-destructive perverseness. In this fashion, a set of messages framed for a particular audience of the eighth century B.C.E. is not just the transcription of a historical document but continues to speak age after age, inviting members of otherwise very different societies to read themselves into the text.

Now, the archetypifying force of vocative poetry in the Prophets can move in two directions beyond the primary mode of accusation, where its general effect is to fix the particular vices within an authoritative, timeless scheme of moral judgment. If the speaker sarcastically invokes the viewpoint of his human objects of reproof, conjuring up the illusory pleasures or power to which they are addicted, he produces a satirical depiction of how the evil are self-deceived. Tonally, the satires tend to jeer where the accusations angrily expose and impugn; substantively, they tend to be evocations of the moral psychology of overweening wickedness. If, on the other hand, the speaker focuses on the cataclysmic consequences of the misdeeds he is stigmatizing, then he produces a vision of the terrible swift force of God in history, wreaking havoc among the nations. The outer limit of archetype is myth, and, for all that has been written about the demythologizing impulse of the Hebrew Bible, prophetic poetry exhibits a certain predilection to mythologize its historical subjects, setting the here and now in cosmic perspectives. This happens most often in the monitory poetry of impending disaster, where warnings about concrete threats to the land and its people easily shade into the vaster terrors of apocalyptic vision. But it can even happen occasionally in satire, as the provoking pretensions of the satiric target invite a mythological scale of mimicry in the satiric poem. The strongest example of such prophetic satire is the sarcastic-triumphal "elegy" over the "king of Babylon" in Isaiah 14:4–21. Its prose introduction (the first half of 14:4) announces the poem as a *mashal*, a literary term of shifting meanings that in the Prophets usually refers to songs of mockery. The poet will then immediately play with the term by referring to the king metonymically as "the rod of rulers" (*moshlim*) and then later invoke still another sense of the root *m-sh-l* when the denizens of the underworld ask the king how he has "become just like" (*nimshalta*) them. The force of this justly famous poem is clear enough without the necessity for much close reading, but it is worth looking at briefly to see how the language of poetry in prophetic satire, as in the other modes of prophetic verses, works in splendid excess of the historical occasion.

1	How is the taskmaster ended,	at end is oppression!
2	The Lord has broken the staff of the wicked,	the rod of rulers.
3	Who struck against peoples in fury,	a blow unrelenting,
4	Who reigned in wrath over nations,	ran them down without stint.
5	All the earth is calm and quiet,	bursts forth into song.
6	The very evergreens are joyed over you,	the cedars of Lebanon:
7	"With you now laid low,	the woodsman won't come up against us."
8	Sheol below stirs for you	to greet your coming
9	It rouses the shades,	all the chiefs of the earth.
10	It raises from their thrones	all the kings of the nations.
11	They all call out	and say to you:
12	"You, too, are stricken like us,	you've become just like us.
13	Your pomp is brought down to Sheol,	the murmur of your lutes,
14	Your bed is spread with worms,	your blankets are maggots.
15	How are you fallen from heaven,	Bright One, Son of Dawn!
16	You are cut down to earth,	master of nations!"

17	And you once thought in your heart:	
	"To heaven will I ascend,	above God's stars I'll raise my throne.
18	I'll sit on the mount of divine council,	in the far reaches of Zaphon.
19	I will ascend to the tops of the clouds,	I will match the Most High."
20	But to Sheol you came down,	to limbo's far reaches.
21	Those who see you, stare,	they look you over:
22	"Is this the man who stirred all the earth,	who made kingdoms tremble?
23	Who turned the world to wasteland,	its towns destroyed,
	and let not its prisoners go home?	
24	All the kings of nations, all,	honorably lie in their tombs
25	And you are flung from your grave	like a loathsome branch,
26	Clothed with the slain,	the sword-slashed,
27	Who go down to the stones of the Pit,	like a trampled corpse.
28	You will not join them in burial,	for your land you ruined, your people you slayed.
29	Let there be no lasting name	for the seed of evildoers!
30	Fix slaughter blocks for his sons	for the sin of their father.
31	Let them not rise to inherit the earth—	and the world will be filled with towns."

The poem begins with the elegy formula ("How is . . .") and the elegy rhythm (three accents in the first verset and two in the second). It is, of course, a mock elegy, and by the end of line 5 it explicitly announces itself as an exultant song (instead of *qinah*, "elegy," *rinah*, "song" or "shout of joy"). By beginning with the designation "taskmaster," the poet assimilates the scepter of imperial authority (line 2) to the slave driver's club or whip (compare Exodus 5 and Job 3) and thus represents the dead king (lines 3–4) less as a ruler than as a batterer of nations. (In the Hebrew, this point is reinforced by sound-play in line 4: "reigned in wrath" is *rodeh be'af* and "run them down" or, literally, the past participle "pursued" is *murdaf*.) There is considerable debate among scholars about which king is actually referred to in the poem, whether it is a Babylonian monarch, as the prose introduction indicates, or an Assyrian, like Sargon, who was not buried in a tomb, or Sennacherib, who was assassinated. Whatever the truth of the matter, or whether or not the prophet had a particular king and an already accomplished historical fact in mind, Christian tradition responded more appropriately to the real point of the poem by rendering "Bright One, Son of Dawn" as Lucifer (that is, light-bearer) and seeing here an account of satanic rebellion against God. That reading, of course, is not entirely accurate, because the poet is concerned with history and politics, not with demonology, but it has the virtue of giving due emphasis to the mythological reverberations of the poem.

The theater for the tyrant's activity and the witness of his downfall is "all the earth" (line 5). The term *'eretz* in its three senses of "earth," "land," and "underworld" is a connecting thread for the whole poem and one way in which the cosmic scope of the satire is intimated. In Sheol "all the chiefs of the earth" (line 9) are roused to greet the dead king who has been "cut down to earth [or, to the underworld]" (line 16). The mocking beholders of the dead king ask whether this can be "the man who stirred all the earth," and we remember that the underworld itself had "stirred" to greet him (line 8). He is denied the dignity of burial (line 28) for having devastated his own land (*'artzekha*), and the poem concludes (line 31) by praying that the line of the evil king be destroyed so that it will "not rise to inherit the earth."

This sort of unifying function of a word-motif is of course extremely common in both biblical poetry and biblical narrative. What needs to be observed here is how it contributes to enlarging the significance of the subject. The poem is a wonderful interaction of vertical movements, first down, then up, then down again. The loftiest members of the natural world, the evergreens and the cedars of Lebanon, rejoice that the woodsman will no longer "come up" against them (lines 6–7), seeing that the tyrant is gone whose armies once cut down whole forests for their siege works and for the imperial buildings of their master. (The line works equally well figuratively, with the lofty trees as epithets for the monarchs of earth and the axman an appropriate emblem for the tyrant himself.) Instead, he himself has been "cut down to earth" (line 16), or, indeed, thrust deeper still into the underworld. The missing pair-term for "earth"—"heaven"—makes its first appearance in line 15: "How are you fallen from heaven, / Bright One, Son of Dawn," which also invokes again the elegy formula that began the poem. Then, the tyrant's arrogant presumption that he could ascend to heaven, sit in the council of the gods, and rival the Most High, is represented in three lines of his direct speech (17–19), which are followed by another violent plunge downward: not only is he hurled into the Pit, but, unburied, his dishonored spirit will linger in limbo (*yarketei bor*). If death is conventionally indicated as sleep or lying down, the tyrant is doomed to have his rest in hell disturbed by the raucous mockery of his enemies, instead of the gentle sound of the lute to which he was accustomed; and instead of the wonted luxury of soft sheets and scarlet coverlets *(tole'ah)* he lies among worms and maggots (also *tole'ah*). Still worse, with his untombed body cast aside like mere offal, his spirit will have no rest at all.

These mordant lines bring us as close as we ever come in the Hebrew Bible to a "Homeric" representation of a colloquy of spirits in the underworld, which is elsewhere in Scriptures imagined as little more than a shadowy hole in the ground into which the dead descend. The point is not what may have been believed in ancient Israel about the underworld but what the poet needed to invent for the requirements of the theme. His motives are similar in regard to the treatment of the celestial upperworld. He would appear to have invoked some archaic myth, for symbolic rather than theological purposes, about a figure who sought to storm the heights of heaven—the epithet "Bright One, Son of Dawn" appears in the Ugaritic documents, but not much is known about the mythological context.

At this point, it becomes irrelevant whether the king who is the object of the poet's satire is Sargon or Sennacherib or somebody else. What is clear is that the language of the poem makes him the very archetype of self-deifying (and hence self-deluding) earthly power. His reign is an unending orgy of violence and murder; even his own people join the roll of his victims. Relentlessly wielding his scepter/bludgeon, he imagines that no limits whatever can be put on his power, that he overmasters the earth as a veritable god. At his ignominious death, the world again rejoices, can envision a future in which, instead of being the wasteland he made it, it will once more be filled with inhabited towns.

From the global perspective through which the poem views the tyrant, his career becomes an exemplary instance of how man overreaches himself in his unslaked thirst for power and by so doing turns civilization into desolation. As a powerful exemplum, the poem possesses a quality of timelessness: though particularly inspired, we may assume, by the historically specific barbarity of Assyrian imperialism in the eighth or early seventh century B.C.E., it gives body and weight to a grim image of political perversion that we have known all too well in the century of Hitler and Stalin. Indeed, when the great Russian poet Osip Mandelstam wrote his famous "Stalin Epigram," in 1933, evoking the mass murderer with "ten thick worms his fingers," who "toys with the tributes of half-men," "rolls the executions on his tongue like berries," he was working in the same genre of deadly serious poetic satire as Isaiah, with the same timeless definition of moral possibility in his rendering of the immediate object of satire—though, alas, without the prophet's ability to envision a happy resolution.

Poetry, as I have been arguing throughout this study, is not just a set of techniques for saying impressively what could be said otherwise. Rather, it is a particular way of imagining the world—particular in the double sense that poetry as such has its own logic, its own ways of making connections and engendering implications, and because each system of poetry has certain distinctive semantic thrusts that follow the momentum of its formal dispositions and habits of expression. In prophetic verse, I think this momentum of the poetic medium is most strikingly evident in the poetry of monitory prediction. The repeated move here from the immediate context to a horizon of ultimate possibility is emphatic and quite awesome. The prophet's discourse begins from the clear-eyed perception of a concrete historical menace—the armies of Assyria or Babylonia, or even a natural disaster like locusts. The prophet, for his own monitory purposes, wants to evoke these actual threats as powerfully as he can. But because this evocation is worked out through the medium of biblical verse, there is a way in which the medium begins to take over, or, at any rate, there is a merging of the logic of the medium with the prophet/poet's own spiritual and political insight.

Specifically, the two impelling forces of narrativity and intensification that govern so much of the movement within lines and within poems in the Bible encourage rather extraordinary developments in this grimly predictive verse. Processes unleashed in history begin to skid forward precipitously toward the brink of the abyss or, alternately, march on implacably, as the narrative development of poetic parallelism is given full play. And on the axis of intensification, the images move from mishap to disaster to comprehensive cataclysm, and the language draws increasingly on the Bible's abundant vocabulary of cosmic catastrophe, shifting from the here and now to the end of things that recalls the beginning. Three short, related examples—each would appear to be a discrete segment within a longer poem—should suffice to illustrate this poetic transformation of history into the stuff of apocalypse.

Here is Isaiah again, conjuring up in his poetry the military threat from Assyria (Is. 5:26–30):

1 He will lift up a banner to the   whistle one in from the ends of
   nations far-off,   the earth,
            and, look, speedily, fleet, he will come.

<table>
<tr><td>2</td><td>None among him is weary or stumbling,</td><td>he does not sleep or slumber.</td></tr>
<tr><td>3</td><td>The belt on his loins will not come loose,</td><td>nor the thong of his sandals break.</td></tr>
<tr><td>4</td><td>His arrows are sharpened,</td><td>his bows are all drawn.</td></tr>
<tr><td>5</td><td>His horses' hooves seem like flint,</td><td>his wheels like the whirlwind,</td></tr>
<tr><td>6</td><td>His roar is like a lion's,</td><td>he roars like the king of beasts.</td></tr>
<tr><td>7</td><td>He growls and seizes his prey,</td><td>carries off, and none can rescue.</td></tr>
<tr><td>8</td><td>He will growl over him on that day</td><td>like the growling of the sea.</td></tr>
<tr><td>9</td><td>One will gaze on the earth,</td><td>and, look, constricting darkness*</td></tr>
<tr><td></td><td colspan="2" align="center">light growing dark in its clouds.*</td></tr>
</table>

This starts as an evocation of an implacable invading army advancing rapidly, but what I have referred to as the logic of the poetic system begins to turn it into a statement about something vaster than that. The whole picture begins with a concrete image of God giving the signal for the attack—in the narrative development of the triadic initial line, first the raising of the ensign, then the whistle, then the surging forward of the armies—and that representation of God mustering armies in itself gives an apocalyptic tilt to what follows. Rhetorically, the invading forces are represented through hyperbole, which jibes nicely with the semantic intensification in some of the lines: not only is the enemy unwearying and surefooted but he never sleeps at all (line 2); not only are his horses' hooves hard as flint but his chariot wheels churn like the whirlwind (line 5). All this transforms the Assyrian hosts into a virtually supernatural agency. The implied clatter of the chariot wheels leads associatively to the roaring of the next three lines, presumably an allusion to battle cries. Though it is conventional in biblical poetry to compare a victorious army to a ravening lion, the simile here has the effect of strengthening the sense of pitiless inhumanity in the invaders, an idea sharpened in the surprising move of intensification between lines 7 and 8 from the growling of a beast to the growling of the sea.

The imagery, in other words, has shifted the action to a cosmic scale, and thus the poem concludes with a vision of light dying in the sky and darkness seizing the earth, imparting a sense of global catastrophe that seems more than just the atmospheric setting for the Assyrian invasion. As my bristling asterisks indicate, the last line—and, in fact, the pronominal references of the preceding line, too—is obscure in the original: the syntax seems jumbled and the meaning of the word rendered as "clouds" is far from certain. Perhaps the apparent confusion has something to do with the apocalyptic pitch the poem reaches at its ultimate moment.

David Noel Freedman has recently proposed in connection with an obscure passage in Micah that the incoherence of the text might be either a transcription or a literary simulation of ecstatic utterance.[5] Although one must of course be cautious in proposing mimetic fidelity where there may be problems of scribal infidelity, I am tempted to invoke Freedman's notion here. At any rate, the poem concludes on a note of encompassing terror that might well be accompanied by frenzy on the speaker's part, whether or not that compelled him to violate ordinary linguistic decorum.

My next example (Is. 24:17–20) is virtually self-explanatory. If in the text we have just considered there is a kind of semantic skid from the historical to the cosmic that becomes entirely evident at the very end, the following lines execute the move in a bold leap at the beginning:

1	Terror and trench[6] and trap	upon you who dwell on earth!
2	Who flees the sound of terror	will fall into the trench.
3	Who climbs up from the trench	will be caught in the trap.
4	For the sluice-gates on high will be opened	and the earth's foundations will quake.
5	Break, the earth will break,	crumble, earth will crumble
	totter, the earth will totter.	
6	Sway, the earth will sway like a drunkard,	will shake like a hut.
7	Its crime will weigh it down,	it will fall, and rise no more.

The emblematic image of the man fleeing from the sound or, perhaps, report, of terror only to fall into some sort of trap, and escaping the trap only to be caught in a snare, is anchored in a historical reference to invading armies that would terrorize the local population and cast a tight net around those attempting to flee. Looking forward to lines 4–7, I have translated *'eretz* in line 1 as "earth," but its immediate meaning could simply be "the land." Having raced through an intensifying sequence from fear to pit to snare, the poet shifts sharply into a cosmic heightening of his theme of destruction. The transition is effected through a literary allusion in a single word, *'arubot*, "sluice-gates" (more traditionally rendered as "windows"), which recalls the sluice-gates of the heavens that were opened to bring on the Deluge recorded in Genesis. But in contrast to Noah's flood, where the waters from above were simply joined by the waters welling up from the abyss below, here what happens below is that the earth itself breaks apart. In order to convey a sense of stark, relentless global havoc, the poet adopts, somewhat uncharacteristically, what amounts to an archaic stylistic device: "earth" is repeated in anaphoric emphasis five times in close sequence, in each instance accompanied by a verb of shattering or shaking, which itself is twice stated, first in the infinitive, then in its conjugated form. The poem will go from here to speak of a punishment God will inflict on the host of heaven as well as on the kings of earth: both the kings and the heavenly luminaries will be shut up in prison until the day the Lord Himself reigns effulgent on Mount Zion (Is. 24:21–23). It has been suggested that the conquest of celestial bodies is an allusion to the pagan deities, who will be revealed as shams when the Lord makes His dominion manifest. But whatever Isaiah may have had in mind historically, it is clear that the sweep of his poetic language has become properly mythological, catching up in its movement the beginning and end of all things, and so quite naturally also envisaging an eschatological triumph of the one God over all competing powers, whether human and actual or celestial and supposed.

My last example, Jeremiah 4:23–27, is a still further step on the road to real apocalypse, since it starts quite explicitly with a vision of first beginnings transformed into the dreaded end:

1	I see the earth, and, look, chaos and void,	the heavens, their light is gone.
2	I see the mountains, and, look, they quake,	and all the hills shudder.
3	I see, and, look, there is no man left,	all the birds of the heavens have fled.
4	I see, and, look, the farmland is desert,	and all its towns are razed.
5	Because of the Lord,	because of his blazing wrath.
6	For thus said the Lord: The whole land will be desolation,	but an utter end of it I will not make.

Lines 1–3 are an obvious and pointed reversal of Genesis 1. The primordial chaos and void are restored; the cosmogonic "let there be light" is retracted; instead of the firmly demarcated "dry land" of Genesis 1, there are quaking mountains, and man, the culmination of creation, is nowhere to be seen (he is designated here generically ʾadam, as in Genesis): the birds of the heavens, a prominent item in the list of living creatures in Genesis, have also vanished. The personal immediacy with which this vision of the end is conveyed through the repetitions of "I see, and, look . . ." (raʾiti vehineh) has an almost surrealistic power to shock: "I see, and, look, there is no man left, / all the birds of the heavens have fled." It is like an ancient Hebrew equivalent of a science-

154

fiction fantasy: What would the world look like if I, the sole unblinking observer/survivor, could walk about it after creation had been canceled?

The prophet, speaking here in his own voice and not for the moment quoting divine speech, takes advantage of that discursive stand to transmit a special sense of dread. Line 4 constitutes a transition. None of the terms here alludes to Genesis. The word for "farmland," *karmel*, evokes contemporary agrarian reality, not a myth of beginnings, and the razing of cities refers to contemporary historical experience, whether actual or imminent. I have rendered *'eretz* in line 6 as "land" because there seems to be a shift—moving in the opposite direction from our two previous poems—from the cosmic (*'eretz* in line 1, which is clearly "earth") to the national-historical. This shift is borne out in the (unquoted) remainder of the poem, where first an invading army is depicted and then we are given an allegorical image of the Daughter of Zion as a promiscuous woman who now finds that her lovers have savagely turned against her (Jer. 4:28–31). Such a reversal of direction obviously makes some difference in the impact of the poem as compared with the other two we have considered, but it may not be a crucial difference. What is arresting and extreme has a way of remaining dominant whether it is first or last, and in the text from Jeremiah *'eretz* as "land" gets caught up in the orbit of *'eretz* as "earth." The prophet is consciously representing a delimited historical disaster that is to befall Judea—as he makes a point of stressing in the last verset of our passage when he goes back to quoting divine speech: "but an utter end of it I will not make." By contagion, however, the land is not dissociated from all the earth, and the desolation that will overtake it is a terrifying rehearsal of the utter end of the created world. Thus, the very attachment to hyperbole and the intensifying momentum of the poetic medium project the prophet's vision onto a second plane of signification.

These prophecies of destruction, it should be noted, are very similar in language when they are directed not to Israel but to an absent third party—that is, in the oracles concerning the foreign nations. The latter poems are, at least by implication, prophecies of "consolation," since they depict the defeat of Israel's sundry ruthless enemies. (In a few prophetic passages, including, perhaps, the one from Isaiah 24 we examined, there is even some ambiguity about whether the object of doom is Israel or an enemy. This uncertainty stems from our inability in some cases to know confidently where a poetic unit begins and ends.) In any event, the more typical prophecy of consolation is a bright positive image closely matching the dark negative of the prophecies of doom. I offer this photographic metaphor not merely because redemption or restoration is the conceptual opposite of destruction but because as poetic structures the poems of redemption correspond to the grim monitory poems in using analogous rhetorical strategies together with pointedly antithetical imagery to that of the doomsaying poems—or, sometimes, the same imagery exploited for opposite effects. If the logic of hyperbole leads monitory poetry ultimately to imagine the historical world turned back into primal chaos, hyperbole in the poetry of consolation leads to a vision of history and nature transformed into harmonious order, unending fulfillment.

Two lines from Amos (9:13) provide a convenient paradigm for this process:

Look, a time is coming, declares
the Lord—
When the plowman will overtake   the treader of grapes, the sower.
the reaper,
The mountains will drip wine,   and all the hills will melt.

The chiastic shape of the first line (planter—gleaner—gleaner—planter) reinforces the manifest hyperbole by suggesting a perfect flow from beginning to end and from end to beginning of the agricultural cycle. That is, the plowman will overtake the reaper because the latter will have so much grain to harvest, while the treader of grapes will scarcely have time to complete the vintage before he finds by his side the eager sowers of a new crop. This does not quite cancel out the curse in Genesis of earning bread by the sweat of one's brow, but it does intimate a smooth and rapid current of fertile production that recuperates through joyful labor something of the Edenic experience. The monitory poems of the prophets are dominated by images of wasteland, uprooting and burning, darkness, enslavement and humiliation, stripping of garments, divorce and sexual abandoning, earthquake and storm. The poems of consolation are dominated by images of flourishing vineyards and fields, planting and building, shining light, liberation and regal dignity, splendid garb, marital reconciliation and sexual union, firm foundations and calm.

In regard to this last set of antithetical images, earthquake against calm, the second line of our paradigm from Amos is especially interesting. The line itself uses interverset heightening to carry a hyperbole to the second power: not only will the mountains drip wine but the hills will melt—presumably because they will overflow with an abundance of wine, fruit, or other succulent things. What should be noted is that the formulaic pair mountains-hills regularly appears in monitory predictions—see, for example, the second line of the passage we looked at from Jeremiah—as a component of earthquake imagery, and the verb *hitmogeg,* which here requires a sense of dissolving in sweet abundance, elsewhere represents the collapse of the hills in seismic shudders. Momentarily invoking the language of apocalypse, the poet has swung the vision of global destruction around to its exact antithesis. (One can set alongside this line another strategy for transforming the seismic mountain-hills pairing, in Isaiah 54:10: "The mountains may move, / and the hills may shake, // But My loving care will never move from you, / and My covenant of peace will not be shaken. . . .") I should add that the remainder of this brief poem of redemption (Amos 9:14–15) offers a much more naturalistic picture of Israel returned from exile, rebuilding its towns, planting its vineyards, and enjoying the fruits of its labors. It is easy enough to conceive of the first two lines of the poem as merely a hyperbolic "embellishment" of the idea of national restoration, but I think that would be an unwarranted reduction of their scope, especially if we compare these lines with visions of redemption in the prophets who came after Amos. The logic of the language of poetry brings Amos to glimpse for a moment a new order of reality. Strictly speaking, this is not yet eschatology as it would be developed seven or eight centuries after Amos, but the imagination in prophetic poetry of restored national existence without want or pain or danger is an important way station to explicit doctrines of a radically new era that will replace earthly life as we know it.

I have been stressing the role of hyperbole in this whole imaginative process, but metaphor in general is equally important. By insistently representing one thing in terms of another, the poet in these prophecies intimates a fundamental transformation of states of being. Such intimations are especially prominent in Deutero-Isaiah, the great master of the poetry of redemption, who is especially given to elaborating and enriching a single key metaphor throughout a poem, bathing his subject in the meanings suggested by its figurative representation. Here is a three-line example (Is. 44:3–4):

As I pour water on parched ground, rivulets on dry land,
I will pour My spirit on your seed, My blessing on your offspring.
And they will sprout from amidst the grass, like willows by streams of water.

157

The Art of Biblical Poetry

For anyone living in the Near Eastern landscape, with its shocking contrasts between desert and oasis, its absolute dependence on winter rains that can turn the wasteland overnight into flower-carpeted gardens, the poignancy of the imagery is perfectly clear. The middle line works with terms that elsewhere sometimes have concrete meanings—"spirit" can mean "wind," and "blessing" can mean "gift"—but that are here used as abstractions. Yet the simile, by fusing spirit and blessing with water, reconcretizes the terms, conveying a physical sense of how God's providential care will vivify and fructify Israel. Thus, "seed" means progeny and is also a concrete vegetal image that leads into the next line, which compounds flourishing with flourishing ("sprout from amidst the grass, / like willows . . ."). And the perfect, unflagging sustenance of growth by water is reinforced with the locative "by streams of water" at the end, which makes a lovely small envelope structure with the pouring out of water that constitutes the beginning of the segment. The metaphoric imagination in this fashion creates a kind of oasis in words, showing us the life of the nation not as it ever has been in the wilderness of this world but as at last it will be in the garden of a time of redemption.

Let me in conclusion offer one full-scale example of the poetry of consolation. In it, the resources of metaphor are deployed with a special effectiveness to evoke that future reality suffused with sweet joy that is the hallmark of Deutero-Isaiah. The passage, Isaiah 49:14–23, has been construed by some as two poems, because of the occurrence of the so-called messenger formula, "thus said the Lord", in verse 22, but it seems to me one continuous and complete poem, for reasons I shall try to make clear in my comments. In my numeration of the lines, I assume that formulas for introducing quoted speech (lines 1, 7, 11, 13) were seen by the poet as extraneous to the lines of verse.

1	Zion says: "The Lord has abandoned me,	my master has forgotten me."
2	Can a woman forget her babe,	reject the child of her womb?
3	Though she forget,	I will not forget you.
4	Look, on My palms I've inscribed you,	your walls are ever before Me,
5	Your children hurry forth—	your ravagers and ruiners will leave you,
6	Lift up your eyes all round and see:	they are all gathered and coming to you.
7	By My life, declares the Lord: You shall wear them like jewels,	bind them on like a bride.

8	Your ruins and your desolation,	your land laid waste—
9	Now you'll be crowded with settlers,	your destroyers gone far-off.
10	Your children deemed lost will yet say in your ears:	"The place is too crowded.

Move over so that I may settle."

11	And you will say in your heart: "Who bore these for me,	when I was bereaved and barren,

exiled and despised?

12	And these, who raised them?	For I was left all alone.

These, where are they from?"

13	Thus said the Lord God: Look, I will lift up My hand to nations,	to peoples I'll raise My banner.
14	And they will bring your sons in their bosoms,	your daughters will be borne on their shoulders.
15	And kings will be their nursemaids,	great ladies give them suck,
16	Face to the ground, they'll bow to you,	the dust of your feet they'll lick.
17	And you shall know that I am the Lord—	Those who hope in Me will not be shamed.

The metaphorical elaboration of redemption takes place here not on the scale of the local figure, as in our preceding example, but in the encompassing symbolic action that dominates the whole poem, in which the people of Israel is addressed, and speaks, as a woman who has lost both husband and children. The loss of husband I would infer from her first words, "The Lord has abandoned me, / my master ['*adoni*, which also means 'my husband'] has forgotten me." God in his answer (lines 3–4) introduces the idea of children in a simile—even the steadfast love of a woman for her baby cannot be compared to God's love for Zion. The biological link between mother and child is stressed and will be important for the rest of the poem. This is even more emphatic in the Hebrew on line 2, which says, literally: "Can a woman forget her babe, / [can she forget] to have compassion [etymologically, womb-feeling] for the child of her belly?" The rather strange image of God's inscribing, or engraving, the name of his beloved on the palms of His hands is a way of continuing this link between love and parts of the body.

In what follows, there is a suggestive interplay between literal and figurative elements. What is literal is the physical setting of the return: first the walls of Zion that God keeps before His mind's eye, then the fleeing ravagers and the ruined countryside that becomes a place crowded with settlers. On the figurative level, symbolic fair Zion discovers, as in the happy ending of a fairytale, that the children of whom she thought herself bereaved are not really dead. Her surprise is conveyed in the touching simplicity of the dialogue given to her: "Who bore these for me, / when I was bereaved and barren, / . . . and these, who raised them? . . . / These, where are they from?" The poem begins with a productive womb, moves through the idea of a womb empty and unable to bear again to the vision of a landscape peopled with the offspring of that supposedly bereaved womb. The notion that Zion will don her children as a bride puts on her ornaments reinforces this sense of the grief-stricken woman returning to an undreamed-of point of renewal.

The final, hyperbolic stage in the working-out of this central metaphor is the last five lines of the poem. God responds to Zion's words of disbelief and amazement—hence the need for the introductory formula "thus said the Lord"—by turning to the historical arena and showing her how triumphant is the return of her sons and daughters. Here, God gives a signal and raises a banner not as in Isaiah 5 to call in invading armies but to begin a grand processional of return from exile. The hyperbolic development of the metaphor at the end, in an impulse toward heightening that we have come to expect in the structure of biblical poems, is that, after what has been said about biological bonds and violent separation between mother and child, the nations of the earth are pressed into the role of mother surrogates, carrying the children in their bosom or on their back, with kings as nursemaids and queens as wet nurses. Perhaps even the faces and feet of the penultimate line contribute to this sense of the primary importance of body parts. In any event, when Zion is told at the end (the unambiguous Hebrew verb is second person feminine singular), "And you shall know that I am the Lord," one hears the undertone of this verb of intimate knowledge in its sexual sense (compare Hosea 2:22), and the psalmodic formula "Those who hope in Me will not be shamed" would seem to have a special point as the end of a poem that began with the voiced shame and despair of a forsaken childless wife.

What difference would it make if this prophecy of restoration—or indeed any of the prophetic poems we have considered—were delivered not as poetry but as prose? There are, of course, as I noted earlier, perceptible elements of continuity between prophetic poetry and prose. Nevertheless, I would contend that as a rule the formal resources of poetry—its pronounced reliance on figurative language; its strong tendency in parallelism to underscore and complicate connections between related sounds, words, images, and motifs; its gravitation toward symbolic structures; its impulse to realize the extreme possibilities of the themes it takes up—all these lead the prophets to a different order of statement when they cast their vision in verse. Let us for a moment try to imagine how this poem from Deutero-Isaiah would read if it were transposed into prophetic prose. If one assumes, at least for the sake of plausible illustration, that such a prose version would be far less likely to make metaphor central to the exposition, it might sound something like this:

Days are coming, the Lord declares, when your exiled children, whose strength was afflicted on the way, and whose ankles were put in chains, will return in exultation to Zion. And your oppressors will flee from your midst, and your people will inherit their land and build its ruined cities, and plant fields and vineyards in place of the desolation. And I will cause them to dwell on their soil, for My loving care will not depart from them. On the day when I return their captivity, nations will bring them tribute, and none will make them afraid.

I have tried to retain certain verse-like elements in my hypothetical version, in keeping with the practice of prophetic prose and in order not to make the differences between poetry and prose too neatly schematic. Readers with a good recall of the Bible will recognize that my version is really a pastiche of different prophetic locutions, and as such I think it is fairly faithful to the style of prophetic prose. All the ideational elements of the poem from Deutero-Isaiah are preserved in this prose paraphrase: God's loyal concern for Israel, the joyous return from exile, the flight of the enemy and the subservience of the nations to Israel, the rebuilding of the desolate land. All this notwithstanding, the poem represents, or creates, an experience quite different in kind from that of the prose paraphrase.

What has been left out in the prose version is the symbolic presence of Zion as a desperate, suffering woman, and the manifestation through God's dialogue with Zion of the Lord's tender, unfaltering love for Israel. The biological immediacy of womb and breast and bosom that contributes to the emotional force of the poem is also absent from the prose. Left out as well is the sense of miraculous surprise in the return to Zion when the bereaved woman suddenly discovers that her children are alive and well, that the very regents of the earth now cradle and care for them. The landscape of the prose version is continuously and perspicuously historical: these, the speaker makes absolutely clear to his audience, are the fine things that will happen when we return from Babylonian exile and reclaim our lost Land. Those same future events are the objects of reference in the poem Deutero-Isaiah actually wrote, but through his strong symbolic language the historical landscape is transfigured—almost displaced—by the metaphorical scene that represents it. Instead of the transcription of an encouraging speech to exiled Judeans about their hopeful future, we have in the poem a vision of national restoration that is also an imaginative enactment of love supremely fulfilled: the mother happily embracing her children, adorned with them like a bride, and God declaring a love for her even more steadfast than maternal affection. The haunting beauty of these lines has not faded two and a half millennia after they were composed.

The prophets, of course, were preeminently poets with a "message," and it is not inappropriate that modern scholarship should have devoted considerable energies to uncovering connections between the forms of prophetic discourse and other kinds of message speeches in the Bible and the ancient Near East. But I think that scholars and others have often construed this notion of message too literally and too restrictively. The prophets had urgent ideas—indictments, warnings, words of consolation—to convey to their audience. The poetic instrument of conveyance, however, generated powers of signification that pressed beyond the immediate occasion; and the imaginative authority with which history was turned into a theater of timeless hopes and fears explains why these poems still address us so powerfully today.

VII

The Poetry of Wit

THE BOOK OF PROVERBS offers a peculiar test case for the role of poetry in biblical literature. In purely formal terms, the poetic character of the text is nowhere more evident than here. Let us set aside for the moment the first nine chapters, which are made up of relatively long poems, four of them (Chapters 5, 7, 8, and 9) occupying a whole chapter, and which are shaped on rather different poetic principles from those governing the material that follows. The book from Chapter 10 onward consists of several discrete collections of proverbs—scholars have variously divided them as seven small anthologies of precepts, or three with a coda of appendices in the last two chapters. Here, with only a few exceptions, the unit of poetic expression is the single, independent proverb. Each proverb takes up one poetic line, and the boundaries of the line are so clearly marked by symmetries of meaning, syntax, and rhythm that for once there is an almost complete congruence between the traditional division into verses and the actual poetic lineation.

But if Proverbs is conspicuously verse, can very much of it be said to be more than the versification of traditional wisdom, a formal means for impressing a message on mind and memory, like an advertising jingle? Indeed, some scholars have speculated that in the Wisdom schools of ancient Israel—whatever such institutions may really have been like—teachers would present students with the initial verset of a proverb, which they were then expected to "cap" with a matching second verset as part of the instructional process. Whether or not such aphoristic word games were actually played by early Hebrew intellectuals, the very fact that a conjecture of this sort could arise suggests a certain quality of predictability, of mechanical variation on a fixed set of themes, in the proverbs passed down to us. Examples of this predictability are not hard to come by: "The aims of the righteous are justice, / the schemes of the wicked, deceit" (12:5); "A gentle answer turns back wrath, / a harsh word stirs up anger" (15:1); "By wisdom a house is built, / by understanding it is founded" (24:3).

We need not linger over lines like these, where, clearly, the general dynamic complexity of semantic parallelism in biblical verse has given way to a didactic and mnemonic neatness of smoothly matched statements clicking dutifully into place. The smoothness, of course, is hardly surprising in a kind of verse devised to transmit the wisdom of the ages. The didactic poet does not want to set up eddies and undercurrents in the unruffled flow of his language, because the wisdom itself derives from a sense of balanced order, confident distinction, assured consequence for specific acts and moral stances. A certain cultivated smoothness of expression also characterizes a good many other proverbs that are considerably more interesting than the ones I have just quoted. In fact, I would argue that, despite the abundant presence of mechanical synonymity and antithesis in our traditional collection, it is the "interesting" proverb that predominates. Some close attention to individual proverbs may give us an idea of where that interest inheres.

One technical problem for a good many readers is that much of Proverbs has become proverbial in English ("Pride goeth before a fall," "Spare the rod and spoil the child," "Train up a child in the way he should go," and so on). Though that may be testimony to the pithiness of the biblical texts, it has the unfortunate effect of isolating one verset from its mate and deflecting our sense as readers that here, too, as elsewhere in biblical poetry, meaning emerges from some complicating interaction between the two halves of the line. The most memorably aphoristic of English poets, Alexander Pope, has suffered, at least in his popular reception, a similar fate. It may be proverbial now in English that "A little learning is a dangerous thing," but in its original context the flatness of authoritative assertion is given a certain imaginative depth, with the intimation of a mythological plot, by the matching line of the couplet: "A *little learning* is a dangerous thing; / Drink deep, or taste not the Pierian spring" (*Essay on Criticism*, II, 215–216). Still more strikingly in the case of Pope, the original meaning of a line is sometimes altogether distorted when it is proverbialized and in this way torn from context. Thus, "Fools rush in where angels fear to tread" has come to indicate the imprudent undertaking of a daunting or dangerous task. In context, the line is part of a snappily colloquial evocation of verbose, pedantic literary critics who will follow you around and harangue you wherever you go, even into the "sanctuary" of St. Paul's Church: "Nay, fly to Altars, there they'll talk you dead; / For Fools rush in where Angels fear to tread" (*Essay on Criticism*, III, 624–625).

The analogy of Pope suggests an essential formal feature of the poetic structure of the biblical proverb that deserves to be kept more clearly in focus than generally has been done. In closed forms, such as the rhyming couplet Pope used or the one-line Hebrew proverb, the two versets of which constitute a kind of couplet, words, syntactic patterns, and repeated or varied cadences have a strong tendency to press closely against one another, generating complications of meaning, by virtue of the sheer tightness of the frame in which they are held. One prominent effect of such closed forms, as Maynard Mack has aptly characterized it for Pope's poetry, is "an inter-animation of words"[1] within the couplet. Even though Pope's heroic couplets occur as part of larger rhetorical movements within the poems, the sense usually requiring that our reading rush through half a dozen or more couplets in one sweep, the end-stopped rhymes have an effect of boxing in terms within the two-line unit and forcing them to confront each other in antithesis or parallel or paradox or some combination of such interrelations. To cite one representative example from among thousands, here is the concluding couplet of Pope's awesome satiric character of Flavia, the relentlessly fashionable, would-be witty, sensualist: "You purchase Pain with all that Joy can give, / And die of nothing but a Rage to live" (*Moral Essay II*, 99–100). The eighteenth-century convention of capitalizing nouns helps make more prominent what is evident enough in the verbal formulation of the couplet—that Flavia has made her life an insidious web of self-frustrating contradictions, the activities meant to confer pleasure turned into occasions for pain, the insatiable hunger for life finally become the cause and tutelary spirit of a pathetic death.

Similar interanimations of key-terms occur with a high degree of frequency within the parallel versets of a biblical proverb, but the difficulties of translation often interpose a formidable barrier to our seeing this. Biblical Hebrew is synthetic rather than analytic like modern Western languages: to cite a central instance, verbs indicate direct and indirect object by a suffix and their pronominal subject by their conjugated form, and there are no compound tenses, so that often a single word in the Hebrew serves for three or four in translation. The poets in Proverbs constantly exploit this terrific compactness to which Hebrew lends itself, and the effect is often blunted or destroyed in the wordiness of translations. In this respect, it is easier to translate Job or Isaiah than Proverbs, for in the poetry of sublime vision, the images, the force of the speaker's voice, and the rhetorical drive from line to line carry one along, even in a language quite unlike the original. In Proverbs, on the other hand, where so often compactness is all, translation frequently flattens a pointed thrust into a clumsy ruler swat.

The typical pattern of the line in Proverbs is an accentual parallelism of three beats in each verset, or four in the first and three in the second verset, which thus pulls up short to clinch the point; and given the compactness of the language, this usually means three or four words in the first verset playing against just three words in the second verset. This rhythmic pattern is here more often accompanied by neat syntactic parallelism than elsewhere in biblical poetry.

The question of translations vis-à-vis the original is not our primary concern, but it may be helpful for the understanding of the intrinsic nature of the poetry of Proverbs to look at one example of how a line fares in translation. The famous proverb that warns against sparing the rod (13:24) takes just four Hebrew words in the first verset, three in the second: *hoséikh shivtó sonéiʾ benó / veʾohavó shiḥaró musár.* A literal accounting for these seven words would be something like this: spares his-rod hates his-son, / and-he-who-loves-him seeks-for-him [or, goes-out-early-for-him] reproof. If one puts this into intelligible English with some attempt to preserve the succinctness of the original, the line might be rendered as follows: "Who spares the rod, hates his son; / who loves him, seeks to reprove." The New Jewish Publication Society version hews close to the lexical values of the Hebrew, but does not hesitate to relax the tautness of the original into a prose amble: "He who spares the rod hates his son, / But he who loves him disciplines him early." This is basically a modernization of the King James Version: "He that spareth his rod hateth his son: but he that loveth him chasteneth him betimes." R. B. Y. Scott, in his translation of Proverbs in the Anchor Bible series, provides a kind of inadvertent parody of the modern translator's scramble for clarity, which here tumbles into clumsy paraphrase: "He who will not punish his son shows no love for him, / For if he loves him he should be concerned to discipline him." From this grotesque transmogrification (Scott does better with other lines), one would hardly guess that a lively point was being made through poetry. The still-current proverbial adaptation of the first half of this verse is actually a much better approximation of the original: "Spare the rod and spoil the child." The dispensing with pronouns imparts to the English much of the compactness of the Hebrew, while the alliteration of "spare" and "spoil" is a real translator's find, for it helps speed the reading along somewhat in the way assonance (*hoseikh/sonei'*) and rhyme (*shivto/beno*) do in the Hebrew.

As far as the poetics of Proverbs is concerned, the succinct formulation within the tight frame of the line here produces a neat little choreography of pointed antonyms. We begin with a paradox: he who spares, or holds back, his rod is doing violence to ("hates") his son. The "hates" (which, syntactically, can also be construed as "hater of") is set side by side with "loves" (or "lover of") in an antithetical chiastic pattern: indulger—hater—lover—discipliner. Thus, the superficially paradoxical notion that true love is manifested by sternness whereas indulgence has the effect of hatred is expressed with a witty sharpness in which the words are palpably interanimated. The verse form compels us to see what it means in moral consequences truly to love or hate one's son.

The Wisdom literature of the ancient Near East, of which the Book of Proverbs is the central biblical instance, assumed that wisdom was a teachable craft: the Hebrew *hakham* means "wise man" but also, in conjunction with nouns indicating trades, "artisan." The other two extended Wisdom texts in the Bible, Job and Ecclesiastes, reflect what has been characterized as radical wings of the movement; and in pursuing their troubling perceptions—Job in richly imaged poetry, Ecclesiastes for the most part in cadenced prose—they do not draw explicit attention to the cunningness of the verbal medium, however artfully it may be employed. Proverbs, on the other hand, as an expression of mainline Wisdom activity, concentrating on the honing of received insights, stresses the presupposition that wisdom is a language craft.

In the verses that introduce the collection as a whole, we are told that the purpose of the book is the enhancement of understanding through an instrument of finely turned language that needs to be properly grasped: "The wise will hear and gain instruction, / the discerning man will acquire astuteness, // to understand proverb and epigram, / the words of the wise and their riddles" (1:5–6). Like the New JPS version, I have translated *melitzah* as "epigram," following the logic of the context, though it could mean "metaphor," "dark saying," or perhaps simply "poem," and it is associated with a verb that elsewhere means to interpret or translate. The main point is that *mashal* and *melitzah*, "proverb" and "epigram," are preeminently literary terms. Which is to say, the transmission of wisdom depends on an adeptness at literary formulation, and the reception of wisdom—we should note, by an audience of the "wise" and the "discerning"—requires an answering finesse in reading the poems with discrimination, "to understand proverb and epigram." The proem of the Book of Proverbs, in other words, at once puts us on guard as interpreters and suggests that if we are not good readers we will not get the point of the sayings of the wise.

I have intimated that semantic parallelism operates somewhat differently in Proverbs than elsewhere in the Bible because of the effects of compression of the one-line frame. This is especially true in many of the lines constructed on antithetical parallelism, where the expressive force seems to come chiefly from the emphatic matching of complementary opposite terms rather than from the interverset patterns for the development of meaning that we have seen in other biblical poems. "Cheating scales are the abomination of the Lord, / an honest weight, His pleasure" (11:1). The vigor of this is largely a matter of word order within the closed form of the one-line poem: "cheating scales" is tightly bracketed with "honest weight," and the compound "abomination of the Lord" (to'avat YHWH) is answered by the succinct "His pleasure" (retzono), which functions as a kind of satisfying "punch-word" at the end of the line. The antonyms "abomination" and "pleasure" are a formulaic pair in Proverbs, but the poet, by repositioning them within the closed line, can stress other lexical-thematic values: "The abomination of the Lord are the crooked of heart, / His pleasure, the blameless of way" (11:20). Here, the form of the parallel versets effects a confrontation between the two compound designations, "crooked of heart" ('iqshei lev) and "blameless of way" (temimei darekh), so that the metaphorical energy of the opposed terms enters into mutually defining play: the crooked, the twisted, and the perverse over against the blameless, the whole, and the perfect and, perhaps also, rightness of action ("way") over against contorted thought and intention ("heart").

Sometimes, the positioning of a final term as punch-word for the line can introduce a small surprise, which is then assimilated into the sense of apt framing of familiar insight that the proverb means to achieve. "When the just man prospers, a town exults, / when the wicked perish— shouts of joy" (11:10). Because of the neat antithetical form of the two versets, we might expect something like, When the wicked perish, they wail; but the semantic parallel (joy/exults) within the antithesis then immediately convinces us of its perfect rightness. At the same time, the answering of a compound term (in this case the small clause "a town exults") by a single, brief term (rinah, "shouts of joy") produces the clinching effect, the sense of a point concluded at the end, which we have seen in other proverbs.

·Though it is important as one reads to keep an eye on these special effects of compression produced by the closed frame of the one-line form, in fact there are also palpable continuities between the treatment of semantic parallelism in Proverbs and elsewhere in biblical poetry. Again and again, the insight the proverb means to convey is driven home through a heightening or intensification in the second verset of an idea or image introduced in the first, or through a narrative progression from the first verset to the second. Some attention to how these principles are worked out may indicate why so many of these one-line poems are lively and inventive, for all the predictability of their didactic messages. Let me propose that in regard to the semantic relation between versets, the one-line proverbs can be divided into three general categories: (1) lines formed on the principle of antithesis (like the three examples we have just considered); (2) lines formed on a principle of equivalence or elaboration between versets; (3) the riddle form, where the first verset is a syntactically incomplete or otherwise baffling statement, which is then explained through the second verset. The last of these categories, for obvious reasons, is distinctively characteristic of Proverbs ("the words of the wise and their riddles") and will require separate attention; in the first two categories, one repeatedly sees the witty exploitation of the underlying principles of poetics that can be detected throughout the biblical corpus.

A good many proverbs prove to be narrative vignettes in which some minimally etched plot enacts the consequences of a moral principle. This happens most frequently in lines based on equivalence, but one sometimes also finds it in a pair of antithetical versets, where the moral calculus of reward for the good and retribution for the wicked is turned into a seesaw of miniature narrative: "The righteous is rescued from straits, / and the wicked comes in his place" (11:8). "Straits" or "trouble" (*tzarah*) means literally "a narrow place," and "rescued" (*neḥelatz*) is a verb that suggests pulling someone out who is stuck or trapped. The two sequenced images, then, that the line evokes are of the good man, first seemingly pinned down and then popped out of the tight squeeze into which he has fallen, and the wicked man slipped into his place. This is very neat, but, we may ask, is that the way the world is? Obviously not—obvious, I think, not only to us but also to the poet in Proverbs, who has chosen these emblematic images to represent an underlying principle of moral causation that he believes to be present in reality but that he knows would never be so perspicuous in the untidiness of experience outside literature. This for him is precisely the advantage of literary expression, the possibility of understanding made available through "proverb and epigram."

Having touched on the effect of these sequenced images, let me comment briefly, before pursuing the issue of narrativity, on the peculiar role of figurative language in Proverbs. One gets the general impression that imagery in this collection is relatively muted, certainly in comparison with the power to shock or dazzle or impress that one feels in the imagery of Job, the Prophets, and much of the Psalms. There are quite a few proverbs that are devoid of figurative languages (including several of the lines we have already glanced at), and in many others, as in our line about the righteous man in straits, the controlling image does not seem very salient. James G. Williams has sketched out a "spectrum" for the occurrence of imagery in biblical gnomic discourse: at one end of the spectrum, images are generally avoided because of a confident concentration on the ideational terms of the maxim; at the other end, statements tend to be bare of images because of the starkness of the paradox expressed, the writer's "doubt regarding the capacity of certain received symbols and doctrines to represent reality."[2] This latter category does not occur in Proverbs but only in the radical Wisdom texts. Thus, embedded in the prose of Ecclesiastes are occasional versified proverbs, or even short sequences of versified proverbs, and each of these proves to be, as James Williams aptly calls it, an "anti-*mashal*": "A good name is better than goodly oil, / and the day of death than the day of birth" (Eccles. 7:1). Here, figurative language is restricted to the conventional simile of the conventional-sounding first verset, which is then wrenched around by the stark assertion of the second verset. More typically, the antiproverbs use no figurative language and instead stress the point-for-point reversal of traditional Wisdom utterances: "For the more the wisdom, the more vexation, / who gets more knowledge gets more pain" (Eccles. 1:18); "Sometimes the righteous perishes in his righteousness, / while the wicked lives on in his wickedness" (Eccles. 7:15).

In the large middle range between these two unfigured ends of the spectrum, the images can on occasion be fresh or playful or striking, as Williams asserts, in their representation of a confidently apprehended moral reality, but I think it is more typical for them to reflect a studied conventionality, to be held to a fairly limited range of familiar semantic fields. Not surprisingly, the recurrent images of Proverbs tend to divide into antithetical clusters. The most frequent metaphor is that of walking on a path or way (that, too, is implied in the image of the good man stuck in a narrow place followed by the wicked). The way may be smooth and straight, or full of pitfalls and crooked or meandering. Other frequent figurative antitheses are riches and jewels over against poverty; life and healing over against death and sickness; sweetness and honey (either real, if associated with wisdom, or meretricious, if associated with a seductress) over against bitterness and wormwood; light against darkness. Water imagery often occurs without antithesis, usually in a positive sense, occasionally to indicate something ambiguous.

All of these images share an aura of familiarity, and that admirably suits the purposes of the Wisdom poets, who typically seek to convey the sort of truth that will seem perfectly "natural" and virtually self-evident once it is well expressed. Some of the images are less metaphor than metonymy, illustrative instances of the way things are: wisdom is actually assumed to confer wealth and physical well-being, ignorance to lead to impoverishment and illness; going on a way is of course an emblematic representation of living, but it is also a common activity we perform, and in the dangers of wayfaring it would not be surprising from the Wisdom point of view to see the good man vindicated, the bad man getting his comeuppance. There is, then, an element of literalism or "realism" in the use of figurative language in Proverbs, the chief exception being the riddle-form proverbs, where much freer play is given to the figurative imagination because the effect of the line consists largely in the use of a striking, perplexing, or surprising image at the beginning, which then requires deciphering. We will have occasion to observe all these aspects of imagery as we consider both the different categories of proverbs and the different principles that link the paired versets.

Narrativity, though it can occur, as we have seen, in lines formed on antithesis, is more frequent in lines based on equivalence because it is so readily used to represent the working-out of process, a course of moral consequentiality, in the subject introduced in the first verset. "A person's folly will twist his way, / and against the Lord his heart will rage" (19:3). The second verset here, as so often in biblical poetry, combines focusing with narrative development. That is, we move from external action to internal state, from the way to the heart, and we move along a trajectory of consequences, from the folly that leads one astray in life to a condition of anger, frustration, alienation from God. Consequentiality is made more schematically clear in the narrative vignettes of proverbs like these two: "Who stops up his ear from the wretched's scream / will himself call out unanswered" (21:13); "A person who strays from the way of prudence, / in the company of ghosts will rest" (21:16). One might note about the second of these lines that the unobtrusive, and avowedly conventional, image of walking on a way becomes the controlling figure for the miniature plot: a man wanders off the path and ends up toppling—perhaps over an unseen precipice or into a hidden pitfall—into the kingdom of the dead, with "strays" at the beginning chiastically matched by "rest," a euphemism for "death," at the end.

There is a good deal of variety in the effects produced through the narrative elaboration of individual proverbs. Occasionally one encounters the surprise of comic exaggeration: "The sluggard buries his hand in the bowl, / he won't even lift it to his mouth" (19:24). This amounts to a witty satiric reversal of narrative expectations: the act that logically follows putting hand in bowl is carrying food to mouth, but in this cameo tale of the lazy fellow, the second narrative moment shows us the hand still buried in the bowl. In a few instances, an unsuspected second party enters the plot in the second verset: "Deep waters, the council in a man's heart, / but a man of discernment will tap them" (20:5). The interverset nexus here is not equivalence but elaboration or completion. This looks a little like the riddle form, but the first verset is actually a perfectly intelligible aphorism in its own right. Its meaning changes, however, in the narrative surprise of the second verset, culminating in the punch-word "tap" (or "draw up")—which is to say, however deep the hidden wells of human designs, the discerning man can fathom them. A similar introduction of an unsuspected personage in the second verset, this time to make a theological point, occurs in the following: "The horse is ready for the day of battle, / but from the Lord is victory" (21:31). The succinctness of the one-line form allows no space for descriptive elaboration, but one easily imagines the stallion pawing the ground, hitched to his chariot or saddled for his rider, and then there is a jolting shift of planes of perception, with the shorter, second verset (only two words in the Hebrew) casting attention forward to the battle's end, which depends not on chargers or armament or soldiers but on the Lord alone.

I have chosen these examples of surprise to give some sense of the expressive range of narrativity in Proverbs. In any case, the predominant use of narrative development is to articulate the perception of orderly process: certain actions, whether because of our psychological constitution or because of the system of retributive morality God has built into reality, will inevitably lead to certain consequences, as surely as second verset follows first. Let me quote without comment five final examples, all from Chapter 22, which is particularly rich in narrativity: "Train a lad in the way he should go, / even in old age he won't swerve from it" (22:6);

"Who sows injustice will reap disaster, / and the rod of his wrath will fail" (22:8); "Banish the mocker, contention departs, / quarrel and insult will end" (22:10); "A deep pit is the strange woman's mouth, / the cursed of the Lord will fall in" (22:14); "Be folly bound in the heart of a lad, / a rod of reproof will remove it" (22:15).

The pointed deployment of interverset intensification within the tight frame of the one-line poem makes still clearer the presence in Proverbs of a pervasive principle of biblical poetics. Indeed, there are several lines in which the second verset actually begins with the phrase "how much more so" ('af-ki) and which thus could serve as paradigms of intensifying parallelism: "It does not suit a dunce to have comforts, / how much more so a slave to rule over lords" (19:10); "Sheol and Perdition are wide open to the Lord, / how much more so the hearts of men" (15:11). The first of these lines, in consonance with the importance accorded to order in Proverbs, stresses both hierarchy and a presumed system of appropriate correspondences: material enjoyments do not suit the dunce, because we know he does not deserve them, will not have the sense to use them properly, and in the end will do himself out of them; but it is an even greater violation of moral propriety—hence the strategic importance of the poetic "how much more so"—to see those fit only to be slaves lording it over princes, and one may assume that the consequences will be even more disastrous than those of putting a dunce in the lap of luxury. The second of the proverbs just quoted is a shrewd combination of spatial focusing and intensification: if God can effortlessly penetrate the vast, murky depths of the underworld, which in biblical poetry only a figure of supreme mythic force can ever do (compare Job 38), then the small compass of the heart, with its proverbial hidden recesses (compare Proverbs 20:5, which we glanced at before), offers no barrier at all to His perfect vision. In another verse, similar terms, this time with the "how much more so" implied but not stated, are used with human rather than divine perception at issue, to make an opposite point: "Heaven for height, earth for depth, / and the heart of kings without fathom" (25:3).

Elsewhere, one detects focusing parallelism without much intensification, the second verset simply "applying" or concretizing the generalization introduced in the first verset: "For mockers, judgments are readied, / blows for the backs of dunces" (19:29). (As an exemplary instance of how textual scholarship of the Bible operates in ignorance of biblical poetics at its own peril, I would cite a gratuitous emendation proposed for this verse by R. B. Y. Scott. He reads *shevatim*, "rods," instead of *shefatim,* "judgments."[3] This change makes the semantic parallelism "better" but flies in the face of biblical poetic practice, where again and again the line moves from general category in the first verset to concrete instance in the second.) Occasionally a proverb exhibits focusing without intensification, as in "A disaster to his father is a stupid son, / a persistent drip, a nagging wife" (19:13). Presumably the general term "disaster" (*havot*) is a more extreme condition than a dripping leak somewhere in the house, but the witty concreteness of the second term makes it more satirically vivid, makes the sense of maddening annoyance more palpable, and enables "nagging wife" at the very end to become a vigorous punch-phrase. In other proverbs, one finds intensification without focusing, as two terms in the same semantic field occur, the stronger following the weaker: "Who troubles his household inherits the wind, / a slave, the fool to the wise of heart" (11:29). It is bad enough, that is, to make trouble for your own family, and you will end by losing your possessions (in the striking phrase "inherit the wind"), but it is still worse to be an outright fool, in which predicament you will not only be without inheritance but also a slave—figuratively or to all intents and purposes—to the wise.

As should be apparent from all these examples, intensification is particularly at home in lines based on equivalence, where the poet can carry us from one instance of a general category (or from the general category itself) to a more extreme or startling or vivid instance. Some antithetical lines as well, however, take advantage of interverset heightening to striking effect, and in some cases with considerable intricacy. A relatively simple maneuver is to match a rather bland simile in the first verset with a more vehement one representing the complementary opposite case in the second verset: "A worthy wife is her husband's crown, / like rot in his bones, she who shames" (12:4). The chiastic shape of this line reinforces the sharpness of the point, interanimates the crucial terms: the worthy wife and the shameful one are the outside terms of the chiasm, and inside, back to back, are the crown, which as an ornament is something exterior, and the bone rot, which eats away from within. A more complicated instance of intensifying antithesis can be seen in the following juxtaposition of the upright and the wicked: "Through the blessing of the upright a city rises, / and the mouth of the wicked destroys" (11:10). "Blessing" is sometimes an abstraction— that is, a condition of prospering and making those around one prosper, as with Joseph in Egypt—and sometimes specifically attached to what is pronounced by the lips, as in the Balaam story. Here, the blessing of the upright remains a little ambiguous until we get to the mouth of the wicked, at the beginning of the second verset, which retrospectively concretizes the initial "blessing" and gives us an antithetical image of destruction that is more focused—again, with a punch-word, "destroys"—than the preceding image of construction because the mouth itself is envisaged as the agency of ruin.

Sometimes the sense of strengthened assertion in the second verset has to do not with the figurative language chosen but with a feeling that, intrinsically, one side of the moral antithesis is more salient than the other, as in this contrasting of the ephemerality of the wicked with the permanence of the righteous: "Storm past, the wicked's gone, / and the righteous is founded forever" (10:25). The Hebrew literally says, "The wicked is not," denying the evil a proper predicate, while the righteous is so substantial that he is said to be, literally, "an eternal foundation," something no storm, no adversity, could sweep away.

What I have tried to show through all these examples is that Proverbs, as the introductory verses in Chapter 1 suggest, requires close reading because within the confines of the one-line poem nice effects and sometimes suggestive complications are achieved through the smallest verbal movements. Occasionally the poet makes his point by a reversal of the prevailing pattern, as in this line, which offers what may be the most complicated punch-word in the whole collection: "Who scorns his friend is mindless, / a man of discernment keeps quiet" (11:12). One might expect here, A man of discernment will bless him (balanced antithesis), or, A man of discernment will crown him with praise (heightening antithesis). "Keep quiet" (one word in the Hebrew) is manifestly not the antonym of "scorn." It brings us up short, makes us absorb what is for Proverbs a rather devious perception about humanity—that, all too often, one's fellow man may in fact behave in a manner worthy of revilement, but that the prudent person will keep his mouth shut about what he sees. As elsewhere in Proverbs, a good deal is going on against the grid of poetic parallelism, and our understanding of how the grid is generally constructed will help us see more sharply this shifting play of wit, perception, and invention.

The one use of the dyadic line that is entirely distinctive of Proverbs is the riddle form. Some scholars, mindful of the allusion to riddles at the beginning of the book, have conjectured that riddling was an established technique of learning in the ancient Wisdom schools. That is, a teacher might have proposed a riddle like the following: What is choicer than much wealth, and better than silver and gold? The student would have then produced the answer: "A good name is choicer than much wealth, / and grace is better than silver and gold" (22:1).[4] My own feeling is that it is idle to speculate about what went on in the Wisdom schools, if in fact they really existed as schools, because we simply don't have enough evidence to go on. In any case, it confuses the issue of poetic form to extend the concept of riddle to lines like the one just quoted, which is a perfectly satisfactory, and rather conventional, case of interverset semantic parallelism. In the riddle form proper, our attention is arrested by some perplexing, startling, or seemingly contradictory statement or image in the first verset, and this tension is then resolved by the solution to the riddle provided in the second verset. Often the relation of the first verset to second, in place of semantic parallelism, is one of predicate to subject (that order, by the way, being quite natural in biblical Hebrew), though, as we shall see, other syntactical patterns are also used.

A characteristic maneuver is to introduce a shocking or illogical metaphor or simile in the first verset: "A golden ring in a pig's snout, / is a lovely woman lacking sense" (11:22); "Like snow in summer, rain in harvest, / so honor suits not a dunce" (26:1); "Clouds and wind and no rain, / is the man who boasts of a gift ungiven" (25:14); "Streams of water a king's heart in the Lord's hand, / wherever He wants, He diverts it" (21:1). What is gained by putting the moral precept in such terms, and in this order of a periodic sentence with the meaning revealed at the end? It is, obviously enough, a way of clinching the point, in which instead of a punch-word the entire second verset becomes a punch-line. But I think it is equally important to stress the special saliency given by the riddle form to the baffling material of the first verset. It is a little shocking to contemplate the image of a gold ring in a pig's snout, and that sense of shocking incongruity then carries over strongly from the metaphor to its referent, making us see with a new sharpness the contradiction of beauty in a senseless woman. The unseasonable snow and rain similarly point up the incongruity of honor for a dunce, as the sound and fury of wind and clouds without rain dramatically expose the emptiness of the lying braggart. The image of streams of water (New JPS, "channeled water") for the king's heart in God's hand works somewhat differently because it is not a paradoxical image, only one that calls for some explanation; the second verset then teases out the implications of the metaphor—the diversion of streams, as by a skilled engineer—and in so doing makes God's mastery over the masters of the earth beautifully perceptible.

As this last example may suggest, the stress in the riddle form on the force—and sometimes the ambiguity—of metaphor can lead to an explicit scrutiny in the proverb of the dynamics of figuration. Occasionally one finds a paradoxical image turned round surprisingly to produce a very different effect from the one it leads to elsewhere, as in the following redeployment of snow in early autumn: "Like the chill of snow on a harvest day, / is a faithful messenger to his senders, / he revives his master's spirits" (25:13). Here, the contradiction of snow in a warm season, instead of conveying outrageous incongruity, is used to express rare and gratifying refreshment (and thus the contradictory nature of the simile also becomes a shrewd comment on the general unreliability of messengers). Despite my disinclination as a matter of methodological prudence to perform surgery on the received text, I am tempted to see the third verset here as an editorial gloss, both because the proverb form is almost always dyadic and because it looks as though someone had difficulty with the appropriateness of the harvest-snow simile and so introduced the refreshing of flagging spirits in order to make the point of the simile clear. But it is, of course, possible that the original poet here exceptionally chose the triadic form so that he could unpack the meaning of his enigmatic initial image in two progressive stages.

In a few proverbs the two versets simply offer two parallel statements and invite us to build a metaphorical relation out of them, as in this wonderful comic characterization of the lazy man: "The door turns on its hinge, / and the sluggard on his bed" (26:14). The beauty of this setting-out of parallel statements is that it leaves the metaphor relatively open-ended. The sluggard is presumably like the door because he constantly turns back and forth without going anywhere, and perhaps also because he is not much more than a senseless slab of inert matter; and then one may begin to muse on the image of the sluggard in bed in a room with an actual door that never turns, because he never goes out, or on the oddly satisfying fit of the vertical door and the horizontal sluggard, both turning.

Elsewhere, the poet exploits the sheer compactness that the closed form encourages in the expression of the figurative relation. Let me render 27:19 quite literally, omitting the explanatory padding that conventional translations add: "As water face to face, / thus the heart of man to man." The terseness makes you work to decipher the first verset. Once it dawns on you that what is referred to is the reflected image of a face in water, further complications ensue: Does each man discover the otherwise invisible image of his own heart by seeing what others are like, or, on the çontrary, is it by introspection (as we say, "reflection"), in scrutinizing the features of his own heart, that a person comes to understand what the heart of others must be? And is the choice of water in the simile merely an indication of the property of reflection, or does water, as against a mirror, suggest a potentially unstable image, or one with shadowy depths below the reflecting surface? If I am reading this proverb right, it is an exemplary instance of how the riddle form can make us attend to the dynamics of figuration even as it exploits the expressive force of the figure.

There are also riddle-form proverbs that use no figurative language or, like the proverb about door and sluggard, that begin with statements that don't appear to be figurative in themselves but are either so odd or so pointless that they need to be linked to something else: "Let a man meet a bear robbed of her cubs, / and not a dunce in his folly" (17:12); "Better to dwell in the corner of a roof, / than with a nagging wife in a spacious* house" (21:9). (In the second of these examples, the first verset could easily be construed in Hebrew as an independent clause—"It is good to dwell in the corner of a roof"—until we arrive at the initial "than" of the second verset.) And here are two examples of riddle-form proverbs without even an implied metaphorical comparison: "He plunders his father, drives out his mother— / a son who disgraces and shames" (19:26); "Two kinds of weights, two kinds of measures, / the abomination of the Lord are they both" (20:10). We can see how much poetic form matters for the emphasis of meaning by setting the second of these two lines alongside another version of the same idea, expressed in antithesis, which we considered earlier: "Cheating scales are the abomination of the Lord, / an honest weight, His pleasure" (11:1). As we noted before, the nice symmetry of the antithesis makes us see the perfect balanced opposition between the sort of commercial behavior that infuriates God and that which gratifies Him. In the riddle form, on the other hand, the first verset boldly focuses what amounts to an enigma: "Two kinds of weights, two kinds of measures" (literally, "weight and weight, measure and measure"). God's decisively negative judgment against crooked business practices is paramount in both versions, but the riddle form makes it possible for us to apprehend more immediately the disturbing contradiction inherent in double standards, weight and weight, measure and measure. Where the parallelistic proverb, whether based on antithesis or equivalence, leads us into a world of confidently generalizing authority, the riddle form frequently assumes a moral reality fissured with contradictions, hiding unexpected comparisons and shocks of extravagant behavior, requiring the surprise of paradox or incongruous imagery in order to be expressed.

Since roughly a third of the Book of Proverbs is taken up with poems ten or twenty lines as long as the one-line aphorisms we have been scrutinizing, it is worth looking at one example of an extended poem in order to get some sense of how else poetry is used in the collection. There are certain connections between the poetics of the one-line proverb and that of the longer poems, but in many respects the latter more closely resemble other kinds of biblical poems than they do the one-liners. Earlier in this study, in a general discussion of narrativity, we had occasion to examine Proverbs 7, the vivid account of the wily seductress and the gullible young man that may be the only clear-cut instance of a full-scale, freestanding narrative poem in the Bible.[5] Let us now consider the poem that constitutes all of Chapter 5, which treats the same theme without prominent narrative development, shifting the burden instead to the elaboration of imagery and the force of direct discourse assigned to both the mentor and the young man.

1	My lad, to my wisdom hearken,	to my insight bend your ear.
2	That you may guard discretion,	and your lips preserve knowledge.
3	For the strange woman's lips drip honey,	her palate is smoother than oil.
4	But in the end she's bitter as wormwood,	sharp as a double-edged sword.
5	Her feet go down to death,	in Sheol her steps take hold.
6	No path of life she traces,	her course wanders, she knows not where.
7	And so, lads, heed me,	swerve not from my mouth's sayings.
8	Keep your way far from her,	approach not the door of her house.
9	Lest you give your vigor to others,	your years to a ruthless one.
10	Lest strangers consume your strength,	your toil—in an alien's house.
11	And in the end you roar,	when your flesh and body waste,
12	And you say: "How I hated reproof,	and rebuke my heart despised!
13	I heeded not the voice of my teachers,	to my guides I bent not my ear.
14	Soon I was caught in utter ruin,	amidst the assembled folk."
15	Drink water from your cistern,	fresh water from your well.
16	Your springs will gush forth streetward,	streams of water in the squares.

17	They will be for you alone,	no stranger sharing with you.
18	Let your fountain be blessed,	and delight in the wife of your youth.
19	A loving doe, a graceful gazelle,	her breasts will ever refresh you.
	in her love you will always dote.	
20	For why dote, my lad, on a stranger,	clasp an alien woman's lap?
21	For before the Lord's eyes are a man's ways,	He traces all his course.
22	The wicked's crime will trap him,	in the ropes of his sin he'll be held.
23	He will die for want of reproof,	in his great folly he will dote.

What remains here of the poetics of the one-line proverb is a certain vestigial presence at a couple of points of the riddle form. The paradox of lines 3–4, quickly resolved by temporal distribution, is one that could be easily cast as a riddle: What is sweeter than honey, smoother than oil, bitter as wormwood, sharp as a sword? A wanton woman when you first encounter her and after you've had dealings with her. Lines 15–19 have the look of an extended riddle form (of which there are a few instances in the collection), elaborating the metaphor of the well without explaining its referent until line 18b, and also introducing a paradox: this is a well whose waters gush out into the streets and yet are enjoyed by you alone. Presumably, the reference of the waters welling outward is to offspring. (Interpreters who render line 16, "*Lest* your springs gush forth . . .," with no warrant from the Hebrew, preserve "logic" by destroying paradox, which happens to be one of the characteristic modes of poetic expression in Proverbs.) Beyond these traces of the riddle form, the poem makes prominent use of formulas of exhortation ("My lad, to my wisdom hearken . . .") that are often employed in much shorter pieces but never in the one-line poem, which of course has room only for the sharp development of a single, pointed precept.

Otherwise, the interlocking set of poetic devices we find here for the imaginative realization of the didactic theme has strong links with structural and stylistic features of biblical poems in other genres. The poem has a formal introduction or exordium (lines 1–2), followed by the specification of the theme (line 3) and a brief narrative elaboration of its consequences (lines 4–6). Then there is a refrain-like resumption in line 7 of the initial language of exhortation ("And so, lads, heed me . . ."), which is tactically useful at this point rather than at the very end of the poem, as in Chapter 7, because the mentor will proceed to quote the discourse of the young man—of course in a prospective and monitory fashion—and that unfortunate figure will be made to confess his own imprudence in having "heeded not the voice" of his teachers.

Like so many biblical poems, this one closes with an envelope structure, though the symmetry is not so explicit as in Chapter 7, and the last four lines answer not to the mentor's exordium in lines 1–2 but to the introductory representation of the dangers of the seductress in lines 3–6. The alien or "stranger woman"—that is, forbidden woman—of the beginning reappears at the end, and if the young man was warned before about the meretricious charm of her mouth or palate (*ḥeikh*), he is now asked why he should embrace her lap (*ḥeiq*). (I will have more to say in a moment about the force of that pun.) Because she did not know how to "trace" the path of life, her "course" wandered (line 6); at the end God "traces" the whole "course" (line 21) that a man follows, with each man's "ways" before the Lord, including the way in line 8 that the young man should have kept far from the seductress's house. Finally, the verb *t-m-kh*, a slightly odd usage in line 5 that I have rendered there as "take hold" ("in Sheol her steps take hold") recurs in the penultimate line's image of the trapped evildoer, "in the ropes of his sin he'll be held [*yitameikh*]." The last line of the poem then closes a local and more obvious envelope structure by concluding with the verb for doting or infatuation that was first used in an antithetical context to suggest the euphoria of consummated marital love.[6]

There are some narrative elements in the poem because a particular course of action is imagined to have particular consequences. If you get entangled with a seductress, she will end up taking you for all you're worth, and you will eventually find yourself with resources depleted and health destroyed, like the young man who confesses his past foolishness, exposed to the eye and the judicial arm of the community (a hint of the latter is introduced in 14b, perhaps in conjunction with the idea that he will be legally deprived of his property). Intensifying parallelism plays an important role in getting this message across. You not only should stay away from such a woman but, more concretely, should not imagine approaching her door (line 8); you will end up giving your substance to others, indeed, to cruel or ruthless strangers (line 9); not only will strangers take their fill of your possessions but, more vividly, all you have worked for will find its way into a foreigner's house (line 10).

Perhaps the best way to see how this poem is a good deal more than a bundle of versified precepts is to observe the operation of its images, which is reinforced by the thematically significant movements from outside to inside and inside to outside. The honey and oil at the beginning refer metaphorically to beguiling speech and metonymically to luscious kisses. There is an interverset progression or movement inward from lips to palate—and the evidence of the Song of Songs should remind us that tongued kisses are a perfectly acceptable activity for poetic representation in the Bible. The framing pun of "palate" (ḥeikh) and "lap" (ḥeiq), the latter euphemistically pointing to the pudenda, suggests that the palate at the beginning is an adumbration by way of analogy of the other orifice where oil-smoothness will turn into a double-edged sword. This pattern of sexual reference is reinforced by the warning to stay away from the door of the seductress's house: the Hebrew says, literally, "opening," petaḥ, not "door," delet, the word used in the proverb about the sluggard turning on his bed.

The evocation of the faithful wife in lines 15–19 works in beautiful counterpoint to this cluster of orificial imagery associated with the seductress. The wife is a well, a synecdochic metaphor that focuses on the womb. A well is the opposite of a pit (the latter image probably being implied in the picture of slipping down into the underworld in line 5, and compare 22:14: "A deep pit is the strange woman's mouth, / the cursed of the Lord will fall in") because it is a cavity that becomes a source of blessing and fertility. The seductress's mouth, like its anatomical analogue, offers honey and oil; the conjugal well offers instead pure running water. In place of the initial spatial orientation from outside to dangerous inside, marital love is firmly situated inside, within the domestic sanctuary, and the fountain's waters—the abundance of blessing it produces—spread outside while the integrity of the fountain is preserved within. As the parallels in the Song of Songs suggest, the poet here does not hesitate to borrow from the stock imagery of Hebrew love poetry both the metaphor of the well for the woman and her secret parts and the delicately erotic animal images of line 19a. "Her breasts will ever refresh you" (19b) may at first glance seem a little surprising, but perfectly catches up the cluster of drinking images that the poem associates with sex. The concrete reference is obviously to love play, but the choice of the breasts complements the metaphor of drinking from a well, and the implied milk is a kind of answer to the honey dripping from the lips of the seductress, perhaps also intimating that there is something nurturing in the delights of this conjugal love. (In the Song of Songs, where there are no moral conflicts, the lover can have both substances together: "Honey and milk are under your tongue . . . ," 4:11.) Some scholars have read for dadim, "breasts," dodim, "love" (or, to convey the difference of connotation from the more general Hebrew term for love, "the pleasure of sensual fulfillment"). In view of the whole context of drinking images, I would prefer to go along with the received text, seeing in the use of *dadim* a deliberate wordplay on *dodim*, so that the explicit evocation of oral pleasure can also intimate other gratifications.

Let me offer one last comment on the formal disposition of the poem. Line 19 is the only triadic line in the entire poem. The third verset, "in her love you will always dote," makes a small A-B-A structure out of the whole line, since the first verset begins with "loving" (in both first and third versets, the root is *'a-h-b*). The third verset also summarizes the whole preceding sequence of five lines, and the triadic line is used, as we have seen repeatedly elsewhere in poems where dyadic lines predominate, to mark the end of a segment. The overlap of "dote" in 19c and 20a (compare the structurally analogous overlap of "lips" in 2b and 3a) neatly ties in the celebration of marital love with the admonitions against the wiles of the loose woman that were the poem's point of departure and, now, its conclusion: man as an erotic creature is drawn by the powerful allure of ecstasy, but there are both salutary and destructive channels for the fulfillment of that urge. In the anatomical imagery that is again invoked as the contrast is made, the "lap" of the forbidden woman is a dubious alternative to the refreshing breasts of the loving gazelle.

In most of what we have been observing, it is clear that the modes of operation of the extended Wisdom poem are different from those of the one-line proverb. Imagery functions differently because it can be elaborated and amplified from line to line and linked with clusters of associated images. Narrativity is not limited to thumbnail illustrative plots, because it can be carried forward in stages, sometimes with the introduction of dramatic dialogue. Symmetries and formal balance of expression are not restricted to the interanimation of a few words within a tight frame but can be distributed with complicating variations over the larger structure and used to indicate interesting shifts of emphasis and complications of thematic development.

There is, nevertheless, an essential connection between the aphoristic poem and its longer counterpart. Each is considerably more than a "translation" into parallel versets of moral precepts because each uses the resources of poetic expression to achieve a fuller apprehension of its subject. The fullness may be simply a matter of catching a moral contradiction more sharply, or envisioning the consequences of some course of action more uncompromisingly, than conventional habits lead us to do. The fullness can on occasion also involve a fresh penetration into the multifaceted or ambiguous character of the subject or, as in Proverbs 5, an imaginative plunge into the experiential enactment of moral alternatives (the life-confirming pleasures of conjugal love against the scheming embrace of deadly lust). Whatever the particular case, the poetic vehicle makes a crucial difference; and an awareness of the nuances of poetic form, seen against the general background of poetic practice and convention in the Bible, will help us grasp the liveliness, the depth of experience-wise reflection, the intellectual vigor, of these didactic texts.

VIII

The Garden of Metaphor

THE SONG OF SONGS comprises what are surely the most exquisite poems that have come down to us from ancient Israel, but the poetic principles on which they are shaped are in several ways instructively untypical of biblical verse. When it was more the scholarly fashion to date the book late, either in the Persian period (W. F. Albright) or well into the Hellenistic period (H. L. Ginsberg), these differences might have been attributed to changing poetic practices in the last centuries of biblical literary activity. Several recent analysts, however, have persuasively argued that all the supposed stylistic and lexical evidence for a late date is ambiguous, and it is quite possible, though not demonstrable, that these poems originated, whatever subsequent modifications they may have undergone, early in the First Commonwealth period.[1]

The most likely sources of distinction between the Song of Songs and the rest of biblical poetry lie not in chronology but in genre, in purpose, and perhaps in social context. Although there are some striking love motifs elsewhere in biblical poetry—in Psalms, between man and God, in the Prophets, between God and Israel—the Song of Songs is the only surviving instance of purely secular love poetry from ancient Israel. The erotic symbolism of the Prophets would provide later ages an effective warrant for reading the Song of Songs as a religious allegory, but in fact the continuous celebration of passion and its pleasures makes this the most consistently secular of all biblical texts[2]—even more so than Proverbs, which for all its pragmatic worldly concerns also stresses the fear of the Lord and the effect of divine justice on the here and now. We have no way of knowing the precise circumstances under which or for which the Song of Songs was composed. A venerable and persistent scholarly theory sees it as the (vestigial?) liturgy of a fertility cult;

others—to my mind, more plausibly—imagine it as a collection of wedding songs. What I should like to reject at the outset is the whole quest for the "life-setting" of the poems—because it is, necessarily, a will-o'-the-wisp and, even more, because it is a prime instance of the misplaced concreteness that has plagued biblical research, which naïvely presumes that the life-setting, if we could recover it, would somehow provide the key to the language, structure, and meaning of the poems.

The imagery of the Song of Songs is a curious mixture of pastoral, urban, and regal allusions, which leaves scant grounds for concluding whether the poems were composed among shepherds or courtiers or somewhere in between. References in rabbinic texts suggest that at least by the Roman period the poems were often sung at weddings, and, whoever composed them, there is surely something popular about these lyric celebrations of the flowering world, the beauties of the female and male bodies, and the delights of lovemaking. The Wisdom poetry of Job and Proverbs was created by members of what one could justifiably call the ancient Israelite intelligentsia. Prophetic verse was produced by individuals who belonged—by sensibility and in several signal instances by virtue of social background as well—to a spiritual-intellectual elite. The psalms were tied to the cult, and at least a good many of them were probably created in priestly circles (the mimetic example of short prayers embedded in biblical narrative suggests that ordinary people, in contradistinction to the professional psalm-poets, may have improvised personal prayers in simple prose).[3] It is only in the Song of Songs that there is no one giving instruction or exhortation, no leader or hierophant, no memorializer of national experience, but instead the voices of two lovers, praising each other, yearning for each other, proffering invitations to enjoy. I shall not presume to guess whether these poems were composed by folk poets, but it is clear that their poetic idiom is one that, for all its artistic sophistication, is splendidly accessible to the folk, and that may well be the most plausible explanation for the formal differences from other kinds of biblical poetry.

To begin with, semantic parallelism is used here with a freedom one rarely encounters in other poetic texts in the Bible. Since virtually the whole book is a series of dramatic addresses between the lovers, this free gliding in and out of parallelism—the very antithesis of the neat boxing together of matched terms in Proverbs—may be dictated in part by the desire to give the verse the suppleness and liveliness of dramatic speech. Thus the very first line of the collection: "Let him kiss me with the kisses of his mouth, / for your love is better than wine" (1:2). The relation of the second verset to the first is not really parallelism but explanation—and a dramatically appropriate one at that, which is reinforced by the move from third person to second: your kisses, my love, are more delectable than wine, which is reason enough for me to have declared at large my desire for them.

In many lines, the second verset is a prepositional or adverbial modifier of the first verset—a pattern we have encountered occasionally elsewhere, but which here sometimes occurs in a whole sequence of lines, perhaps as part of an impulse to apprehend the elaborate and precious concreteness of the object evoked instead of finding a matching term for it. Here, for example, is the description of Solomon's royal palanquin (3:6–10):

1	Who is this coming up from the desert	like columns of smoke,
2	Perfumed with myrrh and frankincense	of all the merchant's powders?
3	Look, Solomon's couch,	sixty warriors round it
	of the warriors of Israel,	
4	All of them skilled with sword,	trained in war,
5	Each with sword on thigh,	for terror in the nights.
6	A litter King Solomon made him	of wood from Lebanon.
7	Its posts he made of silver,	its bolster gold,
	its cushion purple wool,	
8	Its inside decked with love	by the daughters of Jerusalem.

The only strictly parallelistic lines here are 4 and 7. For the rest, the poet seems to be reaching in his second (and third) versets for some further realization of the object, of what it is like, where it comes from: What surrounds Solomon's couch? Why are the warriors arrayed with their weapons? Who is it who has so lovingly upholstered the royal litter?

Now, the picture of a perfumed cloud ascending from the desert, with a splendid palanquin then revealed to the eye of the beholder, first with its entourage, afterward with its luxurious fixtures, also incorporates narrative progression; and because the collection involves the dramatic action of lovers coming together or seeking one another (though surely not, as some have fancied, in a formal drama), narrativity is the dominant pattern in a number of the poems. Such narrativity is of course in consonance with a general principle of parallelistic verse in the Bible, as one can see clearly in single lines like this: "Draw me after you, let us run— / the king has brought me to his chambers" (1:4). The difference is that in the Song of Songs there are whole poems in which all semblance of semantic equivalence between versets is put aside for the sake of narrative concatenation from verset to verset and from line to line. I will quote the nocturnal pursuit of the lover at the beginning of

Chapter 3 (3:1–4), with which one may usefully compare the parallel episode in 5:2–8 that works on the same poetic principle:

1	On my bed at night	I sought the one I so[4] love,
	I sought him, did not find him.	
2	Let me rise and go round the town,	in the streets and squares
3	Let me seek the one I so love,	I sought him, did not find him.
4	The watchmen going round the town found me—	"Have you seen the one I so love?"
5	Scarce had I passed them	when I found the one I so love.
6	I held him, would not loose him,	till I brought him to my mother's house,
	to the chamber of her who conceived me.	

In this entire sequence of progressive actions, the only moment of semantic equivalence between versets is in the second and third versets of the last line, and the focusing movement there from house to chamber is subsumed under the general narrative pattern: the woman first gets a tight grip on her lover (6a), then brings him to her mother's house (6b), and finally introduces him (6c) into the chamber (perhaps the same one in which she was lying at the beginning of the sequence).

This brief specimen of narrative reflects two other stylistic peculiarities of the Song of Songs. Although the collection as a whole makes elaborate and sometimes extravagant use of figurative language, when narrative governs a whole poem, as in 3:1–4 and 5:2–8, figuration is entirely displaced by the report of sequenced actions. There are no metaphors or similes in these six lines, and, similarly, in the description of the palanquin coming up from the desert to Jerusalem that we glanced at, the only figurative language is "like columns of smoke" at the beginning (where the original reading may in fact have been "*in* columns of smoke") and "decked with love" at the end (where some have also seen a textual problem). The second notable stylistic feature of our poem is the prominence of verbatim repetition. Through the rapid narrative there is woven a thread of verbal recurrences that, disengaged, would sound like this: I sought the one I so love, I sought him, did not find him, let me seek the one I so love, I sought him, did not find him, the one I so love, I found the one I so love. This device has a strong affinity with the technique of incremental repetition that is reflected in the more archaic layers of biblical poetry (the most memorable instance being the Song of Deborah). In the Song of Songs, however, such repetition is used with a degree of flexibility one does not find in the archaic poems, and is especially favored in vocative forms where the lover adds some item of enraptured admiration to the repetition: "Oh, you are fair, my darling, / oh, you are fair, *your eyes are doves*" (4:1). One finds the increment as well in the explanatory note of a challenge: "How is your lover more than another, / fairest of women, // how is your lover more than another, / *that thus you adjure us?*" (5:9). One notices that there is a sense of choreographic balance lacking in the simple use of incremental repetition because in both these lines an initial element ("my darling," "fairest of women") is subtracted as the increment is added. In any case, the closeness to incremental repetition is not necessarily evidence of an early date but might well reflect the more popular character of these love poems, folk poetry and its sophisticated derivatives being by nature conservative in their modes of expression.

The most telling divergence from quasi-synonymous parallelism in the Song of Songs is the use of one verset to introduce a simile and of the matching verset to indicate the referent of the simile: "Like a lily among brambles, / so is my darling among girls. // Like an apple tree among forest trees, / so is my lover among lads" (2:2–3). The same pattern appears, with a very different effect, in some of the riddle-form proverbs. In the Song of Songs, such a pattern makes particular sense because, more than in any other poetic text of the Bible, what is at issue in the poems is the kind of transfers of meaning that take place when one thing is represented in terms of or through the image of something else, and the "like . . . / so . . ." formula aptly calls our attention to the operation of the simile. With the exception of the continuously narrative passages I have mentioned, figurative language plays a more prominent role here than anywhere else in biblical poetry, and the assumptions about how figurative language should be used have shifted in important respects.

The fact is that in a good deal of biblical poetry imagery serves rather secondary purposes, or sometimes there is not very much of it, and in any case "originality" of metaphoric invention would not appear to have been a consciously prized poetic value. Let me propose that outside the Song of Songs one can observe three general categories of imagery in biblical poems: avowedly conventional images, intensive images, and innovative images. Conventional imagery accounts for the preponderance of cases, and the Book of Psalms is the showcase for the artful use of such stock images. Intensive imagery in most instances builds on conventional metaphors and similes, with the difference that a particular figure is pursued and elaborated through several lines or even a whole poem, so that it is given a kind of semantic amplitude or powerfully assertive pressure. Intensive imagery occurs sometimes in Psalms, fairly often in Job, and is the figurative mode par excellence of prophetic poetry. Innovative imagery is the rarest of the three categories, but it can occur from time to time in any genre of biblical verse simply because poetry is, among other things, a way of imagining the world through inventive similitude, and poets, whatever their conventional assumptions, may on occasion arrest the attention of their audience through an original or startling image.[5] The highest concentration of innovative imagery in the Bible is evident in the Book of Job, which I would take to be not strictly a generic matter but more a reflection of the poet's particular genius and his extraordinary ability to imagine disconcerting realities outside the frame of received wisdom and habitual perception. Let me offer some brief examples of all three categories of imagery in order to make this overview of biblical figuration more concrete, which in turn should help us see more clearly the striking difference of the Song of Songs.

Stock imagery, as I have intimated, is the staple of biblical poetry, and Psalms is the preeminent instance of its repeated deployment. Here is an exemplary line: "Guard me like the apple of Your eye, / in the shadow of Your wings conceal me" (Ps. 17:8). Both the apple of the eye as something to be cherished and the shadow of wings as a place of shelter are biblical clichés, though the two elements are interestingly connected here by a motif of darkness (the concentrated dark of the pupil and the extended shadow of wings) and linked in a pattern of intensification that moves from guarding to hiding. There may be, then, a certain effective orchestration of the semantic fields of the metaphors, but in regard to the purpose of the psalm, the advantage of working with such conventional figures is that our attention tends to be guided through the metaphoric vehicle to the tenor for which the vehicle was introduced. In fact, as Benjamin Hrushovski has recently argued, there is a misleading implication of unidirectional movement in those very terms "tenor" and "vehicle," coined for critical usage by I. A. Richards some six decades ago,[6] and when we return to the Song of Songs we will see precisely why the unidirectional model of metaphor is inappropriate. In the frequent biblical use, however, of stock imagery, the relation between metaphor and referent actually approaches that of a vehicle—that is, a mere "carrier" of meaning—to a tenor. In our line from Psalms, what the speaker, pleading for divine help, wants to convey is a sense of the tender protection he asks of God. The apple of the eye and the shading of wings communicate his feeling for the special care he seeks, but in their very conventionality the images scarcely have a life of their own. We think less about the dark of the eye and the shadow of wings than about the safeguarding from the Lord for which the supplicant prays.

Since I have pulled this line out of context, let me refer with a comment on the whole poem to the use of cliché in just one other fairly typical psalm, Psalm 94. In the twenty-three lines of this poem, which calls quite impressively on the Lord as a "God of retribution" to destroy His enemies, there are only four lines that contain any figurative language. How minimal and how conventional such language is will become clear by the quoting in sequence of these four isolated instances of figuration: "The Lord knows the designs of man, / that they are mere breath" (11); ". . . until a pit is dug for the wicked" (13); "When I thought my foot had slipped, / Your faithfulness, Lord, supported me" (18); "But the Lord is my stronghold, / and my God is my sheltering rock" (22). Pitfall, stumbling, and stronghold occur time after time in biblical poetry, and their role in this otherwise nonfigurative poem is surely no more than a minor amplification of the idea that security depends upon God. The metaphor of breath or vapor may to the modern glance seem more striking, but it is in fact such a conventional designation for insubstantiality in the Bible that modern translations that render it unmetaphorically as "futile" do only small violence to the original.

We have seen a number of instances of intensive imagery in our discussion of prophetic poetry and of structures of intensification, but since the focus of those considerations was not on figurative language, one brief example from the prophets may be useful. Here is Deutero-Isaiah elaborating a metaphor in order to contrast the ephemerality of humankind and the power and perdurability of God (Is. 40:6–8):

All flesh is grass,	all its faithfulness like the flower of the field.
Grass withers, flower fades	when the Lord's breath blows on them.
Grass withers, flower fades,	and the word of the Lord stands forever.

The metaphor of grass for transience is thoroughly conventional, but the poet gives it an intensive development through these three lines in the refrain-like repetition of the key phrases; the amplification of grass with flower (a vegetal figure that involves beauty and still more fragility and ephemerality, as flowers wither more quickly than grass); and in the contrast between grass and God's breath-wind-spirit (*ruaḥ*). God's power is a hot wind that makes transient growing things wither, but God's spirit is also the source of His promise to Israel, through covenant and prophecy, which will be fulfilled or "stand" (*yaqum*) forever while human things and human faithfulness vanish in the wilderness of time. One sees how a cliché has been transformed into poignantly evocative poetry, and here the frame of reference of the metaphor, ephemeral things flourishing, interpenetrates the frame of reference of Israel vis-à-vis God as the pitfalls and strongholds of Psalms do not do to the objects or ideas to which they allude.

Finally, the Job poet abundantly interweaves with such intensive developments of conventional figures forcefully innovative images that carry much of the burden of his argument. Sometimes the power of these images depends on an elaboration of their implications for two or three lines, as in this representation of human life as backbreaking day labor tolerable only because of the prospect of evening/death as surcease and recompense: "Has not man a term of service on earth, / and like the days of a hireling his days? // Like a slave he pants for the shadows, / like a hireling he waits for his wage" (Job 7:1–2). Sometimes we find a rapid flow of innovative figures that in its strength from verset to verset seems quite Shakespearian, as in these images of the molding of man in the womb: "Did You not pour me out like milk, / curdle me like cheese? // With skin and flesh You clothed me, / with bones and sinews wove me?" (Job 10:10–11). The brilliantly resourceful Job poet also offers a more compact version of the innovative image, in which an otherwise conventional term is endowed with terrific figurative power because of the context in which it is set. Thus, the verb *sabo'a*, "to be satisfied" or "sated," is extremely common in biblical usage, for the most part in literal or weakly figurative utterances, but this is how Job uses it to denounce the Friends: "Why do you pursue me like God, / and from my flesh you are not sated?" (Job 19:22). In context, especially since Job has just been talking about his bones sticking to his flesh and skin (19:20), the otherwise bland verb produces a horrific image of cannibalism, which manages to say a great deal with awesome compression about the perverted nature of the Friends' relationship to the stricken Job.

The innovative image by its forcefulness strongly colors our perception of its referent: once we imagine the Friends cannibalizing Job's diseased and wasted flesh, we can scarcely dissociate the words they speak and their moral intentions from this picture of barbaric violence. What remains relatively stable, as in the two other general categories of biblical imagery, is the subordinate relation of image to referent. We are never in doubt that Job's subject is the Friends' censorious behavior toward him, not cannibalism, or the shaping of the embryo, not cheese-making and weaving. By contrast, what makes the Song of Songs unique among the poetic texts of the Bible is that, quite often, imagery is given such full and free play there that the lines of semantic subordination blur, and it becomes a little uncertain what is illustration and what is referent.

It should be observed, to begin with, that in the Song of Songs the process of figuration is frequently "foregrounded"—which is to say, as the poet takes expressive advantage of representing something through an image that brings out a salient quality it shares with the referent, he calls our attention to his exploitation of similitude, to the artifice of metaphorical representation. One lexical token of this tendency is that the verbal root *d-m-h*, "to be like," or, in another conjugation, the transitive "to liken," which occurs only thirty times in the entire biblical corpus (and not always with this meaning), appears five times in these eight brief chapters of poetry, in each instance flaunting the effect of figurative comparison. Beyond this lexical clue, the general frequency of simile is itself a "laying bare" of the artifice, making the operation of comparison explicit in the poem's surface structure.[7]

The first occurrence of this verb as part of an ostentatious simile is particularly instructive because of the seeming enigma of the image: "To a mare among Pharaoh's chariots / I would liken you, my darling" (1:9). Pharaoh's chariots were drawn by stallions, but the military stratagem alluded to has been clearly understood by commentators as far back as the classical Midrashim: a mare in heat, let loose among chariotry, could transform well-drawn battle lines into a chaos of wildly plunging stallions. This is obviously an instance of what I have called innovative imagery, and the poet—or, if one prefers, the speaker—is clearly interested in flaunting the innovation. The first verset gives us a startling simile, as in the first half of a riddle-form proverb; the second verset abandons semantic parallelism for the affirmation of simile making ("I would liken you" or, perhaps, "I have likened you") together with the specification in the vocative of the beloved referent of the simile. The lover speaks out of a keen awareness of the power of figurative language to break open closed frames of reference and make us see things with a shock of new recognition: the beloved in poem after poem is lovely, gentle, dovelike, fragrant, but the sexual attraction she exerts also has an almost violent power to drive males to distraction, as the equine military image powerfully suggests.

It is not certain whether the next two lines (1:10–11), which evoke the wreaths of jewels and precious metals with which the beloved should be adorned, are a continuation of the mare image (referring, that is, to ornaments like those with which a beautiful mare might be adorned) or the fragment of an unrelated poem. I would prefer to see these lines as an extension of the mare simile because that would be in keeping with a general practice in the Song of Songs of introducing a poetic comparison and then exploring its ramifications through several lines. A more clear-cut example occurs in these three lines (2:8–9), which also happen to turn on the next occurrence of the symptomatic verb *d-m-h:*

Hark! My lover, here he comes!	bounding over the mountains,
	loping over the hills.
My lover is like a buck	or a young stag.
Here he stands behind our wall,	peering in at the windows,
	peeping through the lattice.

This poem, which continues with the lover's invitation to the woman to come out with him into the vernal countryside, begins without evident simile: the waiting young woman simply hears the rapidly approaching footsteps of her lover and imagines him bounding across the hills to her home. What the middle line, which in the Hebrew begins with the verb of likening, *domeh,* does is to pick up a simile that has been pressing just beneath the verbal surface of the preceding line and to make it explicit— all the more explicit because the speaker offers overlapping alternatives of similitude, a buck *or* a young stag. The third line obviously continues the stag image that was adumbrated in the first line and spelled out in the second, but its delicate beauty is in part a function of the poised ambiguity as to what is foreground and what is background. It is easy enough to picture a soft-eyed stag, having come down from the hills, peering in through the lattice; it is just as easy to see the eager human lover, panting from his run, looking in at his beloved. The effect is the opposite of the sort of optical trick in which a design is perceived at one moment as a rabbit and the next as a duck but never as both at once, because through the magic of poetic likening the figure at the lattice is simultaneously stag and lover. What I would call the tonal consequence of this ambiguity is that the lover is entirely assimilated into the natural world at the same time that the natural world is felt to be profoundly in consonance with the lovers. This perfectly sets the stage for his invitation (2:10–13) to arise and join him in the freshly blossoming landscape, all winter rains now gone.

A variant of the line about the buck occurs in another poem at the end of the same chapter (2:16–17), and there is something to be learned from the different position and grammatical use of the verb of similitude:

My lover is mine and I am his,
Until day breathes
Turn, and be you, my love, like a buck,
              on the cleft mountains.

who browses among the lilies.
and shadows flee,
or a young stag

The verb "browses," *ro'eh*, which when applied to humans means "to herd" and would not make sense in that meaning here, requires a figurative reading from the beginning. The only landscape, then, in this brief poem is metaphorical: the woman is inviting her lover to a night of pleasure, urging him to hasten to enjoy to the utmost before day breaks. The lilies and the "cleft mountains"—others, comparing the line to 8:14, render this "mountains of spice," which amounts to the same erotic place—are on the landscape of her body, where he can gambol through the night. What is especially interesting in the light of our previous examples is that the verb of similitude occurs not in the speaker's declaration of likeness but in an imperative: "be you, my love, like [*demeh le*] a buck." The artifice of poetry thus enters inside the frame of dramatic action represented through the monologue: the woman tells her man that the way he can most fully play the part of the lover is to be like the stag, to act out the poetic simile, feeding on these lilies and cavorting upon this mount of intimate delight.

Of the two other occurrences of the verb *d-m-h* in the Song of Songs, one is a variant of the line we have just considered, appearing at the very end of the book (8:14) and possibly detached from context. The other occurrence (7:8–10) provides still another instructive instance of how this poetry rides the momentum of metaphor:

This stature of yours is like the palm,
I say, let me climb the palm,
Let your breast be like grape clusters,
Your palate like goodly wine
              stirring* the lips of sleepers.

your breasts like the clusters.
let me hold its branches.
your breath like apples,
flowing for my love smoothly,*

The speaker first announces his controlling simile, proclaiming that his beloved's stately figure is like (*damta le*) the palm. The second verset of the initial line introduces a ramification—quite literally, a "branching out"—of the palm image or, in terms of the general poetics of parallelism, focuses it by moving from the tree to the fruit-laden boughs. The next line is essentially an enactment of the simile, beginning with "I say," which Marvin Pope quite justifiably renders as "methinks" because the verb equally implies intention and speech. The simile ceases to be an "illustration" of some quality (the stately stature of the palm tree in the woman) and becomes a reality that impels the speaker to a particular course of action: if you are a palm, what is to be done with palm trees is to climb them and enjoy their fruit. The last two lines of the poem sustain the sense of a virtually real realm of simile by piling on a series of images contiguous with the initial one but not identical with it: from clusters of dates to grape clusters, from branches to apples, from the breath of the mouth and from grapes to wine-sweet kisses.

Another reflection of the poetics of flaunted figuration that contributes to the distinctive beauty of the Song of Songs is the flamboyant elaboration of the metaphor in fine excess of its function as the vehicle for any human or erotic tenor. In terms of the semantic patterns of biblical parallelism, this constitutes a special case of focusing, in which the second or third verset concretizes or characterizes a metaphor introduced in the first verset in a way that shifts attention from the frame of reference of the referent to the frame of reference of the metaphor. Let me quote from the exquisite poem addressed to the dancing Shulamite in Chapter 7 the vertical description of the woman, ascending from feet to head (7:2–6).

| 1 | How lovely your feet in sandals, | nobleman's daughter! |
| 2 | Your curving thighs are like ornaments, | the work of a master's hand. |

3	Your sex a rounded bowl—	may it never lack mixed wine!
4	Your belly a heap of wheat,	hedged about with lilies.
5	Your two breasts like two fawns,	twins of a gazelle.
6	Your neck like an ivory tower,	your eyes pools in Heshbon

by the gate of Bat-Rabbim.

| 7 | Your nose like the tower of David, | looking out toward Damascus. |
| 8 | Your head on you like crimson wool, | the locks of your head like purple, |

a king is caught in the flowing tresses.

This way of using metaphor will seem peculiar only if one insists upon imposing on the text the aesthetic of a later age. A prime instance of what I have called the misplaced concreteness of biblical research is that proponents of the theory of a fertility-cult liturgy have felt that the imagery of metallic ornament had to be explained as a reference to the statuette of a love goddess and the looming architectural imagery by an invoking of the allegedly supernatural character of the female addressed. This makes only a little more sense than to claim that when John Donne in "The Sunne Rising" writes, "She'is all States, and all Princes, I, / Nothing else is," he must be addressing, by virtue of the global imagery, some cosmic goddess and not sweet Ann Donne.

Our passage begins without simile for the simple technical reason that the second verset of line 1 is used to address the woman who is the subject of the enraptured description. After this point, the second (or, for the triadic lines, the third) verset of each line is employed quite consistently to flaunt the metaphor by pushing its frame of reference into the foreground. The poet sets no limit on and aims for no unity in the semantic fields from which he draws his figures, moving rapidly from artisanry to agriculture to the animal kingdom to architecture, and concluding with dyed textiles. (In the analogous vertical description of the lover, 5:10–16, the imagery similarly wanders from doves bathing in watercourses and beds of spices to artifacts of gold, ivory, and marble, though the semantic field of artifact dominates as the celebration of the male body concentrates on the beautiful hardness of arms, thighs, and loins.) There is nevertheless a tactical advantage in beginning the description with perfectly curved ornaments and a rounded bowl or goblet, for the woman's beauty is so exquisite that the best analogue for it is the craft of the master artisan, an implicit third term of comparison being the poet's fine craft in so nicely matching image with object for each lovely aspect of this body.

That implied celebration of artifice may explain in part the flamboyant elaboration of the metaphors in all the concluding versets. It should be observed, however, that the function of these elaborations changes from line to line in accordance with both the body part invoked and the position of the line in the poem. In line 2, "the work of a master's hand" serves chiefly as an intensifier of the preceding simile of ornament and as a way of foregrounding the idea of artifice at the beginning of the series. In lines 3–5, as the description moves upward from feet and thighs to the central erogenous zone of vagina, belly, and breasts, the elaborations of the metaphor in the second versets are a way of being at once sexually explicit and decorous through elegant *double entente*. That is, we are meant to be continuously aware of the sexual details referred to, but it is the wittily deployed frame of reference of the metaphor that is kept in the foreground of our vision: we know the poet alludes to the physiology of lovemaking, but we "see" a curved bowl that never runs dry; the wheat-like belly bordered by a hedge of lilies is an ingenious superimposition of an agricultural image on an erotic one, since lilies elsewhere are implicitly associated with pubic hair; the bouncing, supple, symmetrical breasts are not just two fawns but also, in the focusing elaboration, a gazelle's perfectly matched twins.

The geographical specifications of the final versets in lines 6 and 7 have troubled many readers. It seems to me that here, when the poet has moved above the central sexual area of the body, he no longer is impelled to work out a cunning congruity between image and referent by way of *double entente,* and instead he can give free rein to the exuberance of figurative elaboration that in different ways has been perceptible in all the previous metaphors. If, as his eye moves to neck and face, the quality of grandeur rather than supple sexual allure is now uppermost, there is a poetic logic in the speaker's expanding these images of soaring architectural splendor and making the figurative frame of reference so prominent that we move from the dancing Shulamite to the public world of the gate at Bat-Rabbim and the tower of Lebanon looking toward Damascus. As the lover's gaze moves up from the parts of the body usually covered and thus seen by him alone to the parts generally visible, it is appropriate that the similes for her beauty should be drawn now from the public realm.[8] In a final turn, moreover, of the technique of last-verset elaboration, the triadic line 8 introduces an element of climactic surprise: the Shulamite's hair having been compared to brilliantly dyed wool or fabric, we discover that a king is caught, or bound, in the tresses (the Hebrew for this last term is a little doubtful, but since the root suggests running motion, the reference to flowing hair in context seems probable). This amounts to a strong elaboration of a relatively weak metaphor, and an elaboration that subsumes the entire series of images that has preceded: the powerful allure of sandaled feet, curving thighs, and all the rest that has pulsated through every choice of image now culminates in the hair, where at last the lover, through the self-designation of king, introduces himself into the poem, quite literally interinvolves himself with the beloved ("a king is caught in the flowing tresses"). Up till now, she has been separate from him, dancing before his eager eye. Now, after a climactic line summarizing her beauty (7:7), he goes on to imagine embracing her and enjoying her (7:8–10, the climbing of the palm tree that I quoted earlier). It is a lovely illustration of how the exuberant metaphors carry the action forward.

Such obtrusions of metaphorical elaboration are allied with another distinctive mode of figuration of these poems, in which the boundaries between figure and referent, inside and outside, human body and accoutrement or natural setting, become suggestively fluid. Let me first cite three lines from the brief poem at the end of Chapter 1 (1:12–14):

While the king was on his couch,	my nard gave off its scent.
A sachet of myrrh is my lover to me,	between my breasts he lodges.
A cluster of cypress is my lover to me,	in the vineyards of Ein Gedi.

The first line is without figuration, the woman simply stating that she has scented her body for her lover. But the immediately following metaphoric representation of the lover as a sachet of myrrh—because he nestles between her breasts all night long—produces a delightful confusion between the literal nard with which she has perfumed herself and the figurative myrrh she cradles in her lover. Thus the act and actors of love become intertwined with the fragrant paraphernalia of love. The third line offers an alternative image of a bundle of aromatic herbs and then, in the second verset, one of those odd geographical specifications like those we encountered in our preceding text. I have not followed the New JPS and Marvin Pope in translating the second verset as "from the vineyards," because it seems to me that the Hebrew has an ambiguity worth preserving. Presumably the metaphor is elaborated geographically because the luxuriant oasis at Ein Gedi was especially known for its trees and plants with aromatic leaves, and so the specification amounts to a heightening of the original assertion. At the same time the initial Hebrew particle *be*, which usually means "in," leaves a teasing margin for imagining that it is not the cypress cluster that *comes from* Ein Gedi but the fragrant embrace of the lovers that takes place *in* Ein Gedi. Though this second meaning is less likely, it is perfectly consistent with the syntax of the line, and the very possibility of this construal makes it hard to be sure where the metaphor stops and the human encounter it represents begins. There is, in other words, an odd and satisfying consonance in this teasing game of transformations between the pleasure of play with language through metaphor and the pleasure of love play that is the subject of the lines. That same consonance[9] informs the beautiful poem that takes up all of Chapter 4, ending in the first verse of Chapter 5. It will provide an apt concluding illustration of the poetic art of the Song of Songs.

1	Oh, you are fair, my darling,	oh, you are fair, your eyes are doves.
2	Behind your veil, your hair like a flock of goats	streaming down Mount Gilead.

3	Your teeth are like a flock of ewes	coming up from the bath,
4	Each one bearing twins,	none bereft among them.
5	Like the scarlet thread your lips,	your mouth is lovely.
6	Like a pomegranate-slice your brow	behind your veil.
7	Like the tower of David your neck,	built in rows.*
8	A thousand shields are hung on it,	all the heroes' bucklers.
9	Your two breasts are like two fawns,	twins of the gazelle,
	browsing among the lilies.	
10	Until day breathes	and shadows flee
11	I'll betake me to the mount of myrrh	and to the hill of frankincense.
12	You are all fair, my darling,	there's no blemish in you.
13	With me from Lebanon, bride,	with me from Lebanon, come!
14	Descend from Amana's peak,	from the peak of Senir and Hermon,
15	From the dens of lions,	from the mounts of panthers.
16	You ravish my heart, bride,	you ravish my heart with one glance of your eyes,
	with one gem of your necklace.	
17	How fair your love, my sister and bride,	how much better your love than wine,
	and the scent of your ointments than any spice!	
18	Nectar your lips drip, bride,	honey and milk under your tongue,
	and the scent of your robes like Lebanon's scent.	
19	A locked garden, my sister and bride,	a locked pool, a sealed-up spring.
20	Your groove a grove of pomegranates	with luscious fruit,
	cypress with nard.	
21	Nard and saffron, cane and cinnamon,	with all aromatic woods,
22	Myrrh and aloes,	with all choice perfumes.
23	A garden spring,	a well of fresh water,
	flowing from Lebanon.	
24	Stir, north wind,	come, south wind,
25	Breathe on my garden,	let its spices flow.
26	"Let my lover come to his garden,	and eat its luscious fruit."
27	I've come to my garden, my sister and bride,	I've plucked my myrrh with my spice,
28	Eaten my honeycomb with my honey,	drunk my wine with my milk.
29	"Eat, friends, and drink,	be drunk with love."

As elsewhere in the Song of Songs, the poet draws his images from whatever semantic fields seem apt for the local figures—domesticated and wild animals, dyes, food, architecture, perfumes, and the floral world. Flamboyant elaboration of the metaphor, in which the metaphoric image takes over the foreground, governs the first third of the poem (lines 2–4, 7–9), culminating in the extravagant picture of the woman's neck as a tower hung with shields. The very repetition of *ke* ("like"), the particle of similitude, half a dozen times through these initial lines, calls attention to the activity of figurative comparison as it is being carried out. There is a certain witty ingenuity with which the elaborated metaphors are related to the body parts: twin-bearing, newly washed ewes to two perfect rows of white teeth and, perhaps, shields on the tower walls recalling the layered rows of a necklace.[10]

What I should like to follow out more closely, however, is the wonderful transformations that the landscape of fragrant mountains and gardens undergoes from line 11 to the end of the poem. The first mountain and hill—rarely has a formulaic word-pair been used so suggestively—in line 11 are metaphorical, referring to the body of the beloved or, perhaps, as some have proposed, more specifically to the *mons veneris*. It is interesting that the use of two nouns in the construct state to form a metaphor ("mount of myrrh," "hill of frankincense") is quite rare elsewhere in biblical poetry, though it will become a standard procedure in postbiblical Hebrew poetry. The naturalness with which the poet adopts that device here reflects how readily objects in the Song of Songs are changed into metaphors. The Hebrew for "frankincense" is *levonah*, which sets up an intriguing *faux raccord* with "Lebanon," *levanon*, two lines down. From the body as landscape—an identification already adumbrated in the comparison of hair to flocks coming down from the mountain and teeth to ewes coming up from the washing—the poem moves to an actual landscape with real rather than figurative promontories. If domesticated or in any case gentle animals populate the metaphorical landscape at the beginning, there is a new note of danger or excitement in the allusion to the lairs of panthers and lions on the real northern mountainside. The repeated verb "ravish" in line 16, apparently derived from *lev*, "heart," picks up in its sound (*libavtini*) the interecho of *levonah* and *levanon* and so triangulates the body-as-landscape, the external landscape, and the passion the beloved inspires.

The last thirteen lines of the poem, as the speaker moves toward the consummation of love intimated in lines 26–29, reflect much more of an orchestration of the semantic fields of the metaphors: fruit, honey, milk, wine, and, in consonance with the sweet fluidity of this list of edibles, a spring of fresh flowing water and all the conceivable spices that could grow in a well-irrigated garden. Lebanon, which as we have seen has already played an important role in threading back and forth between the literal and figurative landscapes, continues to serve as a unifier. The scent of the beloved's robes is like Lebanon's scent (line 18), no doubt because Lebanon is a place where aromatic trees grow, but also with the suggestion, again fusing figurative with literal, that the scent of Lebanon clings to her dress because she has just returned from there (lines 13–15). "All aromatic woods" in line 21 is literally in the Hebrew "all the trees of *levonah*," and the echo of *levonah-levanon* is carried forward two lines later when the locked spring in the garden wells up with flowing water (*nozlim*, an untranslatable poetic synonym for water) from Lebanon—whether because Lebanon, with its mountain streams, is the superlative locus of fresh running water, or because one is to suppose some mysterious subterranean feed-in from the waters of wild and mountainous Lebanon to this cultivated garden. In either case, there is a suggestive crossover back from the actual landscape to a metaphorical one. The garden at the end that the lover enters—and to "come to" or "enter" often has a technical sexual meaning in biblical Hebrew—is the body of the beloved, and one is not hard put to see the physiological fact alluded to in the fragrant flowing of line 25 (the same root as *nozlim* in line 23) that precedes the enjoyment of luscious fruit.

What I have just said, however, catches only one side of a restless dialectic movement of signification and as such darkens the delicately nuanced beauty of the poem with the shadow of reductionism. For though we know, and surely the original audience was intended to know, that the last half of the poem conjures up a delectable scene of love's consummation, this garden of aromatic plants, wafted by the gentle winds, watered by a hidden spring, is in its own right an alluring presence to the imagination before and after any decoding into a detailed set of sexual allusions. The poetry by the end becomes a kind of self-transcendence of *double entente*: the beloved's body is, in a sense, "represented" as a garden, but it also turns into a real garden, magically continuous with the mountain landscape so aptly introduced at the midpoint of the poem.

It is hardly surprising that only here in biblical poetry do we encounter such enchanting interfusions between the literal and metaphorical realms, because only here is the exuberant gratification of love through all five senses the subject. Prevalent preconceptions about the Hebrew Bible lead us to think of it as a collection of writings rather grimly committed to the notions of covenant, law, solemn obligation, and thus the very antithesis of the idea of play. There is more than a grain of truth in such preconceptions (one can scarcely imagine a Hebrew Aristophanes or a

Hebrew *Odyssey*), but the literary art of the Bible, in both prose narrative and poetry, reflects many more elements of playfulness than might meet the casual eye. Only in the Song of Songs, however, is the writer's art directed to the imaginative realization of a world of uninhibited self-delighting play, without moral conflict, without the urgent context of history and nationhood and destiny, without the looming perspectives of a theological world-view. Poetic language and, in particular, its most characteristic procedure, figuration, are manipulated as pleasurable substance: metaphor transforms the body into spices and perfumes, wine and luscious fruit, all of which figurative images blur into the actual setting in which the lovers enact their love, a natural setting replete with just those delectable things. There is a harmonious correspondence between poem and world, the world exhibiting the lovely tracery of satisfying linkages that characterizes poetry itself. In the fluctuating movement from literal to figurative and back again, both sides of the dialectic are enhanced: the inventions of the poetic medium become potently suffused with the gratifying associations of the erotic, and erotic longing and fulfillment are graced with the elegant aesthetic form of a refined poetic art.

IX

The Life of the Tradition

THESE CHAPTERS have been offered as an effort of loving restoration. Biblical poetry, unlike the remnants we now have of other ancient Near Eastern literatures, never had to be literally unearthed, but in the changing cultural light of three millennia some of its nicely shaded colors have faded, and its intricate designs have by stages been abraded and obscured by the shifting sands of preconception and misconception. In the worst cases, these accreted deposits of later theological and historical views and aesthetic values alien to the original texts have prevented readers from seeing that there was poetry here at all (with the usual exception of Psalms, Job, and the Song of Songs), or have encouraged readers to imagine in the Bible a kind of poetry only distantly related to the actual modes of expression and principles of organization of ancient Hebrew verse.

The discovery by Bishop Lowth in the mid-eighteenth century of the key poetic device of semantic parallelism was an important step toward seeing the original structures of the poems, but much of the work that has followed Lowth has complicated his categories without helpfully refining them or building on them, and that in turn has led to a baby-with-bathwater revisionism on the part of some contemporary scholars. In quite another direction, comparative Semitic philology and continuing archaeological excavation have made their own contributions to the clearing away of the sediment of time by giving us more precise notions of what many biblical words mean and what artifacts, cultural practices, and institutions may be alluded to in the texts, though this admirable enterprise has too often been carried on with no attention, or at best rather misguided attention, to the poetic form in which the words of the texts are cast.

The aim of my own inquiry has been not only to attempt to get a firmer grasp of biblical poetics but also to suggest an order of essential connection between poetic form and meaning that for the most part has been neglected by scholarship. For if I have used the image of brushing away deposits from a beautiful surface to describe the task at hand, I should add that poetry is quintessentially the mode of expression in which the surface is the depth, so that through careful scrutiny of the configurations of the surface—the articulation of the line, the movement from line to poem, the imagery, the arabesques of syntax and grammar, the design of the poem as a whole—we come to apprehend more fully the depth of the poem's meaning.

The choice of the poetic medium for the Job poet, or for Isaiah, or for the psalmist, was not merely a matter of giving weight and verbal dignity to a preconceived message but of uncovering or discovering meanings through the resources of poetry. In manifold ways, some of which I try to illustrate here from chapter 4 onward, poetry is a special way of imagining the world or, to put this in more cognitive terms, a special mode of thinking with its own momentum and its own peculiar advantages. It strikes me that this is a generalization that holds as true for Jeremiah or Proverbs as for Byron or Baudelaire, but the status of the Bible in the Western world as Holy Writ has discouraged the perception of it as a body of literature that uses poetry to *realize* meanings. There have been, of course, perennial admirers of the sublimity of biblical poetry, but such admiration has rarely been accompanied by an understanding that the spiritual, intellectual, and emotional values of the Bible that continue to concern us so urgently are inseparable from the form they are given in the poems.

But if, as I have been arguing, the surface of biblical poetry needs to be delicately brushed so that we can both enjoy its beauty and see its profundity better, I would also like to stress that the object in question has never really been buried. In any poetic system, a good many of the complex effects of the poem are communicated to the reader or listener subliminally, though a conscious awareness of certain salient formal devices may help focus attentiveness. Let us suppose that a literary-philological scholar from another planet, having arrived on earth, had through diligent application achieved a reasonably good control of Elizabethan English and had set himself to the study of Shakespeare's sonnets. With no experience in his own extraterrestrial literature of any poetic phenomenon remotely like rhyme, he would quite fail to see the organization of the sonnets in quatrains and concluding couplets, and he would of course miss the ironies and complications and reinforcements of meaning that Shakespeare concentrates through the binding together of particular rhyme-words. No doubt the academic followers of our visiting scholar on his home planet would continue to miss this crucial feature, until the understanding of the sonnet form would be set right by the appearance of some extraterrestrial Bishop Lowth. In the interim, however, at least some of the beauty and power of Shakespeare would still be seen, if rather askew, whether in the imagery or the forms of address or the development of ideas, or through scarcely visible channels of meaning that the scholars themselves could not have analyzed.

By and large, this has been the fate of biblical poetry over the centuries. Even through the film of misconception and translation, it was not infrequently perceived as a repository of luminous and impressive poetic achievement. This feeling is attested by recurrent encomiums and, more impressively, by volumes of verse like Byron's *Hebrew Melodies* and Else Lasker-Schüler's *Hebräische Balladen,* which are transpositions of biblical materials into a very different poetic key, informed not necessarily by any sure understanding of how the original poems work but by a sense that they are formidably there as poems to be reckoned with.

Since poets, however, are by sensibility and practice adept in the peculiar kinds of thinking that belong to poetry, it is not surprising that through the ages one finds a good deal of fine intuitive understanding of biblical poetry on the part of poets responding to it through their work in various languages. One of the chief ways in which ancient Hebrew poetry has continued to live is in the poems later writers have fashioned out of it. This is most strikingly true for postbiblical Hebrew poetry, which forms a remarkable continuous tradition over nearly two thousand years that again and again recurs to biblical language and biblical images,[1] down to the latest Israeli contemporaries, and that in its "classical" medieval period (roughly, eleventh- to fourteenth-century Spain) seeks to shape its language almost exclusively out of biblical locutions. One instructive testimony to the responsiveness of the poets to the biblical poems is the way the Song of Songs was used in medieval Hebrew love poetry. The official position of Jewish culture on the Song of Songs was, of course, that it was an allegory of the love between God (the male figure) and the Community of Israel (the woman). One may suppose that, on some level, the poets, like other believing Jews, took the allegorical reading quite seriously, and it surfaces in some beautiful liturgical poems in which exiled Israel pleads to God as a once-loved bride who has been driven away by her spouse. But in the thoroughly secular and often boldly explicit erotic poems, one poet after another mines the Song of Songs for idioms and metaphors, demonstrating that the intricate double meanings, the teasing play between figurative foreground and literal sexual background, were as nicely understood then as they are likely to be in any modern analysis.

In certain respects, the Bible was more directly available as a model of poetic emulation in the Middle Ages and the Renaissance because there was a greater congruence then between biblical poetic practice and prevalent conceptions of the purpose of poetry than has existed since. The Bible, that is, knows nothing of the personal lyric; the anonymity of all but prophetic poetry in the Bible is an authentic reflection of its fundamentally collective nature. I of course don't mean to suggest that poetic composition in ancient Israel was a group activity, only that the finished composition was meant to address the needs and concerns of the group, and was most commonly fashioned out of traditional materials and according to familiar conventional patterns that made it readily usable by the group for liturgical or celebratory or educational purposes. This orientation toward collective expression also explains the formal conservatism of biblical poetry. Despite the claims of some scholars, it is not easy to distinguish stylistically between a psalm composed in the tenth century B.C.E. and one written during the Second Commonwealth, because the same conventions, the same poetic norms, the same stockpile of images, were used for psalm composition through the whole thousand-year era of biblical literary productivity, and as late as the Qumran Scrolls. (One has only to contemplate the contrasting example of English poetry, which in little more than a century and a half underwent the startling shifts from Neoclassical to Romantic to Victorian to Modern.)

Now, this collective and traditionalist impulse of biblical poetry accorded nicely with a predisposition of Western poets until the Romantic revolution to conceive of their activity as a transmissible craft, the poet aspiring to be a master artisan rather than a daring explorer of the unique experience of the self. John Hollander has described this notion of poetry quite aptly in an essay on Ben Jonson, whose concerns, he says, "were for creating discourse in an ideal community, within which the literary dialect would be as speech" and for exploiting poetic allusion in a way "recognizable not only to a coterie of poets and gentlemen-scholars, but to a whole culture as well."[2] From a late-twentieth-century perspective, this very notion of the dialect of an ideal community may seem rather alien because so many trends of poetry since the early Moderns, and since Rimbaud and Mallarmé in France before them, have moved in the opposite direction of transforming poetry into a congeries of idiolects. For a long time, however, in many places and languages, poetry was practiced as such a dialect, and the ideal community, which for Western poets included in the first instance the major writers of classical Greece and Rome, was also often extended to the biblical poets, while for those writing in Hebrew the biblical poets were the very founders of that ideal community.

This continuity is most obvious when a poet is composing a hymn of praise to God, a supplication *de profundis,* a Proverb-like aphoristic reflection, or an avowedly liturgical poem. But even when you are writing a love poem or a nature poem, the biblical models will seem more apt if your aim is not to catch a single, unique moment, sensation, or relation but to fashion through your own perception a finely wrought verbal artifact that is intended to be seen as one of a timeless group of such artifacts. Wordsworth looking at the light dawning over Westminster Bridge tries to evoke in words an experience that is uniquely his, though of course he wants to make it intelligible to others through the act of writing. The psalmist, looking up at the moon and stars and pondering the majesty of the heaven and earth God made, uses his own feeling and perception as his point of departure, but they are not really his subject. Rather, in seeing this moment of the natural world's splendor, he is reminded of the timeless truth of the creation story, and he celebrates the created world not as an individual with a unique freight of personal experience but as a member of and eloquent spokesman for the generic category—man.

When I spoke of the "availability" of the Bible as a model for poets, I had in mind something more substantive than the use of the ancient text as a source for allusions. Just as one can write a poem about Leda and the swan without an intrinsic relation between the mode of expression of the new poem and any ancient text, one can easily invoke Leviathan or depth calling to depth without a sense of connection to the distinctive life of the poetry in Job or Psalms. I would suppose that such allusion rather than deep poetic engagement has been the most prevalent use of the Bible by later poets because most of them—again with the notable exception of those writing in Hebrew—have known the Bible from a certain distance, and scarcely as a body of poetic texts, in contrast to Greek and Latin poetry, which poets for so long conned as schoolboys line by line. Nevertheless, moments of deep engagement with the poetry of the Bible do occur, and they reveal how the intrinsic workings of that poetry continued to be grasped, however intuitively, even in ages when the scholars and exegetes had no helpful guidance at all to offer.

Let me propose a rough historical generalization, which I will go on to illustrate with one poem from the Renaissance and one from our own period. Until the watershed in the course of Western poetry that is located around the turn of the nineteenth century, both assumptions about poetry and assumptions of faith made possible, on occasion, an inner congruence between the poetic expression of the later writer and the biblical poets he had absorbed. This congruence might in some instances mean a kind of ventriloquism or, more commonly, an adaptation of the ancient poems in which something of their distinctive poetic movement lived on. Once the sense of "ideal community" broke down— beginning, let us say for convenience' sake, with Blake—for various reasons and with various poetic consequences, it became much more common for writers engaged in the Bible to wrestle with it—as, to cite the central American instance, Melville did in prose in *Moby-Dick*— forcing pieces of its language into radically new contexts, riding with the poetic momentum of the biblical texts toward ends that might be intermittently in consonance with them but more often at cross-purposes with them. These wrestlings with biblical poems are also instructive encounters because as confrontations between poet and poet they generally are not just arguments with an idea or creed but also imaginative responses to a way of saying something, often indeed acts of poetic emulation in the midst of argumentation or ironization.

As an example of a poem clearly congruent with its biblical sources, I should like to quote a brief seventeenth-century text by George Herbert, who is arguably the greatest Protestant poet in English. The poem is called "Antiphon"; the musical conception and allusion are characteristic of Herbert, though the poem does not exhibit the flamboyant virtuoso effects of his more anthologized pieces:

> Let all the world in ev'ry corner sing,
> My God and King.
>
> The heav'ns are not too high,
> His praise may thither flie:
> The earth is not too low,
> His praises there may grow.
>
> Let all the world in ev'ry corner sing,
> My God and King.

The Art of Biblical Poetry

The church with psalms must shout.
No doore can keep them out:
But above all, the heart
Must bear the longest part.

Let all the world in ev'ry corner sing,
My God and King.

The refrain is of course a conflated paraphrase of a number of lines from Psalms (for example, "Let the heavens rejoice and earth exult," Ps. 96:11), and the balanced complementary bracketing of heaven and earth in the first stanza recalls the beginning of many biblical poems, particularly from Psalms, where the heavens are especially associated with the praise of God ("The heavens tell the glory of God, / and His handiwork the firmament declares," Ps. 19:2). The Herbertian fidelity to the concrete image makes the praise "fly" up to the sky and "grow" on the earth, perhaps in oblique reference to the birds of the heavens and the growing things of the field in Genesis. But what is particularly interesting about this simple yet effective poem is the way it reenacts the focusing dynamic of biblical poetry. There is a happy congruence between the tendency of biblical poetry to move from large to small, container to contained, outer to inner, and Herbert's imaginative orientation away from scary spaces and toward enclosures, cozy interiors. (In an exemplary line, he writes elsewhere of nature as "a box where sweets compacted lie.") The poem glides, quite biblically, from heaven to earth to house to heart within the house. The directional force of the songs of praise in this scheme is a little surprising: "No doore can keep them out" suggests that the psalms do not emanate from the church but rather surge into the church, and into the heart, from the great world outside. The "longest part" that the heart must bear is obviously a musical part in the hymn of praise. The heart in Psalms is more often said to exult but can also sing: "My heart and my flesh sing out to the living God" (Ps. 84:3).

The focusing parallelism of the poem, then, is not, as some might imagine, an expression of Protestant inwardness that transforms the background of the Hebrew Bible from which it draws but rather a line of poetic development—or, if you will, poetic thinking—that springs from a sure intuition of the dynamics of biblical poetry and its relation to the life of the spirit. The interlocking structure of creation, "all the world in ev'ry corner," resounds with God's praise because its harmony reveals the perfect handiwork of the Creator, but, as parallel terms move in ordered sequence toward a focus, the human heart stands at the center of the great picture, and precisely as we find again and again in Psalms, man's divine gift of articulateness, his ability to confirm God's majesty in song, is the culmination of the poem and of the whole order of creation. Though stanzaic forms and rhymed couplets are not part of the poetic repertoire of the ancient psalmists, this is nevertheless a poem that re-creates in the idiom of its own age and culture the poetic matrix of many Hebrew psalms.

Herbert's "Antiphon" may seem a special case because it is, after all, a virtually liturgical poem and as such might be expected to have close affinities of feeling and expression with the poems in Psalms that were explicitly framed for use in the celebration of the ancient temple cult. But there are also many poignantly personal notes in Psalms (as in other biblical poetry), for all its anonymity and its collective orientation; and these Hebrew poems have continued to speak through the work of later poets, even as tensions and dissonances have increasingly emerged between the assumptions of the biblical poets and those of their modern counterparts. Again, I should like to stress that in the most interesting cases what is involved is not merely the allusion to an idea or the borrowing of a key phrase but also the partial or extended adoption of a mode of poetic speech, which implies a particular way of imagining the world.

As my modern illustration of the continuing presence of biblical poetics I would like to offer an untitled ten-line poem by the contemporary Israeli poet Tuvia Rübner. The very diction of the poem, which will not be altogether evident in my translation, is a striking testimony to that continuity of poetic tradition in Hebrew of which I spoke before. The poem is written, one would have to say, in modern Hebrew, and there is nothing in it that would strike a cultivated contemporary Hebrew reader as willfully archaic. Yet virtually all the language of the poem is biblical, the sole postbiblical term being the verb "diminish" in the fourth line, accompanied there and in the following line by a postbiblical progressive verb tense. The language of the poem, in other words, would offer few difficulties to the comprehension of the ancient psalmist, just as, conversely, the poetic movement of the millennia-old Psalms remains remarkably accessible to this modern poet.

> Why have You forsaken me? Why have You hidden Your face?
> How can You say without me? For
> it's not enough with worm and tree and dust. I become
> entangled among my words, become diminished
> in a vale with no man by me among the shadows
> I fear the silence I am entangled in words

without You I see only my hands
and they are too heavy to bear my fallen face
without Your eyes
as a candle the flame I seek Your face.

The poem begins with a double citation from Psalms, echoing both the famous "My God, my God, why have You forsaken me?" (Ps. 22:2) and the beginning of another psalm of supplication that we had occasion to examine earlier, "How long, Lord, will You forget me perpetually, / how long will You hide Your face from me?" (Ps. 13:2).[3] The real point, however, as I have been saying, is not citation but poetic assimilation. The poem begins, that is, with a line that is a perfect instance of biblical parallelism, but then the symmetry of parallelism is strenuously broken, as are the demarcations of the end-stopped line and the clarities of an unambiguous syntax. For this is a poem about a man stumbling through a dark wilderness of words ("I become entangled" is literally "I go [or, walk] and am entangled"), and much of the point of the poem's form is the implicit renunciation of that steady biblical progression of parallel utterances moving to a climax of intensification and a turning point of deliverance, as in Psalm 13. The poem, in fact, springs from a radical doubt already reflected in the truncation of the biblical phrase "hide Your face *from me*" to "hidden Your face," intimating a world in which the speaker is in straits but from which, moreover, he feels God's visible presence has been withdrawn.

But if this speaker's argument tears off at a troubling tangent from that of the biblical poet, all the terms through which he imagines his predicament are thoroughly biblical. By "terms" I mean not just the words used but also the conception of reality woven from them. Rübner picks up from Psalms, and behind Psalms from Genesis, the quintessential biblical notion of the nexus of speech that binds man and God. This is not merely an abstract doctrine but, as the framer of these lines knows with a penetration of artistic intuition, an informing poetic principle in Psalms, where so many poems, as we have seen, are built out of an exquisitely self-conscious use of speech, beginning and ending with the praiser's celebration of praise, or moving pointedly from silence to voice, or from the felt efficacy of pleading to a climax of poetic thanksgiving. God speaks the world and man into being, and man answers by speaking songs unto the Lord. In our poem, however, the supplicant is pursued by a dread that a radical break may have occurred, and so he is impelled to ask God whether He can have speech without man's answering speech, whether a world of mute things (the catalogue in the third line obliquely recalls the creation before man in Genesis) can really suffice. The syntactical stammer, the ambiguous spillover of clause into clause, is the precise correlative of this dread that human speech has no theological ground, no divine authentication, and is doomed to be engulfed by the silence that waits in the valley of the shadow.

To the end, the poem is a transposition into a modernist key of Psalm 13. There, we may recall, the speaker begged of God, "Look, answer me, / light up my eyes, / lest I sleep death." The body imagery of Psalms, which is at once part of a series of Hebrew idioms—for example, "hand" for power, "heart" for understanding—and a way of representing human predicaments with physical concreteness, has been deeply assimilated by Rübner. "Face" in the Bible often means presence; a fallen face is dejection or fear. Here, the scrambling and juxtaposition of idioms reconcretizes them with a small effect of shock. Without God's look to light up the eyes, only the outlines of one's own impotent hands can be made out, hands too heavy to lift a fallen face. According to Proverbs, "A candle of the Lord, is the soul of man" (Prov. 20:27), but here "soul" remains an unstated term, barely hinted at in the final candle image, because it is a word that assumes more than the poet is prepared to assume. Nevertheless, something in the speaker, whether fallen face or heavy hand or mouth emitting a confusing tangle of words, longs for the face that gives light, flame, life.

I have felt the need to paraphrase the poem in this fashion in order to suggest how a text that, from one point of view, might be described as a pastiche of phrases from Psalms is in fact profoundly animated by the poetry of Psalms. There is a particular structure of supplication to which the poet alludes but from which he finds it necessary to swerve sharply. There is a particular poetic vocabulary for expressing the human quandary in the midst of daunting existence before the sight of God, and this the poet enlists, fracturing and reassembling its components in an effort to recapture something essential of the ancient eloquent prayers for deliverance after seeming abandonment.

Let me conclude by proposing a musical metaphor to complement the archaeological figure with which I began. There is in all the genres of biblical poetry, even beyond the phonetic system that we now so imperfectly understand, an expressive music whose fine pulsations have continued to be heard through the ages. The most impressive testimony to the continuing ability of many readers to hear that music is in the creations of later writers who have responded poetically to biblical poetry. For less advantaged readers, the sounds of other melodies and a vast volume of mixed background noise have tended to drown out all but the most prominent strains, while poets, by their very relation to their medium, have often been able to tune out the extraneous and tune in the essential music. We cannot all be poets, but what some are privileged to grasp through an act of imaginative penetration others may accomplish more prosaically, step by step through patient analysis. We will of course never be able to hear these poems again precisely as they were once heard in ancient Israel, but the effort to set aside certain literary and religious prejudices and recover what we can of biblical poetics is abundantly warranted. Even a limited success in the enterprise of recovery should help us take in more fully the extraordinary force of these ancient poems, the intricate substantive links between the poetic vehicle and the religious vision of the poets, and the crucial place of the corpus of biblical poetry in the complex growth of the Western literary tradition.

NOTES

CHAPTER I

1. Douglas K. Stuart, *Studies in Early Hebrew Meter* (Missoula, Mont., 1976).

2. Michael O'Connor, *Hebrew Verse Structure* (Winona Lake, Ind., 1980). An equally unconvincing if simpler attempt to make syntax the governing principle is Terrence Collins, *Line-Forms in Biblical Poetry* (Rome, 1978). Having discovered that only a limited number of sentence types appear in a line of biblical verse, Collins concludes, for some unclear reason, that syntax must have determined the line.

3. E.g., Jerzy Kurylowicz, *Studies in Semitic Grammar and Metrics* (Warsaw, 1972).

4. James L. Kugel, *The Idea of Biblical Poetry* (New Haven and London, 1981).

5. Barbara Herrnstein Smith, *Poetic Closure* (Chicago, 1968), pp. 23, 24.

6. Benjamin Hrushovski, "Prosody, Hebrew," *Encyclopaedia Judaica* (New York, 1971), vol. 13, pp. 1200–1202.

7. It is curious, and perhaps revelatory, that Kugel, in a heavily annotated book in which, among hundreds of other sources, he cites two articles of Hrushovski's on modern prosody, should never mention Hrushovski's discussion of biblical versification and yet devote page after page to other approaches that patently won't work.

8. See Samuel R. Levin, *Linguistic Structures in Poetry* ('S-Gravenhage, 1962), especially pp. 49–50, 61–62.

9. T. H. Robinson, *The Poetry of the Old Testament* (London, 1947), p. 21.

10. Ruth apRoberts, "Old Testament Poetry: The Translatable Structure," *PMLA* 92:5 (October 1977), pp. 987–1004.

11. A rather different, Chomskyan use of the concept of deep structure has been applied to parallelism by Edward L. Greenstein in "How Does Parallelism Mean?" *Jewish Quarterly Review Supplement*, 1982, pp. 41–70. He is able to rescue the concept of semantic parallelism in virtually all cases by assuming that where there appear to be semantic discrepancies between versets, the same "deep structure" of meaning is in fact expressed, apparent differences being attributable to the mere surface elaboration of the poem. But surely no real reader of poetry responds to a text in this way. Poetry is significant form—which is to say, its depth and precision of statement, like its beauty, inhere in the elaboration of the verbal surface. It is to particularly chosen words in a particular order that the reader responds. We are thus entitled to be highly suspicious of any theory that ultimately discounts the finely crafted contours of the poem's verbal form.

12. Viktor Shklovsky, "Art as Technique," in *Russian Formalist Criticism*, ed. L. T. Lemon and M. J. Reis (Lincoln, Neb., 1965), p. 21.

13. J. G. Herder, *Vom Geist der erbräischer Poesie* (Dessau, 1782), p. 23.

14. To the extent that one does find stock pairs of words where the sequence is generally the same, there is no reason to assume a single explanation in all cases. It could be because that is the way the pairings were passed on to the poets by pre-Israelite literary tradition, or because of tacit phonetic rules (e.g., putting a bisyllabic before a trisyllabic term), or because of the tendency to place the ordinary term before the literary equivalent.

15. Andrew Welsh, *Roots of Lyric: Primitive Poetry and Modern Poetics* (Princeton, 1978).

16. Kugel, p. 8.

17. It is quite possible to break up these lines differently and attach what I set out here as the first verset of the first line to the end of the preceding line in the text (not quoted here). In point of fact, the verset in question "hovers" between the two lines, serving a

double function; its role in the sequential chain I describe is thus clear no matter how one divides the lines.

18. Kugel, pp. 46–47, makes a similar argument.

CHAPTER II

1. I am indebted to Jack Sasson and Uriel Simon for sharpening my understanding of this point.

2. Shemaryahu Talmon, "The 'Comparative Method' in Biblical Interpretation—Principles and Problems," *Göttingen Congress Volume* (Leiden, 1978), p. 354.

3. Robert Alter, *The Art of Biblical Narrative* (New York, 1981), pp. 23–62.

4. Benjamin Hrushovski, "Prosody, Hebrew," *Encyclopaedia Judaica* (New York, 1971), Vol. 13, pp. 1200–1202.

5. Others, ignoring the immediate context, render this as "stored treasure."

6. It is, admittedly, also possible to construe all these verbs of falling and lying as references, in the pluperfect, to Sisera's going to sleep, in which case the phrase "between her legs" would have to be rendered as "at her feet." But such a reading seems to me strained, in terms of both the narrative context and the semantic range of the crucial verbs.

7. See especially Umberto Cassuto, *A Commentary on the Book of Exodus*, trans. Israel Abrahams (Jerusalem, 1967), pp. 173–181.

8. The Masoretic text at this point is unintelligible. My translation is no more than an educated guess, involving an emended vocalization of one word.

9. William Youngren, "Generality in Augustan Satire," in *In Defense of Reading*, ed. Reuben A. Brower and Richard Poirier (New York, 1962), pp. 206–234.

10. My thanks to Marc Bernstein for this alert observation.

CHAPTER III

1. Jurij Lotman, *The Structure of the Artistic Text*, trans. Ronald Vroom (Ann Arbor, 1977), pp. 126–127.

2. For this observation on the reversal of genre I am indebted to Nitza Kreichman.

3. A striking approximation, however, of this compactness has been achieved by Stephen Mitchell in his bold translation of Job, *Into the Whirlwind* (New York, 1979).

CHAPTER IV

1. For an intelligently argued version of this view, see Robert Gordis, *The Book of God and Man: A Study of Job* (Chicago, 1965). Gordis also offers some apt commentary on the argument of the Voice from the Whirlwind, but without close attention to the links between argument and poetic form.

2. I follow the New Jewish Publication Society translation here, which cites the Aramaic 'oria as warrant for this rendering. The ordinary sense of the Hebrew 'or is simply "light."

3. I am indebted to a valuable conversation with Moshe Greenberg for this general point.

4. Marvin H. Pope, *The Book of Job*, rev. ed. (Garden City, N.Y., 1975).

5. The Hebrew word literally means "tail," but the context of the two lines makes compelling the suggestion of several commentators that here it is a euphemism for the phallus.

Notes

6. My thanks to James Williams for this observation.

7. This feature was called to my attention by Uriel Simon.

8. Some modern translations render this as "glimmerings of the dawn," which has the advantage of smoothness, but the Hebrew word in question does elsewhere mean "eyelids," and I see no persuasive reason not to read it as a bold metaphor for the first gleam of light.

9. The only other occurrence in the Bible of this designation, "proud beasts," *benei shaḥatz,* is also in Job, in the Hymn to Wisdom (28:8), and there it clearly indicates wild beasts, not mythic ones, who live in inaccessible wildernesses.

CHAPTER V

1. Yeshurun Keshet, *The Poetry of the Bible* (Hebrew) (Tel Aviv, 1954), p. 126.

2. A convenient summary of Gunkel's views is available in English translation in *The Psalms: A Form-Critical Introduction,* trans. T. M. Horner (Philadelphia, 1967).

3. Jurij Lotman, *The Structure of the Artistic Text,* trans. Ronald Vroom (Ann Arbor, 1977), p. 23.

4. A related point about the switch from active to passive, and intransitive to transitive verbs, has been made by R. Lack in "Le psaume 1—Une analyse structurale," *Biblica* 57 (1977), pp. 154–167. Lack's article includes several shrewd perceptions about the poem, but, like most Structuralist analyses, it proposes patterns that are altogether too abstract and complicated to reflect the reading experience of real readers, and his argument for eschatological implications in a poem that seems so this-worldly is not persuasive.

5. The Masoretic text reads, ungrammatically, *tenah,* which is presumed to mean "give." I have followed others in vocalizing the word *tunah,* which then makes good sense as "told" or "recounted."

6. Mitchell Dahood, a commentator ever alert to Ugaritic backgrounds, makes the same suggestion, rather more confidently. See his *Psalms I* (Garden City, N.Y., 1966), pp. 50–51.

7. The phrase might mean "the outlying towns of Judea."

8. The verb occurs only here. Others render it "pass through."

9. For a discussion of the sea/land confrontation in Exodus 15, see pp. 50–54 of this book.

10. I vocalize the Masoretic *yordi* ("my going down") as *yordei* ("the goers-down of") because the former construction in the Hebrew is grammatically anomalous.

CHAPTER VI

1. Barbara Herrnstein Smith, *On the Margins of Discourse* (Chicago, 1978), especially Chapter 2.

2. See pp. 40–43 of this book.

3. My categories, of course, are both general and overlapping, but by this point the reader will no doubt have realized that my whole approach to biblical poetry tries to avoid the proliferation of taxonomies, which in my view very rapidly reaches a point of diminishing returns for helpful literary analysis. Those interested in an ambitious attempt to classify the structures of prophetic discourse, including a lengthy review of previous scholarly hypotheses on the subject, may consult Claus Westermann, *Basic Forms of Prophetic Speech,* trans. H. C. White (London, 1967). Westermann's effort to reconstruct the *evolution* of prophetic discourse through form-critical analysis is interesting but, of necessity, highly conjectural. Symptomatically, his analysis of "forms" makes no distinction whatever between poetry and prose and never addresses the fact that the prophets used a poetic vehicle.

Notes

4. Some construe 1:10–21 as the second half of the poem we have been considering. What links the two is Sodom and Gomorrah at the beginning of the second poem and the repetition of the notion of the land being devoured. Otherwise, the concerns of 1:10–21 seem rather different from those of 1:2–9, though there is a complementary relation between the two. One unavoidable complication of dealing with the Prophets is that the boundaries between poems are sometimes ambiguous.

5. David Noel Freedman, "Discourse on Prophetic Discourse," in *The Quest for the Kingdom of God*, ed. H. B. Hoffman, F. A. Spire, and A. R. W. Green (Winona Lake, Ind., 1983), pp. 141–158.

6. The Hebrew actually says "pit," but I have substituted another kind of pitfall to preserve something of the triple sound-play (*paḥad, paḥat, paḥ*).

CHAPTER VII

1. Maynard Mack, " 'Wit and Poetry and Pope': Some Observations on His Imagery," in *Eighteenth-Century English Literature*, ed. J. L. Clifford (New York, 1959), pp. 21–41.

2. James G. Williams, *Those Who Ponder Proverbs* (Sheffield, 1981), p. 68.

3. R. B. Y. Scott, *Proverbs/Ecclesiastes* (Garden City, N.Y., 1965), p. 117.

4. See, e.g., John Mark Thompson, *The Form and Function of Proverbs in Ancient Israel* (The Hague, 1974), p. 75.

5. See pp. 54–61 of this book.

6. R. B. Y. Scott provides a sad illustration of the rage for fragmentation that has characterized so much biblical scholarship in the way he breaks the poem off at verse 14 and reads what follows as a series of brief proverbs unconnected with the poem. It does not seem to occur to him that an evocation of marital fidelity might be the appropriate flip side of a poetic warning about loose women rather than evidence of another poem, and his atomistic assumptions prevent him from seeing the clear signals of an envelope structure in lines 20–23. See Scott, pp. 53–54, 57–58.

CHAPTER VIII

1. For a sensible overview of the highly uncertain dating issue, see Marvin H. Pope, *Song of Songs* (Garden City, N.Y., 1977), pp. 22–34.

2. Beyond allegory, though ultimately related to it, one may see a religious dimension in the Song by referring all its images to archetypal and cosmic realities, as does Francis Landy in *Paradoxes of Paradise: Identity and Difference in the Song of Songs* (Sheffield, 1983). I find this reading intriguing but ultimately strained. Landy's book is also the most imaginative and plausible of recent attempts to see the book as a poetic unity rather than as a collection.

3. For an illuminating study of this phenomenon, see Moshe Greenberg, *Biblical Prose Prayer* (Berkeley and Los Angeles, 1983).

4. Older translations render this "my soul," more recent versions simply "I." Since the Hebrew term serves chiefly as an intensifier, I have, for want of a better solution, added the adverb "so."

5. Intensive development of innovative imagery can also occur, but given the general prevalence of conventional imagery, it is much more common to find such development used to give stock images a force they would not otherwise possess, and so for practical purposes it constitutes a category distinct from innovative imagery.

6. Benjamin Hrushovski, "Poetic Metaphor and Frames of Reference," *Poetics Today* 5:1 (1984), pp. 5–43.

Notes

7. I am grateful to Chana Kronfeld for this last point.

8. For this last observation, I am again indebted to Chana Kronfeld.

9. I am grateful to Ilana Patinkin, whose analysis of this poem in a seminar paper helped draw my attention to the importance of the ambiguous relation between body and landscape.

10. On this see Pope, pp. 467–468, and the illustration he reproduces on p. 454.

CHAPTER IX

1. The reader can get some sense of the fascinating continuity of this tradition from T. Carmi's fine bilingual anthology *The Penguin Book of Hebrew Verse* (New York, 1981).

2. John Hollander, *Vision and Resonance: Two Senses of Poetic Form* (New York, 1975), p. 184.

3. See pp. 63–68 of this book.

GENERAL INDEX

Accusation: direct, in reproof, 141, 142; satire and, 142, 143; in vocative poetry, 146
Ada, 7, 17, 18
Address: direct, prophetic poetry and, 140; modes of, audience and, 143
Advertising jingle, proverb and, 163
Albright, W. F., 185
Alliteration, 53, 78, 166; onomatopoeic, 25
Allusion, 123, 153; sexual, 202
American New Critics, 113
Amos, 76, 140
Analogy, 118
Anaphora, *x*, 65, 75; in prophetic poetry, 144; as repetition, 64
Anat, 46
Ancient Israel, 185, 207; Wisdom schools of, 163; *see also* Israel
Ancient Near East: mourning practices in, 74; verse narrative in, 28; Wisdom literature in, 167
"Antiphon" (George Herbert), 209–11
Antiproverb, 170
Antithesis, 116, 171; intensifying, 174; as proverb category, 169; symmetry of, 178
Antonym, 167, 168
Aphorism, 172
Apocalypse, 147, 154
apRoberts, Ruth, 10
Arabic poetry, of medieval Spain, 113
Argument: didactic, 27; reflective, 27
"Art as Technique" (V. Shklovsky), 10
Art of Biblical Literature, The (R. Alter), *ix*, 28
Assonance, 53, 80
Assyria, 145, 151, 152
Audience, modes of address and, 143
Augustan verse; *see* English Augustan verse

Baal, 119
Babylonia, 151
Balaam, 20, 174
Barak, 48
Bat-Rabbim, 198
Baudelaire, Charles, 205
Behemoth, 94, 105, 106, 107, 108

Beth El, 75, 140
Biblical Hebrew: tense and mood in, 131; translation difficulties from, 165–66
Biblical poetry: actual sound of, 4; formal structure of, 6; Greek versification and, 9, 108; meter in, 9; organizing principle of, 3–5; prosody, *ix*, 8, 9, 18–19, 28; translation of, 9
Binary oppositions, 78, 97; in versets, 29
Birth imagery, 100, 101, 127
Blake, William, 209
Breakup pattern, 72
Byron, George, 205

Cain, 5, 7, 11
Canaan, 54
Canaanites: cosmogonic myth, 99; court ladies, 46; creation myth, 90; literature, 28
Candide (Voltaire), 121
Cause to effect movement, heightening and, 65
Celestial upperworld, 150
Characterization, 49, 57–58
Cherub, 36
Chiasm, 127, 167
Chinese-box construction, 140
Cilicia, 123
Cinema, temporal progression and, 39
Cliches, 190, 191, 192
Climactic structure, heightening and, 62–63
Climax: linear development to, 72; reversal and, 72
Closure, 6, 7, 119
Collective voice, in psalms, 114
Colon, verset and, 9
Complementarity, 29; semantic parallelism and, 56
Concluding couplet, in Shakespearian sonnet, 66
Concretization, 19, 21, 29; *see also* Dramatization; Focusing; Heightening; Intensification; Specification
Confession, 127, 128
Confession of Innocence, 93
Consequentiality, 29, 32, 33, 34

General Index

Consolation poetry, 156, 158
Conventional imagery; *see* Imagery; *see also* Stock imagery
Conventionality, of psalms, 112
Cosmogony, 94, 100; procreation and, 99
Cosmogonic imagery; *see* Imagery
Cosmogonic myth; *see* Canaanites: cosmogonic myth
Cosmogonic verse, 127
Counterpoint, 120
Coupling, linguistic, 9
Creation account, in *Genesis,* 117
Creation myth; *see* Canaanites: creation myth
Creation poetry, in *Psalms,* 117
Crocodile, 94, 105, 106, 107, 108, 109, 110

Damascus, 198
Darkness, 15; light and, 78–80, 97, 171
Daughter of Zion, 155
David, 18, 121, 144
David's victory hymn, 29–38, 39, 50, 60
Day of the Lord, 142
De sacra poesi Hebraeorum (R. Lowth), 3
Deep structure, self-translation and, 10
Defamiliarization, 15
Deluge, the, 153
Demonology, 149
Destruction: metaphorical equivalents of, 144; theme of, 153
Deutero-Isaiah, 84, 137, 157, 158, 161, 162, 191–92; interlinear parallelism in, 20
Dialogue, 61; role in characterization, 57–58; narrative tempo and, 40
Didactic theme, 180
Dinah, 47
Dirge, 27, 74, 135
Discourse: direct, 179; divine, prophetic poetry as, 141; gnomic, 170
Donne, John, 196–97
Double-duty verb, 7, 57, 78
Double entente, 197, 198, 202
Doubling, 14
Dramatization, 19; *see also* Concretization; Focusing; Heightening; Intensification; Specification

Earth, 153; heaven and, 149; in opening formula, 143
Eagle, 102, 103
Ecclesiastes, as Wisdom literature, 167
Ecclesiastian image, 81
Egypt, 174
Egyptians, 50, 53, 54

Ein Gedi, 199
Elaboration, descriptive, 172
Elegy formula, 148–49
Elegy rhythm, 148
Elihu, 87, 91, 92, 93
Eliphaz, 15, 88, 89, 92, 100
Ellipsis, 7, 25; retrospective, 23, 56
Emphasis, anaphoric, 153
English Augustan verse, 35, 58, 113
English literature, generic distinction between poetry and prose in, 7
English poetry, 207
English versions, of *Psalms,* 111
Enigma, 178
Entrapment, prophetic poetry as rhetoric of, 144
Envelope structure, x, 75, 82, 105, 115, 118, 124, 128, 145, 158, 181
Epigram, 167–68
Epithet: relational, 18, 44; substitution, semantic parallelism and, 17
Equivalence, 171, 172; as proverb category, 169
Essay on Criticism (A. Pope), 164–65
Euphemism, 172
Exaggeration, comic, 172
Exhortation, language of, 180
Exordium, 180
Extended riddle form, of proverb, 180
Extended Wisdom poem, one-line proverb and, 183–84

Faith, in *Psalms,* 111–36
Faux raccord, 45, 201
Fertility cult, 185, 196
Fielding, Henry, 7
Figuration, 21, 188, 193; dynamics of, 178
Figurative language, 101, 160, 175, 188; in *Isaiah,* 191–92; in *Job,* 192; in prophetic poetry, 144; in *Proverbs,* 170, 171; in *Psalm 1,* 114; in riddle-form proverb, 178
Figurative meaning, literal meaning and, 17, 22
Fixed pairs; *see* Pairs
Focusing, 19, 20, 21, 29, 33, 34, 38, 52, 80, 82, 94, 101, 120, 123, 135, 171; assertion and, 63; imagistic, 44; intensification without, 174; interverset, 127; parallelism and, 196; semantic parallelism and, 22; spatial, 173; thematic, in psalm, 63–67; temporal sequence and, 63; *see also* Concretization; Dramatization; Heightening; Intensification; Specification
Focusing development, 127
Focusing effect, 24

Focusing impulse, 120
Focusing logic, of biblical poetry, 143
Folk poetry, 189
Foregrounding, 133, 135
Formulaic devices, 113; in Homeric poetry, 13; language, 89; pairing, 13, 157; phrases, 56
Free verse; see Whitmanesque free verse
Freedman, David Noel, 153
Frame-story, 82, 85, 99, 100; poetic argument and, 86
Frame-verse, 56, 60
Framing, static parallelism and, 33

Gazelle, 102, 103
General to specific movement, heightening and, 65
Genesis, creation account in, 117
Ginsberg, H. L., 185
Gomorrah, 146
Greek epic verse, biblical poetry and, 9, 108
Gunkel, Hermann, 112, 133

Halevi, Judah, 67
Heaven: earth and, 149; in opening formula, 143
Hebräische Balladen (Else Lasker-Schüler), 206
Hebrew imagination, anthropomorphism of, 36
Hebrew Melodies (Byron), 206
Hebrew poetry, of medieval Spain, 113
Hebrew prophets, verse and, 76
Heightening, 19, 21, 29, 34, 59, 94, 105, 120, 122, 153; cause to effect movement and, 65; climactic structure and, 62–63; general to specific movement and, 65; interverset, 156, 174; semantic parallelism and, 22; see also Concretization; Dramatization; Focusing; Intensification; Specification
Hemistich, verset and, 9
Hendiadys, 72
Herbert, George, 209–11
Herder, J. G., 10–11
Hippopotamus, 94, 105, 106, 107, 110
Hitler, Adolf, 150
Hollander, John, 207
Homeric poetry, formulaic devices in, 13
Hopkins, Gerard Manly, 84
Horse; see War horse
Hosea, 141

Hrushovski, Benjamin, xi, 8, 9, 19, 28, 190
Hyperbole, 21, 74, 152, 156, 157; cosmogonic, 89; sarcastic, 88
Hyperbolic development, 160
Hymn to Wisdom, 87, 91

Iberian Peninsula, 123
Idea of Biblical Poetry, The (J. L. Kugel), xi, 4, 215n7, 216n18
Ideal king, 132
Iliad (Homer), 125
Imagery: agricultural, 117, 132; anatomical, 183; conventional, 189–90; cosmic, 93, 109; cosmogonic, 79, 119; innovative, 189–90; intensive, 189–90; meaning and, 98; mythological, 79; orificial, 182; in Song of Songs, 186, 189–193, 200–203; see also Birth imagery
Impending disaster, monitory poetry of, 147
Intensification, 11, 12, 19, 21, 23, 29, 32, 33, 34, 36, 40, 52, 61, 69, 75, 126, 151; focusing without, 174; generative principle of, 80, 83; interverset, 22, 173; movement of, in Job, 84; parallelism of, 57, 59; semantic, 72, 152; specification and, 84; structure of, 62–84; temporal sequence and, 78; thematic, 144; see also Concretization; Dramatization; Focusing; Heightening; Specification
Interlinear parallelism; see Parallelism
Interplay, dynamic, between versets, 23
Introductory formula, 160
Irony, 142
Isaiah, 141, 154
Isaiah, figurative language in, 191–92
Isolating, for attention, 24–25
Israel, 20, 21, 44, 50, 52, 74, 123, 124, 140, 143, 145, 146, 155, 157, 158, 159, 161; in parallelism with Jacob, 144
Israelites, 54, 75, 121, 140

Jacob, 16, 47; in parallelism with Israel, 144
Jacob's blessing, 38–39
Jael, 43, 45, 46, 47, 48, 49, 50
Jakobson, Roman, 37
Jehoiakim, 139
Jeremiah, 138, 141
Jerusalem, 50, 53, 67, 121, 122, 123, 124, 145, 188
Joash, 140
Job, 49, 76, 78, 79, 80, 81, 82, 83, 85–111; Friends and, 88, 90, 91, 93, 98, 100, 102, 106, 110

General Index

Job: figurative language in, 192; innovative imagery in, 190; intensive imagery in, 190; structure of, 85; as Wisdom literature, 167, 186
Jonah, 123
Jonson, Ben, 207
Joseph, 174
Judah, 16
Judea, 139, 145, 155
Judgment, justice and, 124
Justice, judgment and, 124

Kenning, 15–16, 121
Keshet, Yeshurun, 112
Key-terms, in proverb, 165
Key-words, thematic, 61, 119, 135; *see also* Leitwörter
Kinesis, stasis *versus*, 117
King; *see* Ideal king
Korah, 54
Kraus, Paul, 4
Kugel, James L., *xi*, 4, 6, 8, 10, 18, 19, 215*n*7, 216*n*18

Lachish, 145
Lamech, 5, 12, 18
Lamech's chant, 8, 11, 12, 17; semantic parallelism in, 9
Landscape, body as, 201
Language, 135–36; of exhortation, 180; paradigmatic axis of, 37; poetic, 141, 147; syntagmatic axis of, 37; *see also* Figurative language
Language craft, wisdom as, 167
Lasker-Schüler, Else, 206
Latin poetry, 208
Leah, 18
Lebanon, 198, 201, 202
Leitwörter, 32, 60, 83; in prophetic poetry, 144; *see also* Key-words, thematic
Levi, 47
Leviathan, 79, 94, 105, 106, 107, 108, 110; *see* Lotan and Sea Dragon
Light, darkness and, 78–80, 97, 171
Limbo, 149
Line; *see* Poetic line
Linear development, of meaning, 83
Linkage, 118
Lion, 102, 106, 107
Liturgy, 27
Locusts, as natural disaster, 157
Lotan, 106, 109; *see* Leviathan and Sea Dragon

Lotman, Jurij, 64–65, 113
Love poetry, *ix*, 182; secular, 185–189, 193–203; *See also* Petrarchan love poetry
Lowth, Robert, 3, 10, 204, 206
Lucifer, in Christian tradition, 148–49

Mack, Maynard, 165
Mallarmé Stéphane, 135, 207
Mandelstam, Osip, 150
Mansfield Park (J. Austen), 117
Mashal, 147
Masoretic text, 7–8; stress in, 4; vocalization of, 4
Matched terms; *see* Terms
Maxim, 170
Meaning: general, specific meaning and, 22; imagery and, 98; linear development of, 83; literal, figurative meaning and, 17, 22; parallelism of, 7; specific, general meaning and, 22; symmetry of, 163
Medieval Spain: Hebrew poetry in, 113; Arabic poetry in, 113
Melville, Herman, 7
Messenger formula, 158
Metaphor, 21, 72, 157, 158, 160, 161, 176, 177, 180, 188, 191, 192, 201; filial, 145; illogical, 176; kenning and, 16; musical, for biblical poetry, 213–14; narrative development of, 39–40; recurrent, 104; referent and, 190–91; sexual, 197–98; tenor and, 145; walking on a path as, 170–71, 172
Metaphorical elaboration, 198; of redemption, 159
Metaphorical equivalents: of destruction, 144; of sin, 144
Meter: in biblical poetry, 9; perceptual psychology and, 6
Metonymy, 42, 71, 143, 171
Michal, 18, 58
Middle Ages, 207
Milton, John, 7
Moab, 16–17
Moby-Dick (H. Melville), 209
Monitory evocation, of impending disaster, in reproof, 141, 142
Monitory poetry, 156; of impending disaster, 147
Monitory prediction, 157; in prophetic poetry, 151
Monitory tale, 57
Moral Essay (A. Pope), 165
Mosaic law, 74
Moses, 52, 53
Moses' valedictory song, 11, 22, 25, 144

Mourning practices, in ancient Near East, 74
Movement: cinematic illusion of, 40; dialectic, 70; diastolic, 103; dynamic, 10; systolic, 103
Myth, 147
Mythology, 106; zoology and, 107

Narrative, 17–18; avoidance of, 27, 49; concatenation, 187; development, 29, 105, 151, 152, 171; dialogue and, 40; elaboration, 172, 180; expectation, satirical reversal of, 172; exposition, 57; incipient, 25; of metaphor, 39, 40; miniature, 60; momentum, 38, 39; movement, 61, 65, 134, 135; poem, 179; poetry and, 28; progression, 63, 128, 187; prose, 40, 46; sequence, 35; sequence of verbs in, 42–43; strategy, 40; structure, specification and, 62–63; summary and, 40; surprise, 172; tempo, 43, 57; time and, 127; verse, 27, 28, 38, 40, 43, 48, 55, 61; of womb image, 99
Narrativity, 171, 172; episodic, 61
Nathan, 144
Nature, inanimate, 102
Nature poetry, in *Psalms,* 117
Near East; *see* Ancient Near East
New Jewish Publication Society translation, 166, 167, 176, 199
Noah's flood, 153
Numbers, in semantic parallelism, 11

"Old Testament Poetry: The Translatable Structure" (R. apRoberts), 10
Olympus, 122
One-line frame, of proverb, 168
One-line proverb, extended Wisdom poem and, 183–84
Opening formula 143; earth in, 143; heaven in, 143
Oracle, 27
Oratory, 27
Organizing principle, of biblical poetry, 3–5
Overlap, 54; interlinear, 127
Oxymoron, 100

Pairing, 14, 18; fixed, 12, 13; formulaic, 58, 131, 168
Paradigmatic axis, of language, 37
Paradox, 167, 176, 177, 180
Parallelism, 3–26, 49, 160, 195; accentual, 166; antithetical, 168; complementary, 75,

78; complete, 10; dynamic, 33; elliptical, 24; focusing, 173, 210; focusing and, 196; of intensification, 57, 59, 173, 181; interlinear, 14, 20, 37, 40, 52, 75, 81, 101, 124; semantic, *ix*, 4, 8, 9, 10, 11, 17, 19, 22, 28, 29, 35, 37, 39, 53, 56, 69, 75, 83, 123, 134, 164, 169, 174, 176, 186, 193, 204; of specification, 57, 58, 59; static, 22, 33, 120; of stress, 7; synonymous conception of, 10, 12, 18; syntactic, 7, 116, 166; theory of, 8; in Ugaritic literature, 28
Pharaoh, 52
Pit, 134, 135, 149; *see* Sheol and Underworld
Perceptual psychology, meter and, 6
Peregrine Pickle (T. Smollett), 13
Petition, 128
Petrarchan love poetry, 113
Poetic argument, frame-story and, 86
Poetic closure; *see* Closure
Poetic genre, prosodic system and, 62
Poetic line, 9, 14; breaks, 5
Poetic structure, 63
Poetic system, logic of, 151
Poetry: boundaries between prose and, 5, 6; narrative and, 28; prophecy and, 137–162; religious, 125; *see also* Prophetic poetry
Political speeches, prophetic poetry and, 141
Pope, Alexander, 7, 35, 164–65
Pope, Marvin, 106, 195, 199
Postbiblical Hebrew poetry, 201, 206
Procreation, 101; cosmogony and, 99
Proem, 127
Progression, narrative, 169
Prophecy, 27; of consolation, 155; of doom, 140, 155; expository nature of, 138; poetry and, 137–62; prose, 137
Prophetic castigation, 142
Prophetic poetry, *ix*, 137–162, 186; anaphora in, 144; direct address and, 140; as divine discourse, 141; figurative language in, 144; *Leitwörter* in, 144; monitory prediction in, 151; prophetic prose and, 160; *Psalms* and, 140; reproof in, 141, 142; as rhetoric of entrapment, 144; structure of intensification in, 73; vocative character of, 139, 141
Prophetic prose, 161; prophetic poetry and, 160
Prose: boundaries between poetry and, 5, 6; oracular vision and, 137
Prosody; *see* Biblical prosody
Prague Structuralists, 133
Proverb, 167–168; advertising jingle and, 163; compression in, 169; key-terms in, 165; one-line frame of, 168; in riddle

Proverb (*continued*)
form, 171, 175–79; as unit of poetic expression, 163
Proverbs: 163–184; figurative language in, 170, 171; semantic parallelism in, 169; Wisdom poetry of, 186
Psalmodic structure, 67
Psalms, *ix*, 186; collective voice in, 114; conventionality of, 112; definition of, 133; historical, 27, political, 121; royal, 121, 129; of supplication, 64, 126; of thanksgiving, 133; thematic focusing in, 63–67; typological study of, 112
Psalms: 111–136; conventional imagery in, 189; creation poetry in, 117; intensive imagery in, 190; nature poetry in, 117; prophetic poetry and, 140; *Sea Poems* (Judah Halevi) and, 67; semantic parallelism in, 8; stock imagery in, 190–91
Pun, 143
Punch-line, 176
Punch-word, 168

Qumran Scrolls, 207

Rachel, 18, 58
Rebecca, 58
Reed Sea, 54, 124
Referent, metaphor and, 190–91
Refrain, 118, 119, 120
Renaissance, 207
Repetition, 6, 18, 118; anaphora as, 64; dynamics of, 11; emphatic, 64–65; implied, 23; incremental, 23, 33, 34, 43, 44, 45, 52, 57, 60, 64, 188, 189; literal, 23, 44; symmetrical, 41; synonymity and, 9; verbatim, 29, 45, 65, 188
Reproof: monitory evocation of impending disaster in, 141, 142; in prophetic poetry, 141, 142; satire in, 141, 142; in vocative poetry, 146
Revelation, 87
Reversal: climax and, 72; satirical, of narrative expectations, 172
Rhetorical structure, 125
Rhyme, 53, 73
Rhythm: free, 8, 19; semantic-syntactic-accentual, as basis of biblical poetry, 8; symmetry of, 163
Richards, I. A., 190
Riddle form, 172; of proverb, 169, 171, 175–79, 178, 189; *see also* Extended riddle form, of proverb

Rimbaud, Arthur, 207
Robinson, T. H., 9
Rübner, Tuvia, 211–13

Saul, 18
Sarcasm, 142
Sargon, 148, 150
Satire: accusation and, 142, 143; poetic language in, 147; prophetic, 147; in reproof, 141, 142; in vocative poetry, 146
Scott, R. B. Y., 166, 173–74
Sea dragon, 106; *see* Leviathian and Lotan
Sea Poems (Judah Halevi), *Psalms* and, 67
Semantic development, 34
Semantic equivalence, 187, 188
Semantic movement, 120
Semantic relations, between versets, 29; *see also* Complementarity; Consequentiality; Focusing; Heightening; Intensification; Specification; Synonymity; Repetition
Semitic philology, 204; poorly understood words and, 4
Sennacherib, 145, 148, 150
Sequence of verbs, in narrative, 42–43
Sequentiality, 38, 120, 123; as cause to effect movement, 38
Serpent, 75
Shakespeare, William, 7, 77
Shakespearian sonnet, 62, 205–6; concluding couplet in, 66
Sheol, 75, 89, 149; *see* Pit and Underworld
Shklovsky, Viktor, 10, 15
Shulamite, 198
Sievers, Eduard, 4
Silence, theme of, 70, 71
Simile, 21, 42, 51, 72, 152, 158, 159, 170, 174, 188, 189, 195, 196; agricultural, 114; illogical, 176
Similitude, 193
Sin, metaphorical equivalents of, 144
Simeon, 47
Sisera, 43–49
Smith, Barbara Herrnstein, 6, 141
Smollett, Tobias, 13
Sodom, 146
Solomon, 129, 187
Song, 74; celebratory, 27
Song of Deborah, 23, 27, 43–49, 188
Song of Songs: 185–203; allegorical reading of, 206–7; dating of, 185; genre of, 185; imagery of, 186
Song of the Sea, 27, 50–54, 123, 124
Sonnet, biblical verse and, 84; *see also* Shakespearian sonnet

Sound-play, 77
Soviet literary semioticians, 113
Spain; see Medieval Spain
Specification, 19, 20, 23, 29, 32, 80, 120; intensification and, 84; narrative structure and, 62–63; parallelism of, 57, 58, 59; see also Concretization; Dramatization; Focusing; Heightening; Intensification
Speech, theme of, 70–71
Stalin, Joseph, 150
"Stalin Epigram" (O. Mandelstam), 150
Stasis, kinesis versus, 117
Stock imagery, 190–91; in Psalms, 190–91; see also Imagery, conventional
Story, frame and, 60
Stress: in Masoretic text, 4; parallelism of, 7
Structure: climactic, heightening and, 62–63; formal, of biblical poetry, 6
Summary, narrative tempo and, 40
Supplication, 65; collective penitential, 126; formulaic conclusion of, 71; psalm of, 68
Symmetry, 6, 181; of antithesis, 178; of meaning, 163; of rhythm, 163; of syntax, 163
Synecdoche, 74
Synecdochic substitution, 20
Synonymity, 29, 38, 120, 135; approximate, 58; parallelism and, 10, 56; repetition and, 9; true, 10, 13
Synonymous conception, of parallelism, 18
Synonymous substitution, 44
Syntagmatic axis, of language, 37
Syro-Palestinian tradition, in Ugaritic poetry, 12, 13
System, formal, of biblical versification, 18–19

Talmon, Shemaryahu, 28
Tamar, 58
Tarshish ships, 123
Tarsus, 123
Telescoping effect, 50, 53
Temporal progression, 40, 42, 43; cinema and, 39
Temporal sequence, 38, 53; focusing and, 63; intensification and, 78; movement, 118
Temporal terminology, 128
Tenor, metaphor and, 145
Tense and mood, in Biblical Hebrew, 131
Terms, matched, 14
Textual incoherences, biblical poetics and, x
Thanksgiving, psalm of, 67, 133

Thematic development, 67
Theodicy, 92, 96; in Job, 76, 86
Thought-rhymes, 9
Time: narrative movement and, 127; perception of, 129; poetic redefinition of, 125; space and, 124, 133
Translation difficulties, from Biblical Hebrew, 165–66
Triadic lines, 56, 69, 145, 177; function of, 35
Transience: human, 127, 128; theme of, 71, 72
Typological study, of psalms, 112

Ugaritic literature, 13, 16, 27, 28, 45; parallelism in, 28; Syro-Palestinian tradition in, 12; verse narrative in, 27; word-pairing in, 28
Underworld, 150; see Pit and Sheol
Utopianism, 130

Verb: of aggression, 132; of similitude, 193–96; see also Double-duty verb
Verb tense, ambiguity of, 131
Verse, Hebrew prophets and, 76
Verset, 9; colon and, 9; hemistich and, 9
Vision, oracular, prose and, 137, 138
Vocalization, of Masoretic text, 4
Vocative force, of prophetic poetry, 141
Vocative poetry: accusation in, 146; in Prophets, 146; reproof in, 146; satire in, 146
Voice from the Whirlwind, 86–89, 91–94, 97, 98, 99

Walking on a path, as metaphor, 170–71, 72
War horse, 102, 105, 107
Wedding songs, 186
Whitmanesque free verse, 62
Wilderness stories, 54
Williams, James C., 170
Wisdom, as language craft, 167
Wisdom literature, 54; of ancient Near East, 167; Ecclesiastes as, 167; Job as, 167

Wisdom poetry, *ix;* of *Job,* 186; of *Proverbs,* 186
Wisdom psalms, 87, 114
Wisdom schools, of ancient Israel, 163, 176
Word games, aphoristic, 163
Word-motif, *x,* 149
Word order, 7, 45, 53, 168
Word-pair, fixed, 45
Word-pairing, in Ugaritic literature, 28
Wordplay, 70–71, 77
Wordsworth, William, 208

Yeats, William, 83–84
Youngren, William, 58

Zilla, 7, 17, 18
Zion, 122, 123, 124, 145, 154, 160, 161; God's love for, 159
Zoology, 94, 106; mythology and, 107; mythopoeic, 94
Zophar, 89, 92
Zaphon, 122

BIBLICAL REFERENCE INDEX

Genesis, 153, 155, 156, 210, 212, 213; 1, 70, 117, 120, 154; 4:15, 7; 4:23–24, 5, 7–8, 9, 11–12, 13, 17–18; 34:31, 47; 49:11, 16; 49:17, 38–39

Exodus, 1, 148; 15, 125; 15:1–18, 50–54; 15:14–16, 123

Numbers, 24:4, 20

Deuteronomy, 32, 144; 32:10, 25; 32:13, 24; 32:30, 11

Judges, 5:22, 46; 5:23, 23; 5:24–31, 43–49

I Samuel, 12, 144; 22, 29–38, 109

Isaiah, 1:2–9, 142–46; 1:3, 25; 1:10, 146; 1:23, 146; 1:31, 39; 5:26–30, 151–53, 160; 10:2, 22; 11, 130; 14:4–21, 147–51; 17:1, 20; 24:17–20, 153–154; 24:21–23, 154; 26:17, 38; 28:13, 38; 40:6–8, 191–92; 44:3–4, 157–58; 45:12, 20; 48:20–21, 20; 49:14–23, 158–62; 49:23, 21; 54:10, 157; 58:10, 21; 59:9–10, 14–15; 59:10, 23; 61:4, 25

Jeremiah, 84, 137; 1:13–14, 138; 1:13–19, 137; 2:15, 21; 4:23–27, 154–56; 4:28–31, 155; 7: 34, 19; 9:7, 22; 20:7–13, 142; 36:27–31, 138; 46:10, 38; 48:11, 16

Ezekiel, 137

Hosea, 2:22, 160

Joel, 1:5, 15; 1:13, 15; 2, 40–43, 142

Amos, 7, 140; 8:9–10, 73–74; 9:1–4, 74–76; 9:13, 156–57; 9:13–15, 130; 9:14–15, 157

Micah, 153; 6:7, 15

Zechariah, 137

Psalms, 22, 61, 84, 111–36, 185; 1, 114–17, 128; 2:9, 21; 3:8, 21; 8, 117–21, 143; 11:2, 39; 13, 63–67, 68, 69, 73, 75, 213; 13:2, 213; 17:8, 190; 18, 29–38; 19, 119; 19:2, 210; 22:2, 212; 22:10, 38; 30, 133–36; 36: 7, 131; 39, 67–73; 48, 121–25, 130; 72, 129–33; 72:9, 21; 78, 27; 84:3, 210; 88:12– 13, 14; 90, 125–29; 94, 191; 96:11, 210; 100:4, 38; 104:2, 143; 104:5, 143; 105, 27; 106, 27; 137:2, 19; 139, 74; 139:13, 100; 145, 22–23

Proverbs, 56, 61, 92, 140, 163–84; 1:5–6, 167; 1:14, 20; 1:16, 38; 2:16, 25, 60; 2:17– 19, 25–26; 3:10, 19; 4:3, 21; 5, 179–82, 184; 7, 55–61, 179, 181; 10:25, 175; 11:1, 168, 178; 11:8, 169; 11:10, 168, 174; 11: 12, 175; 11:20, 168; 11:22, 116; 11:29, 174; 12:4, 174; 12:5, 164; 13:24, 166; 15:1, 164; 15:11, 173; 17:12, 178; 19:3, 171; 19:5, 22; 19:9, 22; 19:10, 173; 19:13, 174; 19:24, 172; 19:26, 178; 19:29, 173; 20:5, 172, 173; 20: 10, 178; 20:27, 213; 21:1, 176; 21:9, 178; 21:13, 171; 21:16, 171; 21:31, 172; 22:1, 176; 22:6, 172; 22:8, 173; 22:10, 173; 22:

14, 173; 22:15, 173; 24:13, 20; 25:3, 173; 25:13, 177; 25:14, 176; 26:1, 176; 26:14, 177; 27:19, 177

Job, 22, 29, 68, 74, 112, 137; 1:10, 82; 3, 96, 97, 98, 99, 100, 101, 102, 103, 104, 106, 109, 148; 3:3–26, 76–83; 3:6, 103; 3:18, 104; 3:19, 104; 3:24, 102; 4:10–12, 88; 5: 10, 19; 7:1–2, 192; 9:2–3, 90; 9:5–10, 89– 90; 9:12–13, 90; 10:10–11, 192; 11:7–9, 89; 11:10–11, 89; 12, 91; 12:7, 107; 12:7–25, 89–90; 12:22, 91; 12:25, 91; 15, 100; 15:7– 8, 88; 15:9–10, 89; 15:14, 15; 16:9–14, 39– 40; 19:20, 192; 19:22, 192; 27:4, 22; 28, 87, 92, 94, 125; 28:7, 93; 28:20–28, 93; 29:23, 21; 29:31, 93; 30:10, 21; 30:27, 22; 32:37, 87; 37:14–24, 92; 37:26–33, 91; 38, 89, 90, 95–96, 97, 98, 99, 101, 103, 109, 173; 38: 2–3, 94; 38:2–38, 95–102; 38:4, 104; 38:4– 21, 94; 38:5–12, 104; 38:7, 98, 99; 38:9, 98, 99; 38:10, 99; 38:12, 98; 38:12–15, 98; 38: 16, 110; 38:17, 98; 38:21, 100; 38:22, 101; 38:22–38, 94; 38:23, 100; 38:27, 101; 38:28, 101; 38:28–29, 100–01; 38:28–30, 101; 38: 30, 101; 38:31–33, 98; 38:36, 101; 38:39, 88; 38:39–40, 102; 38:39–39:30, 94; 38:41, 103; 38:39, 104; 38:41, 88, 103, 104; 39:1– 4, 103; 39:5–7, 104; 39:13–18, 103; 39:17, 103; 39:18, 105; 39:19–25, 105; 39:29–30, 102; 40, 94; 40:1–5, 94; 40:2, 110; 40:4–5, 110; 40:6–13, 94; 40:7–14, 106; 40:16–17, 108; 40–41, 107; 41:5–26, 108–09; 41:13– 24, 109; 41:16, 19, 23; 41:25–32, 109; 42: 2–6, 110

Song of Songs, 59, 140, 182, 185–203; 1:9, 193; 1:10–11, 193–94; 1:12–14, 199; 2:2–3, 189; 2:8–9, 194; 2:10–13, 194; 2:16–17, 194; 3:1–4, 188; 3:6–10, 187; 4, 199–203; 4:1, 189; 4:11, 182; 5:2–8, 188; 5:9, 189; 5: 10–16, 197; 7:2–6, 196–98; 7:7, 198; 7:8– 10, 195–96, 198; 8:14, 195

Lamentations, 1:2, 20

Ecclesiastes, 68, 70; 1:18, 170; 7:1, 170; 7:15, 170